Manufacturing
in the
Corporate Strategy

MANUFACTURING MANAGEMENT: A WILEY SERIES

Series Editors: **STEVEN C. WHEELWRIGHT**
Harvard Business School

MICHAEL A. JENSEN
Corning Glass Works

Materials Management Systems: A Modular Library
By Robert Goodell Brown

Manufacturing in the Corporate Strategy
By Wickham Skinner

MANUFACTURING
IN THE
CORPORATE STRATEGY

WICKHAM SKINNER
Harvard University Graduate School of Business Administration

A WILEY-INTERSCIENCE PUBLICATION

JOHN WILEY & SONS, New York • Chichester • Brisbane • Toronto

This publication is designed to provide accurate and authoritative information in regard to the subject matter covered. It is sold with the understanding that the publisher is not engaged in rendering legal, accounting, or other professional service. If legal advice or other expert assistance is required, the services of a competent professional person should be sought.

From a Declaration of Principles jointly adopted by a Committee of the American Bar Association and a Committee of Publishers.

Library of Congress Cataloging in Publication Data:

Skinner, Wickham.
   Manufacturing in the corporate strategy.

   (Manufacturing management)
   Includes index.
   1. Production management.   I. Title.

TS155.S55   658.5   78-602
ISBN 0-471-01612-8

TO

ALICE BLACKMER SKINNER

Series Preface

Given the large number of books and journals on production and operations management and on manufacturing, one might well ask: why a *manufacturing series*? Existing books cover a wide range of topics in manufacturing management—inventory control, production planning, material requirements planning, logistics, and work force management—as well as the analytical techniques for dealing with problems in these areas.

Manufacturing, like many other functional areas of business, has gone through several cycles both in terms of the practitioner's orientation to its management task and its role in corporations. The most recent phase over the past two decades has focused on operations research and management science as the essence of production and operations management. Numerous volumes of literature have appeared on a wide range of quantitative techniques applied to production problems.

Unfortunately, the emphasis on techniques and methodologies has tended to crowd out some of the critical aspects of manufacturing management. This is perhaps nowhere better illustrated than in a review of the required course offerings in general management curricula or in MBA programs. By the late 1970s the vast majority of such programs did not require a production course (though frequently requiring courses in operations research/quantitative methods). Few schools maintained a faculty group in the production/manufacturing area, and only rarely were more than one or two electives offered on these subjects. Our own experience and discussions with manufacturing managers indicate that there is much more to this functional area than can be adequately addressed by quantitative models and methods, no matter how useful those may be.

The major focus missing in many of the approaches described in recent literature might be described by the concept of effectiveness: meeting the overall goals and objectives of the organization through the appropriate design and utilization of manufacturing resources and capabilities. The changes in the general corporate environment over the past two decades, particularly for manufacturing-based firms, have been significant. These changes have highlighted the need to consider effectiveness and the general goals of the organization if manufacturing is to be used as a competitive tool, rather than simply fulfilling a reactionary role in the organization.

This series on Manufacturing Management is based on the premise that materials about the functions of manufacturing management in the context of their role in the organization and their interrelationship to other parts of the company are urgently needed. Only then can major manufacturing management tasks be effectively designed and carried out so as to comple-ment the effectiveness of other functional areas and better aid the organiza-tion in meeting its objectives and goals. Matching such an orientation with an understanding of the basic methodologies and techniques currently available can significantly affect manufacturing performance.

Contributors to this series must have extensive experience in applying available techniques and concepts and in dealing with the realities of the manufacturing manager's functions. Out of such experience come guidelines on the framework and individual concepts in various subparts of manu-facturing management. In relating traditional approaches to manufacturing management examples are used to tell the practicing manager how the framework and concepts relate to him or her and how to use them most effectively in the environment of one's own organization.

It is particularly appropriate that Professor Wick Skinner of the Harvard Business School prepared the first book in this series. Harvard is one of the few academic institutions that has continuously maintained a substantial group of faculty and researchers in the production and operations manage-ment area, independent of the quantitative methods and operations research disciplines. Following the standards and focus established and illustrated for this series through Professor Skinner's book, titles dealing with work force management, technology selection, facilities planning, capacity planning, purchasing/procurement, inventory management, materials control, logis-tics, quality control, production planning, process management, maintenance, and many other areas are sought. However, new volumes are published only as new materials become available that fit our desired func-tional and "effectiveness orientation" toward manufacturing management.

Boston, Massachusetts
Corning, New York
January 1978

STEVEN C. WHEELWRIGHT

MICHAEL A. JENSEN

Acknowledgments

I am grateful to my wife, Alice, for her enthusiasm and ever-willing availability to react to my experiences and their significance with perceptive questions and encouragement.

To the Harvard Business School, Deans George Baker and Lawrence Fouraker, the Division of Research, and the Associates Program of the School, I acknowledge with gratitude the financial support that made this research possible. Suzanne Tyrer, Carole Whittemore, Kathleen Miller, and Vic Burford provided production and editorial services with great skill. The *Harvard Business Review* graciously released a number of my articles for use in this book.

I have been enormously influenced by the ideas and frequent interplay of discussion and reactions to drafts by my colleagues at the Harvard Business School. I am especially indebted to the following colleagues: Professors Franklin Folts, Arch R. Dooley, Philip Thurston, Richard Rosenbloom, Robert Hayes, Steven Wheelwright, Stanley Miller, David Rogers, Joel Goldhar, Curtis Jones, Robert Ackerman, Edward Davis, Lawrence Bennigson, John Rosenblum, Earl Sasser, Chris Argyris, Roger Schmenner, William Abernathy, William Fulmer, Jeffrey Miller, Richard P. Olsen, Robert Stobaugh, Richard Walton, Raymond Vernon, and Bert Wood. The length of this list attests to the emphasis on production and operating management at the Harvard Business School, an emphasis that has created an environment that was most favorable for working on a book on manufacturing. While I take full responsibility for the conclusions reached and judgments made, each of the above has contributed significantly to the development of my thinking.

I acknowledge with great thanks the contributions of the large number of exciting and vital people in manufacturing management who cooperated with me in research and case-writing endeavors and in many exchanges of ideas. Too numerous to mention individually, they are well remembered for their stimulation, ideas, and accomplishments.

I thank the publishers who have granted me permission to reprint or adapt their material:

Chapter 2: an adaptation of my article, "Production under Pressure," *Harvard Business Review,* November–December 1966, p. 139.

Chapter 3: an adaptation of my article, "Manufacturing—Missing Link in Corporate Strategy," *Harvard Business Review,* May–June 1969, p. 136.

Chapter 4: an adaptation of my article, "The Anachronistic Factory," *Harvard Business Review,* January–February 1971, p. 61.

Chapter 5: an adaptation of my article, "The Decline, Fall, and Renewal of Manufacturing Plants," *Industrial Engineering,* October 1974, p. 32.

Chapter 6: an adaptation of my article, "The Focused Factory," *Harvard Business Review,* May–June 1974, p. 113.

Chapter 10: An adaptation of my article with W. Earl Sasser, "Managers with Impact: Versatile and Inconsistent," *Harvard Business Review,* November–December 1977, p. 140.

Chapter 11: Copyright © 1973 by the President and Fellows of Harvard College. Distributed by the Intercollegiate Case Clearing House, Soldiers Field, Boston, Mass. 02163. All rights reserved to the contributors.

Chapter 12: Copyright © 1967 by the President and Fellows of Harvard College. Revised 1971. Distributed by the Intercollegiate Clearing House, Soldiers Field, Boston, Mass. 02163. All rights reserved to the contributors.

Chapter 13: Copyright © 1967 by the President and Fellows of Harvard College. Revised 1968. Distributed by the Intercollegiate Case Clearing House, Soldiers Field, Boston, Mass. 02163. All rights reserved to the contributors.

Chapter 14, pp. 000–000: Reprinted, with express permission of the publisher, from Harold B. Meyers, "The Great Nuclear Fizzle at Old B. & W.," *Fortune,* November 1969, p. 123.

Chapter 15: based on research conducted for the Division of Research at the Harvard Business School; an adaptation of my article, "Management of International Production," *Harvard Business Review,* September–October 1964, p. 125.

Chapter 16: From H. B. Maynard, *Handbook of Business Administration,* McGraw-Hill, New York.

Chapter 17: From Wickham Skinner, *American Industry in Developing Economics,* John Wiley, New York.

Chapter 18:

WICKHAM SKINNER

Concord, Massachusetts
January 1978

Contents

INTERNATIONAL MANUFACTURING

PERSPECTIVES

Manufacturing
in the
Corporate Strategy

INTRODUCTION

The purpose of these two chapters is to introduce the reader to what the book is all about and how it came to be written. They describe some of the author's concerns about manufacturing and how it is generally managed. The second chapter, in particular, makes the point that production has come under new and mounting pressures and that new approaches to its management are fast becoming essential.

CHAPTER 1

Manufacturing
in
Corporate Strategy

The American production system has been hailed in the United States and around the world for nearly 100 years because of its productivity, capacity, innovations, and contributions to our amazing standard of living. About 15 years ago, the picture began to change. Our number one position in world industrial capability is not what it used to be on most measures. Comparative proportions of the world's manufacturing, leadership in technological and process innovation, ability to compete in world markets, and a dozen sick industries signal that somehow United States industry may be slipping or at least that we are no longer clearly outstanding.

Cracks in our industrial base are being blamed in part for high costs, high imports, trade imbalances, and heavy unemployment. Stagnant productivity, labor unrest, consumer complaints over shoddy workmanship and sometimes unsafe products have caused a loss in prestige and credibility for our industrial establishment. As a place to work the factory can hardly rank lower in the appeal to most of our young. Even unemployed young seem to hesitate before factory gates because they see factories as an entry into a regimented, subhuman quality of working life.

Fair and rational or not, these criticisms reflect the fact that somehow things are not working so well in industry as they did. This book is written as the result of concern over these problems. Are our premises, our tools, our approaches, our basic concepts in industrial management realistic or adequate? These are questions pursued in this book.

In the middle 1960s, I became increasingly aware of growing difficulties and frustrations of manufacturing executives in the United States. As I visited various companies, I became gradually aware of a new set of circumstances that were surrounding and invading the world of manufacturing and making a successful manufacturing operation increasingly difficult. The primary cause seemed to be a new environment—an environment in which there was more competition, more pressure from management, labor, stockholders, consumers, and the public. The environmental changes were characterized by growing foreign competition, an accelerating rate of technological change, and new modes of competition. Competition was resulting in more advertising, narrower profit margins, a flood of new products, pressures toward integrating forward and backward, and broadening product lines. Amidst this frenetic background, the manufacturer was being hit with new forms of federal regulation and threatened with drastic exposure by the courts' new interpretations of company liabilities for product failures.

Controlling the old, conventional problems—to produce at lower cost, to achieve satisfactory quality constantly, to meet delivery promises, to cut down the time necessary to deliver each order, to get new products into production more quickly, and to maintain investment, facilities, and inventories at low levels while adjusting flexibly to changes in volume—became even more difficult. This set of conflicting requirements intensified the fact that no matter what manufacturing managers attempt to do, they have always been easily susceptible to criticism by top management. This is inherent in the nature of the manufacturing world: The successful manufacturer must produce quickly and deliver on schedule a quality product at a minimum of cost and investment.

The added pressures from outside made the management tools available for coping with these problems seem more and more inadequate. Feeling cut off from top management, many manufacturing vice presidents felt that not only were their management tools inadequate, but they were regularly criticized for unacceptable costs, delivery, quality, or investment.

Their impressions of being cut off were indeed true, for during the 1950s and 1960s the typical major emphasis was on growth in sales and market share, and top management seemed to be dominated and influenced more by executives who were especially competent in marketing and finance and less by those with a manufacturing point of view. Manufacturing people felt that they were being asked to "do their duty and perform as good soldiers," doing what was asked without complaint. In spite of the fact that they were entrusted with responsibility for typically 75% of the firm's investment, 80% of the firm's personnel, and 85% or more of the firm's expenditures for materials and equipment, manufacturing issues were often treated by top management as perfunctory and operational rather than strategic. Manufacturing was considered essential, but seemed to offer little intellectual or managerial challenge. Conceptually, manufacturing was considered a management area in which adequate theory and techniques were available and in which the complex problems of planning and control that had challenged management science pioneers had been solved. Paradoxically, in the very field in which scientific management had started—that is, with Frederick Taylor in industrial engineering—professional management had somehow apparently run out its string and developed itself to the point where successful manufacturing required only doing what the book—written half a century before—said. Manufacturing was perceived by many top managers and most professors in well-known schools of business as relatively routine, standardized, and unexciting. The function was no longer attracting many of the most able members of the young generation as workers, technicians, or managers.

Clearly something was basically wrong. The old tools did not seem to work in a new environment. Able, highly professional, experienced managers felt themselves unfairly criticized no matter what they did, and their whole function seemed cut off from the enterprise as a whole. The enigma was that it was cut off in terms of involvement and communication with the enterprise, yet its impact on the enterprise was as pronounced as ever—if not more—in the new competitive world. Finally, manufacturing had somehow drifted into becoming a necessary evil in the corporation; it had become a function that was more often than not holding back the entire corporation.

In the middle of this research into what was going on in United States industry, of course I came across some companies whose manufacturing functions were extraordinarily well-managed. The outstanding feature of these companies seemed to be that in some way or another they had forged manufacturing into a major and formidable competitive weapon. They competed not only with new products, marketing, advertising, and skillful financing, but also with unique approaches to a competence in manufacturing. They competed with manufacturing because they had exceptionally short deliveries, or remarkably low costs, or could move fast in developing new products, or produced the same volume with much lower investment than their competitors.

I ran across some of these situations while teaching a course called Advanced Production Problems. I asked students to study a group of companies within a single industry, comparing them and their performance over the industry as a whole and then looking at the ways they structured and operated their manufacturing enterprises. Somewhat to my surprise, we found that within a given industry, companies would have entirely different approaches to manufacturing. For example, different companies could employ quite different technologies in their equipment and process decisions; or one company would have a number of small plants, whereas another company would concentrate its manufacturing in one or two big plants. The organizational structure or scheduling, inventory management, or management of work force differed among companies. So we discovered that in spite of common technology, a common set of competitors, and a common industry structure, and common market practices, different companies often would have developed quite different manufacturing policies.

The next logical step was to analyze which manufacturing policies seemed to work best. After thorough study, it became clear that there was no principle or formula that would suggest which worked best in a given industry. The surprising fact was that the company's corporate competitive strategy was the salient factor. If the manufacturing policy was consistent with and supported the company's competitive corporate strategy, it worked well and became a competitive weapon. If the policy was not consistent with the corporate competitive strategy, it became a negative influence in the company's performance.

About this time I had a telephone call from the president of a medium-sized manufacturing firm. He asked me if I could come down and go over his manufacturing operations. I asked him what the trouble was, and he replied, "Everybody here is upset, disappointed, and frustrated with manufacturing. Sales are mad at them for poor deliveries, and the marketing people are angry because they are so slow at getting new products in production. The treasurer is put out with them because they seem to require so much in the way of inventories and capital equipment. The personnel manager feels that they do a lousy job with their people. No matter who you talk with, no one is very happy with our manufacturing."

I asked him why he thought this was happening and what was the basic trouble. He hesitated a moment and then said, "I think it's because we don't have a manufacturing philosophy." I said, "A manufacturing philosophy? What's that?" His reply was, "Professor Skinner, I don't know what it is, all I know is we don't have one."

A "manufacturing philosophy"—that was a new term for me as well. But after visiting his operations, I came to agree that indeed they did not have a manufacturing philosophy. Instead of a consistent set of manufacturing policies that were all focused in one direction and were mutually supportive, their approaches were conflicting and at cross purposes internally. Their equipment, for example, promoted low costs but made product changeover difficult. Their production control system favored short deliveries on standard items at the cost of high inventories. Their work force management approaches made flexibility for volume changes difficult. Across the whole span of the decisions they had made one by one, almost everything in their manufacturing pulled a different way. In fact, they were attempting to serve five markets, five technologies, and five strategic requirements within the same factory.

All of these events led me to produce—usually for the *Harvard Business Review*—a series of articles in which I cited the basic problems in American manufacturing and offered some ways of solving them. The articles led me from study of what seemed to be going wrong to a different way of looking at manufacturing from within the corporation. Essentially, what I recommended was an approach to manufacturing from the top down that is based on the recognition that manufacturing can become a major corporate competitive weapon. These articles, which started with problems and led into some broad new ways of looking at them, have been developed, over the past few years into a sequence in which I have gone from the broad to the more specific. This book follows the sequences. The reader will note that the early chapters give the broad point of view and the later chapters become more specific, in the sense of "how to do it." For this purpose, I have also included four cases that illustrate some of the problems about which I have written. Each case is followed by a short analysis from the point of view of the "older approaches to manufacturing," which are then contrasted with a newer approach to manufacturing management. The book also includes several chapters about international production management in which I discuss some of the new challenges of making manufacturing a competitive weapon on the international scene. I have also included one chapter dealing with some of the pedagogical and management development aspects of the new approach to manufacturing.

This book offers a new way for top management to perceive and manage manufacturing. It does not demean the older, from the bottom up, detailed type of tools, which in most cases are just as useful as ever. These old tools—for example, time and motion studies, operation research techniques, and the more traditional approaches in industrial engineering—are useful for optimizing one facet or another of a manufacturing operation. They cannot be thrown away, and indeed, they must be used more than ever. But top management in manufacturing must decide which tools to use and which facets of their operations to attempt to optimize, because in a technologically based system, it is almost virtually impossible to optimize one tool or facet of business without penalizing another. The better the management, the less the penalty; but some type of penalty always takes place. The new approach starts with the role of manufacturing in the corporate strategy, a link that had been missing, and it leads to a strategy for making consistent and focused basic policy decisions in the design and management of manufacturing operations.

This book is submitted with profound and heartfelt respect to my hundreds of friends in manufacturing. These are the men and women who have the difficult job of managing resources in our factories: people, capital assets, and logistics. It is exciting work. This book is offered to them with great admiration in the hope that it will make their lives even more exciting by making explicit the links between their work, the success of their enterprises, and the productive lives of the millions who produce goods for their people.

CHAPTER 2

Production
Under
Pressure

In spite of high employment and output levels, I find it difficult to be complacent about manufacturing in the United States today. Production managers—attempting to cope with pressures from the marketing and engineering departments, the union, the treasurer, and the controller—give an impression of being on the defensive, plagued by recurrent crises. According to many informed observers, our position as the world leader in industrial technology is deteriorating. In many industries we appear to be losing ground to foreign competition. Are we doing better than a mediocre job of coping with and taking advantage of automation? Are not inferior product quality and lack of reliability astoundingly common, considering our proven accomplishments in space technology? Are not strikes and serious industrial conflicts ordinary events of the day?

As I examine the United States manufacturing scene, it appears to me that these obvious and immediate concerns are symptomatic of an underlying process of change which is of major significance. The fact is, we have begun the painful process of replacing the techniques, skills, facilities, and even the managers of an already outmoded concept of production, which I call, for want of a better name, "mass production."

NEW DEMANDS

The concept of mass production was characterized by certain factors:

- Long runs.
- Stabilized engineering designs.

9

- Concise product lines.
- Repetitive operations by each worker.
- A high proportion of the total costs spent for direct labor.
- Intensive use of labor standards and incentives.
- Many identical machines in the factory.
- Batch processes, job-shop layouts, disconnected flows, and a substantial amount of materials handling done by employees.
- Industrial engineering based on breaking a job down into its parts.
- Production management selected and promoted largely on the basis of experience and proven supervisory talents.

These factors are changing, with the extent and rate of change varying with the industry and the company. Increased competition, social change, and new technology are transforming both the factory and the job of the production manager. These changes are increasing the demands on managers and expanding the complexity and risk of their decisions.

One consequence is that many manufacturing departments are on the defensive. Another result, interestingly enough, is that the potential role of the production function in corporate strategy is being *enlarged*. The production function no longer has the relatively routine assignment of prior years: Turn out the product in volume at a reasonable quality level, and keep costs down. In most industries such an elementary definition of this task is fast becoming insufficient for corporate success.

In visits to plants and in discussions with manufacturing managers from many industries, I have observed:

1. Many top managements and many production managers appear unaware of the scope, nature, and significance of the changes.
2. Production managers are under increasing stress, and too many are not coping adequately with growing pressures and demands.
3. Educators and researchers are only partially effective in meeting the needs of production managers for improved knowledge and practical skills.
4. The kind of people who are needed in United States manufacturing are not being attracted in sufficient numbers.

What seems to be the trouble? To distinguish cause from effect is sometimes difficult, but one thing that stands out is the variety of *new* problems that are making the production manager's job more complex. These problems fall into three classes:

1. New pressures from outside the firm.
2. New problems within the firm.
3. The impacts of accelerating technology.

Let's look at each of these categories.

PRESSURES FROM OUTSIDE

One of the most noticeable sources of problems is new trends in the industry and marketplace. Their impact on corporate planners and marketing strategists has been dramatized many times. Not so widely recognized is the fact that they have a profound effect on production management.

Increasing Competition

In most United States industries, competition has become more severe during the past 10 years. Overcapacity has been the cause in some industries, and in other industries competition has been intensified by a management emphasis on growth and diversification as a corporate objective. Companies in the defense industry diversify into consumer products; consumer goods producers see advantages in military contracts. New products and materials capture consumer dollars from older, established products. Aluminum fights steel; plastics threatens aluminum.

Foreign competition, originally based primarily on price, has added quality in function and style to its advantages. The initial lack of distribution and service facilities has been overcome in many industries. Once established—as in textiles, typewriters, bicycles, and watches—the foreign-made product competes on an equal basis in a marketing sense, often with the advantage of lower production costs due to traditionally lower wages. Such trends are putting production executives under even more pressure to produce efficiently than in the past.

Marketing Pressures

Increased competition has naturally brought greater pressures from the marketing side of the business. "Our competition is offering 10-day delivery," states a Midwestern plastics manufacturer. "It is taking us three weeks to deliver. We've got to completely revise our production planning and control system." New products and new models are introduced more often; product life is shorter; product changes are more frequent and more drastic as research and competition combine to thwart the factory manager's traditional goal: uninterrupted long runs.

The marketing manager also insists on improved quality because the company's quality image depends in large part on the service record of its product. Higher quality in appearance and function is demanded. Tolerances are shrinking as specifications grow more exacting under demands for better performance and longer, trouble-free product life.

In many industries the manufacturing facility has been forced to produce more "specials"—short-run, special-purpose, or customer-designated items necessary to make the sale. A paper manufacturer in Ohio has added 30% to the number of products in his line in the past five years. These products all involve special setups, paper work, control, and the conversion of a mammoth paper-making machine to the special run. Special runs, of course, require more setups, different worker skills, special purpose tools, unique processes and equipment, and quality and production control techniques that are quite different from those used for the long, continuous runs of the mass production era.

The insistence on shorter lead times and more immediate deliveries is a sales demand that seldom can be ignored. But how to accomplish it without further increasing costs and inventories is the production manager's dilemma. These outside-generated problems represent trends that may be expected to continue, bringing further pressure on the production system to produce more products better, cheaper, often in shorter runs, and with less time allowed for delivery.

PROBLEMS FROM WITHIN

A second set of problems is complicating life in the factory. By and large they are actually old problems made critical by the outside pressures and the accelerating rate of technology. Their urgency makes them new.

Reevaluating Cost Control

Increased mechanization, shorter runs, and higher quality generally result in a higher proportion of indirect labor and fixed costs relative to direct labor and variable costs. How does a production manager cope with "stickier," less variable costs? How are indirect labor costs evaluated? Not long ago a time-study department could provide the tools and information necessary for appraisal and effective action regarding the productivity of the bulk of the work force. Today this is often not so. More direct labor time is machine controlled. Many jobs are less repetitive. Financial incentives are generally less effective in motiving workers. More technicians, maintenance men, material handlers, and paperwork personnel are required to service a shrinking direct labor group. The old concepts and techniques of job measurement, time standards, and control are becoming progressively more inadequate.

Manning the Operation

The United States factory labor force is tending to divide into two divergent classes: (1) the highly skilled "knowledge workers" who handle setups, equipment adjustment and overhaul, daily scheduling, and quality inspection; and (2) the relatively unskilled, trained workers who perform routine assembly work or are trained to "push the red button" if the automatic machine starts to make a strange noise. Fewer semiskilled workers are needed.

The changing mix of jobs brought about by mechanization is combining with changes in both employee qualifications and expectations. The availability of low-cost college education and widespread recognition of its advantages is drawing the cream of the potential candidates for highly skilled positions in maintenance, toolmaking, and machine setup at the very time that automation requires increasing numbers of people with such skills.

The handling of "knowledge workers" in relation to the unskilled workers has brought problems and unanswered questions to personnel management and labor relations. For example, what skill level is needed to run a tape-controlled machine? How should the operator be paid? Are incentives useful? How can capable "knowledge workers" be found and trained? (One appliance manufacturer in the Midwest, whose apprentice program had dwindled almost to oblivion, has found a new source of candidates in college dropouts. These people are proving to be able and enthusiastic trainees for the kind of factory jobs that demand highly skilled operators.)

Production management's answers must revolve around the achievement of higher productivity, but the factory world by no means agrees on the best approaches to this objective. The market, the product, the equipment, the job, the people—all are changing. Work force management must change in response.

Handling Paperwork

The growing of paperwork and of employees associated with paperwork is a common phenomenon, involving enormous costs. Planned, integrated data processing systems have begun to attack the paper monster created by shorter runs, product diversification, and the clamor for better deliveries and quality, but they have necessarily upset many traditional approaches and procedures. The resultant systems and communications problems in the factory further change the nature of the production manager's job. It is no longer a question of "men, machines, and material" as the classic definition runs; the job now requires the management of an increasingly complex information system.

ACCELERATING TECHNOLOGY

Finally, a whole set of new problems has been produced by invention and product development.

Equipment Decisions

In the "old days" equipment decisions were generally less complex and involved a smaller investment than they do today. Today the equipment under consideration is likely to span larger, integrated, linked systems rather than single machines. One tape-controlled milling-drilling-tapping combination costs $250,000 in contrast to a milling machine at $15,000. The purchase of one of these new systems typically has a substantial effect on the whole factory—on product design, quality, maintenance requirements, materials handling, plant layout, wage systems, employee morale, production scheduling, and work-in-process inventories.

With rapidly changing technology, a high degree of uncertainty over the reliability, feasibility, and economic life of new equipment is common. How well will it work? When will something better be coming along? Would it be better to invest now or wait for the next generation of technological improvements?

Engineering Changes

The factory is being transformed by the need to introduce new products more quickly and to handle a flood of engineering changes brought about by market pressures and enlarged research and engineering budgets.

Under "mass production," when a product's design was accomplished, one complete stack of blueprints and specifications was "released" to the production department. Typically, the production department had a methods-engineering group that proceeded to design the necessary tooling and to detail the exact process by which the product was to be made. This was communicated to the foremen on the "process sheets," and when the various jigs and fixtures were ready and material was available, production started.

In contrast, the new product in today's plant often is released in bits and pieces as each part is designed. In the case of one computer manufacturer, the commercial model followed the first prototype down the assembly line only two days later—an experience that is not unusual. Equally common is the fact that, in an effort so save time and improve the product, the company was making engineering changes on the product at a rate of 100 per day! The defense industry is famous for this kind of pressure for delivery of new products, but no longer are crash programs confined to defense production. Manufacturing managers in many industries have been forced to try to produce a product while it is still being designed.

Materials and Processes

Another source of problems for today's production manager rises from challenges and opportunities brought about by a flood of new developments in materials and processes. The vast outpouring of research and development laboratories and engineering groups is deluging production with decisions to be made on a scale never before seen.

New materials and new processes are coming along at a rate old-timers consider fantastic. Each much be considered and accepted, or rejected or ignored. The diverse properties and higher strengths of these materials often require new processes and equipment. New manning, maintenance, and control approaches may also be implied.

CAUSES FOR CONCERN

These trends and pressures contribute substantially to the spotty performance of manufacturing. They have serious implications. They are causal forces behind the evolution that makes mass production concepts outmoded.

The combination of shrinking factory profit margins, more pressure from the marketing side of the business, and the accelerating pace of technology have made the production manager's job more exacting. Present tensions are due to new and more stringent demands coupled with inadequate improvements in the means of handling them.

Outmoded Tools

Many production managers are attempting to function with outmoded tools. The management concepts and techniques being used in manufacturing are frequently inadequate for today's problems. Some available techniques, both old and new, are ignored by firms that would find them helpful.

Present circumstances and conditions also require new management tools that are not yet perfected.

Given the complexity of today's demands, production manager's must think comprehensively. They must be able to think in terms of *systems* of needs to be met and jobs to be done. From the very start of a project, they must be able to plan and coordinate the technological functions, the work of people, and informational procedures. With more continuous processes, mechanization, linked or integrated flows, specialized equipment, highly paid indirect workers, and fewer discretely separable pieces of equipment, materials-handling and communications systems must be built into the production system.

In the past the techniques of Taylor, Gilbreth, and other industrial engineering pioneers were generally sufficient for planning and control. These techniques were based on analyzing a job, breaking it down into its parts, improving each part, and setting standards. The techniques of time and motion study, work analysis, job evaluation, job standards, piece-rate wages, quality sampling, Gantt charts, simple payback calculations, and computation of economic order quantity for lot-size calculations were adequate for cost control, equipment planning, and production scheduling.

But these tools alone are not adequate today. Indirect labor is less susceptible to time and motion study and standards, and mechanization has changed the nature of so many direct labor jobs that present job-evaluation bases are often inappropriate. Planning for expensive, integrated yet flexible systems can seldom be accomplished with Gantt charts. The introduction of complex new products that are still in the design stage cannot be handled with a simple release system.

New management tools that help managers to cope with some of these problems are being used in many companies. But my observations indicate that in industry generally progress in introducing the new tools and techniques is slow. In fact, it is surprising and even alarming to note that many companies are just now learning the "old" tools and techniques developed in the early days of industrial engineering. For instance, I visited a well-known company that had just discovered the enormous potential of savings in economic-order-quantity formulas. Executives' excitement was almost boastful as they discussed reductions in costs of setup labor and improved equipment utilization using a technique which had been available fully 30 years before they discovered it!

What accounts for lags like this? Perhaps the explanation is that production management in the mass production era required more emphasis on work force management than on conceptual skills.

Actually, some approaches with which companies have not caught up do not require specialized knowledge at all. Consider work simplification—a rudimentary application of common sense applied in an orderly process to almost any job. Ignoring its simplicity and potential, our plants are full of wasteful methods and systems. Go into any plant or office and analyze an operation picked at random. In my experience the chances are nine out of 10 that one can develop an improvement within 30 minutes that will save 10% or more worker time.

Useful New Methods

Many relatively new tools are available to managers. They include techniques such as work sampling, linear programming, heuristic algorithms, PERT, statistical quality control, computer process control, learning curve theory, queuing theory, simulation, inventory models, investment policy models, and others. However, these tools are complex and take training to understand and put into practice. It is no wonder then that their use is developing slowly. The potential benefits in better decisions and better design of production systems are tremendous, however, because these concepts are designed to solve and handle more complex problems. One characteristic of the new family of management techniques is that they are designed to integrate, to consider systems as a whole, rather than to take jobs apart and analyze the parts—the approach that was the basis of mass production industrial and engineering techniques.

While complexity alone might explain why the new tools are spreading so slowly, there are usually very real problems in their application. Mathematical models that include enough variables to be realistic can become fantastically difficult to formulate and program. And oversimplified models, eliminating vital factors, are inaccurate and misleading. Research in new techniques and theoretical concepts is apparently far outrunning the study needed for developing practical applications.

THE TALENT SHORTAGE

If I am correct that industry is losing ground, that transitions to automation and the computer are unnecessarily expensive and painful, that quality is often unsatisfactory, and that many production managers posses inadequate tools for coping with their mounting problems, what can be done?

Underlying the whole problem is the point stressed earlier: The job of production management in most industries is greatly different today from what it was 15 years ago. With the mechanization of part of direct labor and much of management's paperwork and short-term scheduling decisions, managers may now spend more of their time on tomorrow's equipment and systems and less on today's personnel assignments and grievances, parts shortages, and one-at-a-time machine choices. Here is an opportunity, but it comes at a price. To take advantage of it, more planning and system-designing skills are needed. There is an increasing requirement for specialists, and the production manager must be able to direct these experts and not be overwhelmed by them.

This is a tall order, and there seem to be too few people in industry who can fill it. As a result, the production group in many companies is constantly on the defensive—criticized for late deliveries, high inventories, shoddy quality, automation and computer fiascoes, crippling strikes, and low profit margins. These companies have to compete without the benefit of a crack manufacturing function. Their poor manufacturing performance becomes a corporate millstone.

We are not getting enough of the kind of people needed in manufacturing, either from the lower ranks of industry or from the graduate schools of business. A generation ago those with ability but without the means for college became skilled mechanics and craftsmen; many moved up to become foremen and managers. Now there are far too few who train themselves for manufacturing management.

The manufacturing life typically has had little appeal for college graduates. My talks with students indicate that factories still represent grease and sweat and unimportant trivia; the minutiae of a multitude of small details; and the confrontation with rough, uneducated people and a militant union. A factory career is expected to begin at the bottom and proceed at a slow and boring pace, dealing with small decisions and uncooperative masses, and learning to work under "bull of the woods" kinds of superintendents. Presumably missing is the glamour and breadth of exposure in marketing, the big dollar deals in finance, and the precision and sense of the overall business felt in the field of control. "Factories are for engineers" is the theme of most business school graduates.

But too few engineers see it that way. Manufacturing engineers are accurately perceived by the engineering graduate as being comparatively low in prestige and pay, while research and development is seen as offering more freedom and enlarged opportunity for individual, creative work. Besides, engineering training by itself is not enough for the production manager today. Managerial education and broad training in new concepts and techniques are becoming more vital, while strictly technical training is probably less essential than it used to be.

QUESTIONS AND GUIDELINES

Although pressures of competition and economic survival have already begun to bring about changes needed on the production scene, they are coming too slowly. Many companies, industries, and people are being hurt in the process. Beyond the recognition of the pressures, problems, and trends I have mentioned, top management, production managers, and educators might well consider various steps to facilitate changes and adjustments.

Corporate Policy

In my experience many top management groups are unaware of the potential power of a top-flight production organization as a competitive weapon. Companies dominated by any one functional point of view are liable to find themselves in trouble, but too often production is perceived as less critical to corporate survival and growth than is marketing, finance, or engineering. When this happens, manufacturing people play subordinate roles in strategic planning, and the agrressive quality of performance usually deteriorates.

Top management must ask itself whether production is being developed and deployed to competitive advantage. It must look at the management approaches employed, appraising, for example:

- The use of well-established industrial engineering tools.
- The use of new concepts and techniques of operations management.
- The source and quality of production management people.
- The evaluation, compensation, and promotional policies used for production managers.

A vital question is whether the company recognizes the need and is developing a contemporary breed of managers in manufacturing.

Production Management

How can production people take the offensive and get away from a defensive posture? Often a critical self-appraisal of results and the establishment of new objectives can help. Key performance standards may be measured in terms of delivery responses, inventories, cycle time, costs, and quality. Top management can be asked: What improvements in these standards would give us a significant competitive advantage? The detailed appraisal involved in initiating revision of standards of performance generally leads to searching reexamination of basic systems, procedures, and processes and even challenges fundamental assumptions that have been accepted for years without question.

But production management people must go even further in self-appraisal today, inquiring into two key areas: (1) new kinds of managers, and (2) new analytical and planning techniques.

Executives might ask themselves whether they are employing and developing people who have a broad, integrative point of view; who can perceive the production system as a whole, take a company rather than a department point of view, and supervise the new breed of specialists. And does the company have or have access to the specialists—the highly trained people who can put the new, improved quantitative techniques to work? Do factory promotional and personnel policies encourage or discourage such people? Do the manufacturing engineers compare favorably in ability, potential, and pay to the company's research engineers?

Do we understand the potential of new analytical and planning techniques, and are we taking advantage of their existence? The new techniques are still being developed, and needed refinements and practical improvements are coming; but a company cannot afford to wait until new tools are "perfected." It will take a company many years to acquire, absorb, and practice pertinent new concepts and techniques. Lead times are long, and the crash programs sometimes attempted are liable to be dangerous and ineffectual. Each company must get started in a pattern appropriate to its means and needs, and regard self-education and renewal as a continuing process.

Business Education

As a teacher in a graduate school of business I am both proud and self-critical. I am proud of the progress being made in many schools in developing the new, quantitative techniques that can help hard-pressed production managers to cope with their more demanding environment. However, I am critical of United States business schools on three counts:

1. We have done much more to develop new techniques than to help business bridge the gap between theory and application.
2. In the intellectual excitement of developing quantitative concepts, business education may tend to ignore or slight the development of the generalist—the executive whose chief skill is broad judgment and leadership—in favor of educating the quantitative specialist.
3. We educators have failed to communicate effectively to students that life in the factory is changing, and that the needs and opportunities for creative and skilled production managers are going to increase dramatically in the next 20 years; that the production management decisions will be big ones; that promotion to positions of responsibility will not be weighted solely in favor of operating or line experience; and that the old excitement of managing a complex mix of men, machines, and materials is now being supplemented with a major new challenge, that of systems

planning and control. When we begin to communicate this better, we can start to attract more good people into manufacturing life, people whom industry badly needs.

CONCLUSION

Technology, competition, and social change have brought serious problems for manufacturing. Further technological and social changes will take place and, in combination with the natural competitive processes, will, I believe, continue to force an accelerating evolution in the factory. Mass production as we have known it is an outmoded concept. Changes in production management are essential. The corporations and managers that lead in bringing about changes in manufacturing management will gain an important competitive advantage.

CONCEPTS
OF
MANUFACTURING
STRATEGY

The three chapters in this part offer a new approach to manufacturing management that may help to meet some of the increasing challenges of these times. The concepts suggested are a kind of top-down approach that may end the isolation from the corporate strategy and top management that is typical of manufacturing and form it into a competitive weapon.

Chapter 3 focuses on the key concepts of a manufacturing strategy. Chapter 4 deals with some preventive applications of these concepts. Chapter 5 refines the application of these concepts and concentrates on the long-term, often implicit changes that, if not recognized, make "white elephants" out of formerly excellent facilities.

Manufacturing: Missing Link in Corporate Strategy

A company's manufacturing function typically is either a competitive weapon or a corporate millstone. It is seldom neutral. The connection between manufacturing and corporate success is rarely seen as more than the achievement of high efficiency and low costs. In fact, the connection is much more critical and much more sensitive. Few top managers are aware that what appear to be routine manufacturing decisions frequently come to limit the corporation's strategic options, binding it with facilities, equipment, personnel, and basic controls and policies to a noncompetitive posture that may take years to turn around.

Top management unknowingly delegates a surprisingly large portion of basic policy decisions to lower levels in the manufacturing area. Generally, this abdication of responsibility comes about more through a lack of concern than by intention. And it is partly the reason that many manufacturing policies and procedures developed at lower levels reflect assumptions about corporate strategy that are incorrect or misconstrued.

MILLSTONE EFFECT

When companies fail to recognize the relationship between manufacturing decisions and corporate strategy, they may become saddled with seriously noncompetitive production systems that are expensive and time-consuming to change. Here are several examples:

Company A entered the combination washer-dryer field after several competitors had failed to achieve successful entries into the field. Company A's executives believed their model would overcome the technical drawbacks that had hurt their competitors and held back the development of any substantial market. The manufacturing managers tooled the new unit on the usual conveyorized assembly line and giant stamping presses used for all company products.

When the washer-dryer failed in the market, the losses amounted to millions of dollars. The plant had been "efficient" in the sense that costs were low, but the tooling and production processes did not meet the demands of the marketplace.

Company B produced five kinds of electronic gear for five different groups of customers; the gear ranged from satellite controls to industrial controls and electronic components. In each market a different task was required of the production function. For instance, in the first market extremely high reliability was demanded; in the second market rapid introduction of a stream of new products was demanded; in the third market low costs were of critical importance for competitive survival.

In spite of these highly diverse and contrasting tasks, production management elected to centralize manufacturing facilities in one plant in order to achieve "economies of scale." The result was a failure to achieve high reliability, economies of scale, or an ability to introduce new products quickly. What happened, in short, was that the demands placed on manufacturing by a competitive strategy were ignored by the production group in order to achieve economics of scale. This production group was obsessed with developing "a total system, fully computerized." The manufacturing program satisfied no single division, and the serious marketing problems which resulted choked company progress.

Company C produced plastic molding resins. A new plant under construction was to come on-stream in eight months, doubling production. In the meantime the company had a much higher volume of orders than it could meet.

In a strategic sense, manufacturing's task was to maximize output to satisfy large, key customers. Yet the plant's production control system was set up—as it had been for years—to minimize costs. As a result, long runs were emphasized. Although costs were low, many customers had to wait, and many key buyers were lost. Consequently, when the new plant came on-stream, it was forced to operate at a low volume.

The mistake of considering low costs and high efficiencies as the key manufacturing objective in each of these examples is typical of the over-simplified concept of "a good manufacturing operation." Such criteria frequently get companies into trouble, or at least do not aid in the development of manufacturing into a competitive weapon. Manufacturing affects corporate strategy, and corporate strategy affects manufacturing. Even in an apparently routine operating area such as a production scheduling system, strategic considerations should outweigh technical and conventional industrial engineering factors invoked in the name of "productivity."

Shortsighted Views

Manufacturing is seen by most top managers as requiring involved technical skills and a morass of petty daily decisions and details. It is seen by many young managers as the gateway to grubby routine, where days are filled with high pressure, packed with details, and limited to low-level decision making—all of which is out of the sight and minds of top-level executives. It is generally taught in graduate schools of business administration as a combination of industrial engineering (time study, plant layout, inventory theory, etc.) and quantitative analysis (linear programming, simulation, queuing theory, etc.). In total, a manufacturing career is generally perceived as an all-consuming, technically oriented, hectic life that minimizes one's chances of ever reaching the top and maximizes the chances of being buried in minutiae.

These perceptions are not wholly inaccurate. The technically oriented concept of manufacturing is all too prevalent; and it is largely responsible for the typically limited contribution manufacturing makes to a corporation's arsenal of competitive weapons, for manufacturing's failure to attract the top talent it needs and *should* have, and for its failure to attract more young managers with general management interests and broad abilities. Manufacturing is generally perceived in the wrong way at the top, managed in the wrong way at the plant level, and taught in the wrong way in the business schools.

These are strong words, but change is needed, and I believe that only a more relevant concept of manufacturing can bring change. I see no sign whatsoever that we have found the means of solving the problems mentioned. The new, mathematically based "total systems" approaches to production management offer the promise of new and valuable concepts and techniques, but I doubt that these approaches will overcome the tendency of top management to remove itself from manufacturing. Ten years of development of quantitative techniques have left us each year with the promise of a "great new age" in production management that lies "just ahead." The promise never seems to be realized. Stories of computer and "total systems" fiascoes are available by the dozen; these failures are always expensive, and in almost every case management has delegated the work to experts.

I do not want to demean the promise—and indeed some present contributions—of the systems/computer approach. Close observation of the problems in industry has convinced me that the "answer" promised is inadequate. The approach cannot overcome the problems until it does a far better job of linking manufacturing and corporate strategy. What is needed is some kind of integrative mechanism.

PATTERN OF FAILURE

An examination of top management perceptions of manufacturing has led me to some notions about basic causes of many production problems. In each of six industries I have studied, I have found top executives delegating excessive amounts of manufacturing policy to subordinates, avoiding involvement in most production matters, and failing to ask the right questions until their companies are in obvious trouble. This pattern seems to be due to a combination of two factors:

1. A sense of personal inadequacy on the part of top executives in managing production. (Often the feeling evolves from a tendency to regard the area as a technical or engineering specialty or a mundane "nuts-and-bolts" segment of management.)
2. A lack of awareness among top executives that a production system inevitably involves trade-offs and compromises and so must be designed to perform a limited task well, with that task defined by corporate strategic objectives.

The first factor is, of course, dependent in part on the second, for the sense of inadequacy would not be felt if the strategic role of production were clearer. The second factor is the one we concentrate on in the remainder of this article.

Like a building, a vehicle, or a boat, a production system can be designed to do some things well, but always at the expense of other abilities. It appears to be the lack of recognition of these trade-offs and their effects on a corporation's ability to compete that leads top management to delegate often-critical decisions to lower, technically oriented staff levels and to allow policy to be made through apparently unimportant operating decisions.

In the balance of this article I:

• Sketch out the relationships between production operations and corporate strategy.

- Call attention to the existence of specific trade-offs in production system design.
- Comment on the inadequacy of computer specialists to deal with these trade-offs.
- Suggest a new way of looking at manfacturing, which might enable the nontechnical manager to understand and manage the manufacturing area.

STRATEGIC IMPLICATIONS

Frequently the interrelationship between production operations and corporate strategy is not easily grasped. The notion is simple enough—namely, that a company's competitive strategy at a given time places particular demands on its manufacturing function, and conversely, that the company's manufacturing posture and operations should be specifically designed to fulfill the task demanded by strategic plans. What is more elusive is the set of cause-and-effect factors that determine the linkage between strategy and production operations.

Strategy is a set of plans and policies by which a company tries to gain advantages over its competitors. Generally a strategy includes plans for products and the marketing of the products to a particular set of customers. The marketing plans usually include specific approaches and steps to be followed in identifying potential customers; determining why, where, and when they buy; and learning how they can best be reached and convinced to purchase. The company must have an advantage, a particular appeal, a special push or pull created by its products, channels of distribution, advertising, price, packaging, availability, warranties, or other factors.

Contrasting Demands

What is not always realized is that different marketing strategies and approaches to gaining a competitive advantage place different demands on the manufacturing arm of the company. For example, a furniture manufacturer's strategy for broad distribution of a limited, low-price line with wide consumer advertising might generally require:

- Decentralized finished-goods storage.
- Readily available merchandise.
- Rock-bottom costs.

The foregoing demands might in turn require:

- Relatively large lot sizes.
- Specialized facilities for woodworking and finishing.
- A large proportion of low- and medium-skilled workers in the work force.
- Concentration of manufacturing in a limited number of large-scale plants.

In contrast, a manufacturer of high-price, high-style furniture with more exclusive distribution would require an entirely different set of manufacturing policies. While higher prices and longer lead times would allow more leeway in the plant, this company would have to contend with the problems implicit in delivering high-quality furniture made of wood (which is a soft, dimensionally unstable material whose surface is expensive to finish and easy to damage), a high setup cost relative to running times in most wood-machining operations, and the need to make a large number of nonstandardized parts. While the first company must work with these problems too, they are more serious to the second company because its marketing strategy forces it to confront the problems head on. The latter's manufacturing policies will probably require:

- Many model and style changes.
- Production to order.
- Extremely reliable high quality.

These demands may in turn require:

- An organization that can get new models into production quickly.
- A production control group that can coordinate all activities to reduce lead times.
- Technically trained supervisors and technicians.

Consequently, the second company ought to have a strong manufacturing-methods engineering staff; simple, flexible tooling; and a well-trained, experienced work force.

In summary, the two manufacturers would need to develop very different policies, personnel, and operations if they were to be equally successful in carrying out their strategies.

Important Choices

In the example described, there are marked contrasts in the two companies. Actually, even small and subtle differences in corporate strategies should be reflected in manufacturing policies. However, my research shows that few companies do in fact carefully and explicitly tailor their production systems to perform the tasks that are vital to corporate success.

Instead of focusing first on strategy, then moving to define the manufacturing task, and next turning to systems design in manufacturing policy, managements tend to employ a less effective concept of production. Most top executives and production managers look at their production systems with the notion of "total productivity" or the equivalent, "efficiency." They seek a kind of blending of low costs, high quality, and acceptable customer service. The view prevails that a plant with reasonably modern equipment, up-to-date methods and procedures, a cooperative work force, a computerized information system, and an enlightened management will be a good plant and will perform efficiently.

But what is "a good plant"? What is "efficient performance"? And what should the computer be programmed to do? Should it minimize lead times or minimize inventories? A company cannot do both. Should the computer minimize direct labor or indirect labor? Again, the company cannot do both. Should investment in equipment by minimized—Or should outside purchasing be held to a minimum? One could go on with such choices.

The reader may reply: "What management wants is a combination of both ingredients that results in the lowest *total* cost." But that answer too is insufficient. The "lowest total cost" answer leaves out the dimensions of time and customer satisfaction, which must usually be considered. Because cost *and* time *and* customers are all involved, we have to conclude that what is a "good" plant for Company A may be a poor or mediocre plant for its competitor, Company B, which is in the same industry but pursues a different strategy.

The purpose of manufacturing is to serve the company—to meet its needs for survival, profit, and growth. Manufacturing is part of the strategic concept that relates a company's strengths and resources to opportunities in the market. Each strategy creates a unique manufacturing task. Manufacturing management's ability to meet that task is the key measure of its success.

TRADE-OFFS IN DESIGN

Few executives realize the existence of trade-offs in designing and operating a production system. Yet most managers will readily admit that there are compromises or trade-offs to be made in designing an airplane or a truck. In the case of an airplane, trade-offs would involve matters such as cruising speed, takeoff and landing distances, initial cost, maintenance, fuel consumption, passenger comfort, and cargo or passenger capacity. A given stage of technology defines limits of what can be accomplished in these respects. For instance, no one today can design a 500-passenger plane that can land on a carrier and also break the sonic barrier.

Much the same thing is true of manufacturing. The variables of cost, time, quality, technological constraints, and customer satisfaction place limits on what management can do, force compromises, and demand an explicit recognition of a multitude of trade-offs and choices. Yet everywhere I find plants that have inadvertently emphasized one yardstick at the expense of another, more important one. For example, an electronics manufacturer with dissatisfied customers hired a computer expert and placed manufacturing under a successful engineering design chief to make it a "total system." A year later its computer was spewing out an inch-thick volume of daily information. "We know the location of every part in the plant on any given day," boasted the production manager and his computer systems chief.

Nevertheless, the customers were more dissatisfied than ever. Product managers hotly complained that delivery promises were regularly missed—and in almost every case they first heard about failures from their customers. The problem centered on the fact that computer information runs were organized by part numbers and operations. They were designed to facilitate machine scheduling and to aid shop foremen; they were not organized around end products, which would have facilitated customer service.

This had come about largely because the manufacturing managers had become absorbed in their own "systems approach"; the fascination of mechanized data handling had become an end in itself. Top management had more or less abdicated responsibility. Because the company's growth and success had been based on engineering and because top management was R&D-oriented, policy-making executives saw production as a routine requiring a lower level of complexity and brainpower. Top management argued further that the company had production experts who were well paid and who should be able to do their jobs without bothering top-level people.

Recognizing Alternatives

To develop the notion of important trade-off decisions in manufacturing, let us consider *Exhibit 3.1,* which shows some examples.

In each decision area—plant and equipment, production planning and control, and so forth—top management needs to recognize the alternatives and become involved in the design of the production system. It needs to become involved to the extent that the alternative selected is appropriate to the manufacturing task determined by the corporate strategy.

Making such choices is, of course, an on-going rather than a once-a-year or once-a-decade task; decisions have to be made constantly in these trade-

Exhibit 3.1 Some Important Trade-Off Decisions in Manufacturing—or "You Can't Have It Both Ways"

Decision area	Decision	Alternatives
Plant and equipment	Span of process	Make or buy
	Plant size	One big plant or several smaller ones
	Plant location	Locate near markets or locate near materials
	Investment decisions	Invest mainly in buildings or equipment or inventories or research
	Choice of equipment	General-purpose or special-purpose equipment
	Kind of tooling	Temporary, minimum tooling or "production tooling"
Production planning and control	Frequency of inventory taking	Few or many breaks in production for buffer stocks
	Inventory size	High inventory or a lower inventory
	Degree of inventory control	Control in great detail or in lesser detail
	What to control	Controls designed to minimize machine downtime, labor cost, time in process, or to maximize output of particular products or material usage
	Quality control	High reliability and quality or low costs
	Use of standards	Formal, informal, or none at all
Labor and staffing	Job specialization	Highly specialized or not highly specialized
	Supervision	Technically trained first-line supervisors or nontechnically trained supervisors
	Wage system	Many job grades or few job grades; incentive wages or hourly wages
	Supervision	Close supervision or loose supervision
	Industrial engineers	Many or few such men
Product design/ engineering	Size of product line	Many customer specials, few specials or none at all
	Design stability	Frozen design or many engineering change orders
	Technological risk	Use of new processes unproved by competitors or follow-the-leader policy
	Engineering	Complete packaged design or design-as-you-go approach
	Use of manufacturing engineering	Few or many manufacturing engineers
Organization and management	Kind of organization	Functional or product focus or geographical or other
	Executive use of time	High involvement in investment, production planning, cost control, quality control, or other activities
	Degree of risk assumed	Decisions based on much or little information
	Use of staff	Large or small staff group
	Executive style	Much or little involvement in detail; authoritarian or nondirective style; much or little contact with organization

off areas. Indeed, the real crux of the problem seems to be how to ensure that the continuing process of decision making is not isolated from competitive and strategic facts, when many of the trade-off decisions do not at first appear to bear on company strategy. As long as a technical point of view dominates manufacturing decisions, a degree of isolation from the realities of competition is inevitable. Unfortunately, the technical viewpoint is all too likely to prevail.

TECHNICAL DOMINANCE

The similarity between today's emphasis on the technical experts—the computer specialist and the engineering-oriented production technician—and yesterday's emphasis on the efficiency expert—time-study expert and industrial engineer—is impossible to escape. For 50 years management relied on efficiency experts trained in the techniques of Frederick W. Taylor. Industrial engineers were kings of the factory. Their early approaches and attitudes were often conducive to industrial warfare, strikes, sabotage, and militant unions, but that was not realized then. Also not realized was that their technical emphasis often produced an inward orientation toward cost that ignored the customer and an engineering point of view that gloried in tools, equipment, and gadgets rather than in markets and service. Most important, the cult of industrial engineering tended to make top executives technically disqualified from involvement in manufacturing decisions.

Since the turn of the century this efficiency-centered orientation has dogged manufacturing. It has created that image of "nuts and bolts," of greasy, dirty, detail jobs in manufacturing. It has dominated "production" courses in most graduate schools of business administration. It has alienated young people with broad management educations from manufacturing careers. It has "buffaloed" top managers.

A group of industrial engineers asked me to offer an opinion as to why so few industrial engineers were moving up to the top of their companies. My answer was that perhaps a technical point of view cut them off from top management, just as the jargon and hocus-pocus of manufacturing often kept top management from understanding the factory. In their isolation they could gain only a severely limited sense of market needs and of corporate competitive strategy.

The Computer Expert

Today the industrial engineer is declining in importance in many companies and is being overshadowed by a new technical expert, the computer specialist—an individual who specializes in computer systems design and programming.

I do not deny, of course, that computer specialists have a very important job to do. I do object, however, to any notion that computer specialists have more of a top management view than was held by their predecessors, the industrial engineers. In my experience the computer experts have been forced to master a complex and all-consuming technology, a fact which frequently make them parochial rather than catholic in their views. Because they are so preoccupied with the detail of a total system, someone in top management must give them objectives and policy guidance. In their choice of trade-offs and compromises for their computer systems, they need to be instructed and not left to their own devices. Or, stated differently, they need to see the entire corporation as a system, not just one corner of it—the manufacturing plant.

Too often this is not happening. The computer is a nightmare to many top managers because they have let it and its devotees get out of hand. They have let technical experts continue to dominate; the failure of top management truly to manage production goes on.

How *can* top management begin to manage manufacturing instead of turning it over to technicians who, through no fault of their own, are absorbed in their own arts and crafts? How can production management be helped to cope with the rising pressures of new markets, more rapid product changes, new technologies, larger and riskier equipment decisions, and the swarm of problems we face in industry today? Let's look at some answers.

BETTER DECISION MAKING

The answers I suggest are not panaceas, nor are they intended to be comprehensive. Indeed, no one can answer all the questions and problems described with one nice formula or point of view. But surely we can improve on the notion that production systems need only be "productive and efficient." Top management can manage manufacturing if it will engage in the making of manufacturing policy, rather than considering it a kind of fifth, independent estate beyond the pale of control.

The place to start is with the acceptance of a theory of manufacturing which begins with the concept that in any system design there are significant trade-offs (as shown in *Exhibit 3.1*) that must be explicitly decided on.

Determining Policy

Executives will also find it helpful to think of manufacturing policy determination as an orderly process or sequence of steps. *Exhibit 3.2* is a schematic

Exhibit 3.2 The Process of Manufacturing Policy Determination

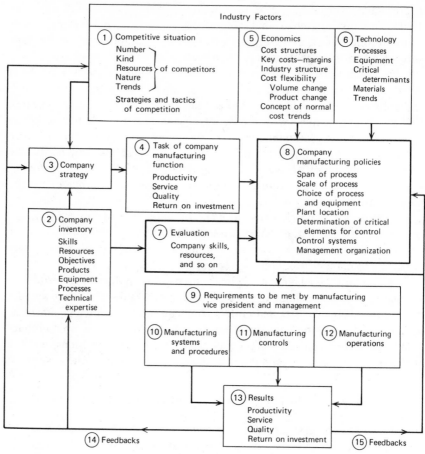

Key

1. What the others are doing
2. What we have or can get to compete with
3. How we can compete
4. What we must accomplish in manufacturing in order to compete
5. Economic constraints and opportunities common to the industry
6. Constraints and opportunities common to the technology
7. Our resources evaluated
8. How we should set ourselves up to match resources, economics, and technology to meet the tasks required by our competitive strategy
9. The implementation requirements of our manufacturing policies
10. Basic systems in manufacturing (e.g., production planning, use of inventories, use of standards, and wage systems)
11. Controls of cost, quality, flows, inventory, and time
12. Selection of operations or ingredients critical to success (e.g., labor skills, equipment utilization, and yields)
13. How we are performing
14. Changes in what we have, effects on competitive situation, and review of strategy
15. Analysis and review of manufacturing operations and policies

portrayal of such a process. It shows that manufacturing policy must stem from corporate strategy and that the process of determining this policy is the means by which top management can actually manage production. Use of this process can end manufacturing isolation and tie top management and manufacturing together. The sequence is simple but vital:

It begins with an analysis of the competitive situation, of how rival companies are competing in terms of product, markets, policies, and channels of distribution. Management examines the number and kind of competitors and the opportunities open to its company.

Next comes a critical appraisal of the company's skills and resources and of its present facilities and approaches.

The third step is the formulation of company strategy: How is the com-

Exhibit 3.3 Illustrative Constraints or Limitations That Should Be Studied

A. Economics of the Industry

Labor, burden, material, depreciation costs
Flexibility of production to meet changes in volume
Return on investment, prices, margins
Number and location of plants
Critical control variables
Critical functions (e.g., maintenance, production control, personnel)
Typical financial structures
Typical costs and cost relationships
Typical operating problems
Barriers to entry
Pricing practices
"Maturity" of industry products, markets, production practices, and so on
Importance of economies of scale
Importance of integrated capacities of corporations
Importance of having a certain balance of different types of equipment
Ideal balances of equipment capacities
Nature and type of production control
Government influences

B. Technology of the Industry

Rate of technological change
Scale of processes
Span of processes
Degree of mechanization
Technological sophistication
Time requirements for making changes

pany to compete successfully, combine its strengths with market opportunities, and define niches in the markets where it can gain advantages?

The fourth step is the point where many top executives cut off their thinking. It is important for them to define the implications or "so-what" effects of company strategy in terms of specific manufacturing tasks. For example, they should ask: "If we are to compete with an X product of Y price for Z customers using certain distribution channels and forms of advertising, what will be demanded of manufacturing in terms of costs, deliveries, lead times, quality levels, and reliability?" These demands should be precisely defined.

The fifth and sixth steps are to study the constraints or limitations imposed by the economics and the technology of the industry. These factors are generally common to all competitors. An explicit recognition of them is a prerequisite to a genuine understanding of the manufacturing problems and opportunities. These are facts that a nontechnical manager can develop, study, understand, and put to work. *Exhibit 3.3* contains sample lists of topics for the manager to use in doing his or her homework.

The seventh and eighth steps are the key ones for integrating and synthesizing all the prior ones into a broad manufacturing policy. The question for management is: "Given the facts of the economics and the technology of the industry, how do we set ourselves up to meet the specific manufacturing tasks posed by our particular competitive strategy?" Management must decide what it is going to make and what it will buy; how many plants to have, how big they should be, and where to place them; what processes and equipment to buy; what the key elements are that must be controlled and how they can be controlled; and what kind of management organization would be most appropriate.

Next come the steps of working out programs of implementation, controls, performance measures, and review procedures (see Steps 9–15 in *Exhibit 3.2*

CONCLUSION

The process just described is quite different from the usual process of manufacturing management. Conventionally, manufacturing has been managed from the bottom up. The classical process of the age of mass production is to select an operation, break it down into its elements, analyze and improve each element, and put it back together. This approach was contributed years ago by Frederick W. Taylor and other industrial engineers who followed in his footsteps.

What I am suggesting is an entirely different approach, one adapted far better to the current era of more products, shorter runs, vastly accelerated product changes, and increased marketing competition. I am suggesting a kind of "top-down" manufacturing. This approach starts with the company and its competitive strategy; its goal is to define manufacturing policy. Its presumption is that only when basic manufacturing policies are defined can the technical experts, industrial and manufacturing engineers, labor relations specialists, and computer experts have the necessary guidance to do their work.

With its focus on corporate strategy and the manufacturing task, the top-down approach can give top management both its entrée to manufacturing and the concepts it needs to take the initiative and truly manage this function. When this is done, executives previously unfamiliar with manufacturing are likely to find it an exciting activity. The company will have an important addition to its arsenal of competive weapons.

CHAPTER 4

The Anachronistic Factory

The conventional factory is fast becoming an anachronism. Many of the values and assumptions on which its productivity has depended are now running head-on into changing beliefs and expectations in our society. The effect of this collision is rising worker dissatisfaction and repugnance toward the factory as a place to work. Conventional methods of managing and making decisions in manufacturing are equally out of touch with the times. In many instances the result is low utilization and efficiency of expensive equipment. As a final measure of industrial ineffectiveness, total productivity is frequently inadequate for meeting return-on-investment needs amidst the facts of worldwide competition.

Some call the problem one of "productivity." Others label it as "blue-collar blues." Or it elicits the question, "Can the United States stay competitive?" The fact is that United States industry is in trouble on all three related counts. Unless managers begin to recognize this and take corrective action, the situation may gradually spiral into a genuine national industrial emergency.

Combining to produce a powerful impact on industry are three environmental factors: (1) accelerating foreign competition, (2) technological changes in production and information-handling equipment, and (3) social changes in the work force. The massive effect of these rapidly moving, simultaneous changes is rendering the typical factory an obsolete institution. Changes in our conventional management methods of accomplishing improved manufacturing plant performance are becoming mandatory.

In this chapter I report on the anachronistic status of the factory system by first arguing that changes are essential in the factory infrastructure. I show that the normal approach of attempting to improve factory results by pecking away at the various elements of the plant complex—that is, making modifications one by one—can no longer be tolerated by owners, employees, and society at large. Then in the balance of the chapter I offer my recommendations on the changes needed in conventional concepts of managing manufacturing and meeting human needs in manufacturing careers.

PRESSURE FOR CHANGE

An indisputable fact is that as worldwide competition spreads, United States companies in a steadily increasing number of industries are finding the going rough, with high wages placing producers at a comparative disadvantage. American industry is also wrestling with some puzzling and stubborn internal problems, such as assimilating new technology, the will to work, and shortages of highly skilled workers—all key elements in achieving better productivity.

Like it or not, we are being forced to challenge from the ground up all pieces of conventional wisdom concerning every facet of industrial management from individual job definitions, work force management, the foreman's job, and equipment and process design to scheduling and inventory control.

In sum, innovative, even radical, changes in the factory as a total social and technological institution are already necessary because rapid obsolescence of the factory as an institution has already set in. And wholesale, broad, sweeping changes are in order because whatever is done must be internally consistent.

Piecemeal Syndrome

Industrial leadership and competitive productivity in the United States are eroding so quickly that manufacturing executives in many industries can no longer permit themselves the luxury of what I call the "piecemeal syndrome." Let me illustrate what I mean:

The XXX Company, concerned over low profit, set out to modernize its plant. Over a two-year period new automated, highly mechanized machines were anlayzed, justified, and purchased one by one. But productivity improved very little. Since low utilization of equipment was one obvious culprit, a computer-based information, planning, and scheduling system was installed. This system clearly revealed that changes in plant layout and materials handling were needed.

All this took several more years, and profit margins improved somewhat. But absences, workmanship, effort, and morale were being adversely affected by the earlier changes in physical facilities and the information system.

Further analysis suggested that the pay system was apparently inappropriate to the new production and scheduling methods and that an inconsistent span of individual jobs was contributing to poor morale. Supervisory assumptions and practices were challenged, along with employment procedures. These changes spanned another year and a half.

About that time, the company's strategic approaches to competing in worldwide markets were revised, pracing an emphasis on fewer standard items and on more customer specials and model changes. Management realized that not only would the scheduling and information system need changes but much of the basic production equipment as well, if the plant was to fulfill the revised manufacturing task imposed by the new corporate strategy.

The entire period of time represented six and a half years of frustration, inadequacy, and the constant pressure of making changes. In the end the system needed as much revision as in the beginning. During no single year were results even marginally satisfactory. Stockholders, managers, employees, and engineers shared only one mutual sentiment—that of unrelenting dissatisfaction.

This common example represents a reasonably accurate model of how most factories are being managed. To manage manufacturing differently will be a difficult undertaking because of the obvious problems in developing planned and coordinated systems that require long lead times and heavy capital investments and involve little-understood sociological phenomena. And it will also be difficult because of the problem of keeping the whole "show" going while changing it.

These are not impossible tasks. They seem entirely "doable" once a manager knows what to do. First, however, manufacturing executives must begin to develop—admittedly at some personal and corporate risk—new concepts in organizing and managing factories as complete social and technical institutions.

But what is to be done, more precisely, to update our industrial system and to improve our productivity?

It is puzzling to many people that increased mechanization, automation, and computerization in industry have not been more effective in boosting industrial productivity. The temptation of seizing on new technology as the answer to our industrial dilemmas is appealing. For surely one way out of the growing difficulties in remaining competitive lies in the possibilities of increased mechanization and automation. As James Bright wrote several years ago, our problem is not that we are mechanizing too fast but that we are mechanizing too slowly.[1]

Thus, if mechanization, automation, and computerization can do any good at all in the factory, they should help to reduce costs and improve quality. They should also help to reduce boredom from dull jobs, and by their very complexity to attract, as the factory formerly did, bright and able young people into new knowledge and skill-oriented jobs in industry.

This sounds promising—and it is—but the gap between promise and payoff is proving to be very wide. Increased mechanization is coming about neither smoothly nor quickly enough to meet the cost and productivity improvements that are apparently needed. Automation is not a consistent success, nor does it lack confusing and paradoxical elements. Consider:

- In the face of a pressing need to change the factory, increasing both its mechanization and its humanization, we are apparently making slow progress.
- In the face of an increasing rate of technological change and potential for automation, actual applications are surprisingly cautious.
- In the face of expanding uses for the computer, its effects in reducing lead times and costs and in improving quality of output are disappointing.
- In the face of what appear to be enormous opportunities for retooling with modern numerically controlled gear, we see a slowdown in orders.

In the meantime a combination of growing competition and changing social expectations threatens to make obsolete many plants and many industries. One effect is on the appeal of factory life to able men and women. I am concerned that the problem of attracting better employees to the factory will multiply unless industrial managers are able to perform several orders of magnitude better in introducing computer-based systems and automated industrial equipment. They must also somehow change the time-hardened image of the factory as an undesirable workplace for intelligent, independent, and resourceful people. But changing over the American factory is proving to be a sticky and sluggish problem, fraught with stubborn internal resistances that block progress.

What is going wrong? Why is progress so slow and painful? Why is it so

[1] "Are We Falling Behind in Mechanization?" *Harvard Business Review* (November–December 1960).

difficult to meet the problems, to change over and renovate the factory, and to employ without nightmare the fruits of amazing technologies?

RESEARCH FINDINGS

I have analyzed many situations that involve the introduction of numerically controlled machine tools and other complex automated equipment and the use of the computer in the factory. Some tentative findings are beginning to emerge from this research.

First, the complexities involved in achieving successful, large-scale increases in mechanization and computerization are simply enormous—in number as well as in potentially devastating effects—and they are typically much greater than anticipated. This finding may hardly be news to industrialists, but its significance is not inconsequential.

The warning is clear: Automation and computer-aided production must not be undertaken without extensive and exhaustive planning. Even then, start-up problems and side-effect falldowns are going to occur. More is involved than mere technology. Side effects are often more important (for better or worse) than the primary goals contemplated for the technological change.

Interesting Patterns

My study of the anatomy of automation/mechanization/computerization experiences is turning up some interesting patterns. To illustrate:

A typical problem is the case of one company in which expensive new automated equipment took a year and a half to become fully operational, and even then its utilization was about half of that on which acceptable paybacks had been based. Why? The reason was a complex myriad of cause-and-effect relationships: inadequate operator and programming skills, unrealistic demands for precision, and difficulties in matching market demands with shop scheduling.

In another company a computer-aided, automated line of process equipment proved unable to handle the process it was designed to control. The problem was finally traced to the operators, who prior to mechanization had been handling certain material and process-introduced variables with a kind of experience-developed intuition that was too complex for the computer and sensor to handle.

In still another company, a new multimillion-dollar plant performed according to specifications, but it was ruining the company's ability to compete. The problem was a lack of flexibility in the process which resulted in lead times for new products and special product variations that were significantly longer than those offered by the competition.

Case examples such as these prove a kind of Murphy's Law—if something can go wrong, it will. An inconsistency or lack of congruence in any one of dozens of ingredients in the system will often ruin the performance and utility of the whole. These are not just technical or engineering problems, but also problems of marketing, scheduling, engineering, inventory, changeover, cost control, accounting, volume sensitivity, worker acceptance, training, supervision, safety, wage system, motivation, union contract, utilities, maintenance, pollution/effluents, community relations, vendor requirements, plant organization structure, executive performance evaluation, and communications and information flows. In short, everything counts. One subtle flaw may immobilize or neutralize the benefits of an otherwise marvelously planned and conceived project. This interconnectedness signals the need for a "total systems" approach, which will surprise few. But the massive inertia and complexities attendant to bringing about change also say something about the kind of system the factory is: a complex network of social and technological factors with both economic and strategic payoffs.

Infrastructure Problem

My analysis of companies that have invested in new technology as a means of overcoming competitive disadvantage suggests that the potentially positive results of automation and computer technology are being largely neutralized by failings or inconsistencies in other elements of the factory institution. By this I mean the internal systems through which work is carried on—what I call the "infrastructure" of the factory. The infrastructure includes elements such as organizational levels, wage systems, supervisory practices, production control and scheduling approaches, and job design and methods concepts.

By analogy, we are learning that a new engine does not make an old automobile new. Any one part—such as the transmission, body, suspension, or electrical system—dates the vehicle's performance and can render it inadequate. To carry on this analogy, the new engine may in fact bring out new problems that make total performance worse than before the old engine was replaced.

The entire factory must be planned and renovated as a unit lest any one element undermine the entire structure. To introduce advanced mechanization successfully and to achieve full productivity the entire makeup of the factory in all its interconnected intricacies must be retooled to make it internally consistent with the new process.

Without substantial changes in equipment and technology, we will not be able to withstand foreign competition; but without changes in methods of work, concepts of supervision, control and direction, and promotion and salary practices, I doubt very much whether the factory can ever again have the appeal it once did to sufficient numbers of competent employees. In a nutshell, our methods of decision making, communicating, scheduling, and supervising make up the infrastructure of our plants; and these internal elements are proving more resistant to change than the purely technological ingredients on which factory managers and engineers tend to focus.

One way of looking at the present situation is shown in *Exhibit 4.1.* Changes in technology, society, and the economic situation are impinging on the factory system—all at the same time.

Exhibit 4.1   How Pressures Impinge on the Factory System

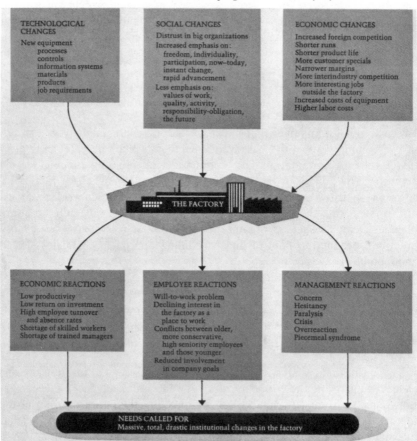

By no means is it surprising that production executives with orders to fill, schedules to meet, budgets to hold, and unions to negotiate with are hesitant to "start changing everything around." The stability of evolutionary change is demanded by the practical person, and this is eminently reasonable. But my view of the scene today is that there is a great deal of paralysis and hesitancy, a real sense of crisis and floundering in many industries, and frequently a sluggishness and failure of nerve among top managements. All of this is ominous for the overhauling of our factory institutions and the raising of productivity levels.

RECOMMENDED CHANGES

How might top managers of manufacturing go about making profound changes in the stubborn infrastructure of the conventional factory to make it less anachronistic, more productive, and more relevant to today's social and economic facts of life?

Analysts of the current scene approach such a difficult question with a humble confession of their own inadequacies and uncertainties. Who knows, really, how to solve the complex problems of our times? Nevertheless, I move to the other side and offer my opinion that there is a great deal that managers responsible for manufacturing can do to make their factories more productive and less anachronistic.

My recommendations are simple yet vital, and fall into two groups:

1. Changes *in conventional concepts* of managing manufacturing.
2. Changes *in meeting human needs* in manufacturing careers.

Conventional Concepts

Manufacturing management was derived in a conceptual sense from engineering and technologically oriented variables. Because manufacturing requires specialized expertise and constant improvement of often complex equipment and processes, its foci as a sector of management have been on technology, efficiency, and equipment. As a result of this legacy, manufacturing executives have typically been more expert in those areas of their work than in other parts.

Indeed, the potential of manufacturing as a competitive weapon and the concept of using manufacturing as a strategic asset have been almost always overlooked in management's single-minded attention to efficiency, costs, and engineering.

Manufacturing can be managed quite differently from the way most companies manage it. What is required are three fundamental changes to bring about (a) the recognition and banishment of a number of fallacious myths and assumptions about manufacturing, (b) the management of manufacturing as a corporate strategic weapon, and (c) the widespread acceptance of a concept of manufacturing as an institution, with an extensive and influential infrastructure of internally consistent technological and sociological elements.

Let me take each of these three conceptual changes in manufacturing management in turn.

Myths and Assumptions

By having led us into planning and managing plants in ways that result in disappointments and unnecessary hard work and away from more fruitful approaches, myths and assumptions have seriously hurt our progress.

The main criterion for evaluating factory performance is efficiency and cost.

This statement is wrong. Manufacturing can also be a competitive weapon when it is less "efficient" but more flexible in terms of product change, in managing inevitable ups and downs in volume, in getting new products into production quickly, in providing for and consistently meeting short-delivery promises, and in producing with a minimum investment in inventory and fixed assets.

Criteria for judging a factory should not be limited to efficiency and cost, for these criteria ignore the fact that in the context of a particular company's competitive strategy, other criteria may be vastly more important.

A good factory can simultaneously accomplish low costs, high quality, minimum investment, short-cycle times, high flexibility, and rapid introduction of new products.

Wrong again. A factory system—like an airplane or a building—can be designed to do only certain things well. The failure to clearly identify design objectives or to compromise among many criteria results in manufacturing systems which do not perform well by any criteria.

The management of factories is essentially a task for engineers.

This assumption is a grievous mistake—blindly employed since the turn of the century and now made even more seductive by advancing technology—that has generally entrusted the direction of manufacturing to people conditioned with a technical point of view. The technical dimension is important, but time is proving that social and strategic dimensions are at least equally important. Moreover, the technical obsession often delegates the production function to those who are inadequately trained and oriented toward human and social factors, financial problems, and the strategy and markets of the entire firm.

Increasing mechanization is a job for industrial engineers and operations researchers.

Another wrong assumption. Tackling complex multidimensional problems with the limited array of disciplines offered by even those broadly intentioned professionals is simplistic.

The systems approach and a high level of conceptualization are a substitute for experience and substantive knowledge.

This fallacy is implicit in excessively theoretical and conceptual planning exercises which have caused a multitude of errors in judgment and swarms of "bugs" in automated factories.

The ultimate objective of automation is to reduce the numbers of people required; problems with and costs of people can be avoided and overcome with automation and mechanization; people problems can be bypassed with good equipment.

These three interrelated misconceptions should have been demolished by the experiences of the past 10 years.

Economics always favors machines.

This is a myth because the fantastic abilities of people to plan, remember, and use judgment, wisdom, and intelligence extend far beyond the capabilities of computers and mechanization. To try to make such facilities substitute for people has repeatedly proved expensive, especially when reliable back-ups are built in to achieve a hands-off operation. When a skilled person is to be replaced by a machine, the cost of the equipment replacing the person may run into hundreds of thousands of dollars. Therefore, economics often favors the use of people.

In total, these myths and assumptions about plants and people have led us into an excessively technically oriented point of view of the factory. They have allowed us to overlook key dimensions in industrial change and to attempt to introduce machines and equipment without changing organizations, responsibilities, job contents, information systems, promotion and pay systems, and control and motivational approaches—in short, the stubborn total infrastructure of the factory as an institution.

The simplistic view of the factory as measured largely by efficiency not only drives away good men and women, but fails to use the factory as a competitive weapon to meet specific manufacturing tasks demanded by corporate strategy. Delegation of their own responsibility by top managers allows too many plants to be managed by technologists who do not have a general management point of view.

Wise managers recognize the multidimensional complexity of the problems with which they deal. To bring about change in the infrastructure of manufacturing involves a great deal more than new technology and technological innovation. Production managers are asking for heartache, frustration, and frequent defeat when they attempt to go it alone.

We walk innocently into an ambush when we attempt to develop new production systems without looking at their strategic and social implications as well as their technological aspects. Present know-how and skills will be multiplied enormously, and failures and delays will be prevented when we recognize that factory problems are just as complex and demanding as all the other problems involved in renewing major social institutions. They require a multidimensional team approach.

Strategic Weapon

Here I can be more brief since I covered this subject in the preceding chapter. Suffice it to say at this point that the concept of manufacturing as a strategic weapon is powerful in my experience because, once understood and assimilated, the concept has a dynamic effect on managers. Its use automatically lifts them out of any narrow, parochial corner into a broad, total view of the production system and its relation to the corporation and its strategy. The concept gives them a means and a framework for thinking about the design of manufacturing and requires them to think of the production process in policy—rather than solely operational—terms.

Concept of Manufacturing

Seen as a major institution, manufacturing at once takes on new dimensions which have existed often unrecognized all along. Certain conclusions then follow:

- Elements of the infrastructure must be mutually and internally consistent.
- Everything counts, since one overlooked element may ruin the total.
- Manufacturing decisions must span the infrastructure; changes can no longer be made piecemeal if they are to be successful.
- The span of changes must be broader and take in more elements.

The interaction between the various elements of the infrastructure is complex and often not easily understood; but their resulting effects warrant attention and improved expertise.

Meeting Human Needs

A different kind of recommendation from those representing conceptual changes involves the organization and operation of production systems in terms of societal and personal values. If an institution is to be productive in the short run and viable over the long run, it must (a) meet or change the felt needs and expectations of employees so as to be generally satisfying, and (b) develop an image that attracts sufficient numbers and varieties of people to allow for the selection of an able total cadre of employees and managers.

As stated earlier, we have much evidence that the factory as a social institution may be rapidly growing outdated. Who, after all, wants to work in a factory these days? And what does the common answer, "Not very many," mean? To me it suggests that the values and demands that today's factory institution imposes on its members are beginning to conflict with the values and expectations of an increasing fraction of modern Americans.

Specifically, *Exhibit 4.2* suggests a number of these conflicts and growing incongruencies and anachronisms.

What can be done with this vital "people segment" of the factory infrastructure? While it is probably the most difficult element with which to cope, I suggest, albeit cautiously, that the people area is not so impossible to deal with as is often assumed. It can be resolved more satisfactorily, but it will take some daring and innovative management nerve, for changes in people policies can be explosive; and this means that top management must take responsibility and be involved.

But the picture is not all negative, for the factory can offer a great deal that employees want and need. Employees, particularly in metropolitan, big-city environments, are often lonely in the crowd; do feel needs for group memberships and cooperative, nonaggressive, nondefensive, fulfilling experiences; wish to identify with a successful organization and quality products; and seek outlets for their ideas and opinions.

Seen in this sense, the factory can be attractive if it meets some of these

Exhibit 4.2 Conflicts Between Current Factory and Societal Viewpoints

Factory Expectations and Values	Social Expectations and Values
Employees are to perform jobs designed by management.	Employees know better than their boss how to do their own work.
Advancement is to be by seniority and long-proven performance.	Employees want continued and steady advancement.
Experience is important.	Experience is overemphasized.
Time is important.	Time is pressure.
Work, activity, achievement on one's job are to come first	Family, leisure, and balanced life are most important.
Decisions are to be made quickly and efficiently.	Employees don't want anyone to decide anything that concerns them as individuals without first getting their opinions.
Employees are to adjust to the demands of expensive machinery.	Employees don't want to be treated like machines.
Following orders is essential.	Freedom is essential.
The individual is to be paid what he or she is worth.	Employees are entitled to a decent standard of living.
Productivity is essential to economic well-being.	Friends, conversation, and social interaction are essential to human well-being.
Employees are to perform well (even under adverse physical conditions).	Employees don't want to work under adverse physical conditions.
Seniority entitles employees to job protection and privileges.	Each person has one vote.
Loyalty to the company is owed by employees.	Loyalty to one's beliefs is more important than loyalty to the corporation.
The corporation cares for its people.	The corporation cares little about its employees.
Employees are to perform work per schedules, quotas, and budgets.	Schedules, quotas, and budgets are mechanisms to exert control over people.

needs. Some factories are already doing a superb job in certain facets. In fact, it appears to me that the factory is in an ideal position to meet many of today's unfulfilled social needs and expectations.

But to do so, what must be changed? Consider these anachronistic elements of many conventional factories:

- Pay systems based on hours worked.
- Physical arrangements that treat employees with disrespect and supervisory assumptions that fail to treat them as individuals.
- Decision-making processes that leave out the opinions and ideas of involved employees.
- Promotion and job security policies that emphasize only experience and seniority.
- Communications practices that withhold information or present only one point of view.
- Job designs and work content that focus solely on motor-mechanism/physiological aspects of an employee's capacities and leave out the emotional and spiritual dimensions.
- Union contracts and governance systems that restrict change and stifle initiative.

Innovative Examples

Lest the foregoing discussion strike the reader as recommendations from an ivory tower, let me cite several real-life examples of changes going on now in manufacturing management. These are typical of what some few innovative companies are doing in the light of the kinds of problems I have been discussing here.

Company A is a $50 million annual sales manufacturer of capital equipment whose manufacturing vice president and president became concerned enough about late deliveries, high costs, shortages of skilled technicians, and rising labor problems to decide that total organization—rather than piecemeal—changes were in order. Their factory in now being overhauled from top to bottom.

The changeover process started with a determination of the specific manufacturing task required by the company's competitive strategy, which the executives identified as offering short lead times on an ever-increasing number and variety of products with a trend toward shorter runs of more customer specials. Subsequently, they tackled each element of the factory infrastructure, such as analyzing scheduling and information systems, supervisory and wage policies, equipment, and layout.

In short, all of this factory's operations were reexamined and rethought

(a) to be mutually consistent, (b) to provide short lead times on new product development and delivery, and (c) to cope with today's social and economic environments.

Company B is one of our industrial giants. At one decentralized division where labor productivity has been marginal at best, a totally new approach to supervision and work-force management has been installed on a pilot basis. The approach features a "self-determining work group," consisting of about 30 workers in a general purpose, job shop, machine area who are permitted to govern themselves. The group members set their own rules and regulations within the framework of only the general and functional company objective of making parts as needed, per blueprint, and on schedule. Quality controls, scheduling of machines, discipline and work rules, and productivity are all under the control and direction of the group itself with the help of a "trainer," who functions as a nondirective, consultive coordinator.

Companies C and D are pursuing a less drastic approach to a new kind of supervision and work-force management. Entirely independent of each other—they are located 1200 miles apart and are in different industries—both have restructured traditional foremen jobs.

Concluding that the typical foreman's job is "impossible," Company C took four sections of 30 men each under four foremen and set up an enlarged section of 120 men with a team of the four former foremen in charge. One member of the team was asked to focus on quality, the second on training, the third on technical problems, and the fourth on scheduling, planning, and reporting.

In Company D the same kind of change took place, but with a three-man team in which the role of the quality specialist was omitted.

In each of these four companies positive responses to its innovative approaches and changes are taking place. Perhaps a kind of "Hawthorne effect" (in which experiment and change always seem to produce beneficiary results regardless of the particular change) is at work. Then, again, perhaps the experiments are sound in themselves and will become models for other companies.

In any event, the climate for innovation and experimentation in manufacturing management has never been better. The recommendations in this article are derived in large part from actual cases. Real progress is taking place among a relatively small number of companies whose managers are recognizing the seriousness of problems in industry and courageously taking the risks of bringing about substantial change.

CONCLUSION

The factory system is anachronistic on two counts:

1. Its management concepts are outdated, focusing on cost and efficiency instead of strategy, and on making piecemeal changes instead of changes that span and link the entire system.
2. Its infrastructure contains such conflict and paradox that the expectations and desires of its people are too often incongruent with the imperatives of its technology, the demands of its markets, and the strategies of its managers.

This internal inconsistency marks a failure to adapt to environmental change in a key functional area of business—the production function.

How ironic that in production, where scientific management techniques began, these conventional approaches now seem out of date and out of tune with the social and economic facts of the times. Production management is perhaps bringing to an end a long cycle that began with innovation and new concepts for accomplishing productivity, developed in maturity of ideas, subsequently grew into a "conventional wisdom," and finally arrived at the point where we now see obsolescence.

Looking ahead, the changes in economics, technology, and society that now affect the factory may, if we dare, lead us to new kinds of production infrastructures that could absorb and harness new technology and new social values. With creative and substantial change, led by the more intrepid, the factory institution could begin to achieve the productivity breakthrough our economy so sorely needs.

CHAPTER 5

The
Decline, Fall, and
Renewal of
Manufacturing Plants

A successful manufacturing plant seldom stays successful for long. Somehow, competitive, efficient operations decline, to become corporate liabilities. One day its owners discover that it is no longer performing successfully. It has become a target of criticism for high costs, poor quality, and unreliable deliveries and is no longer a competitive asset.

Why should a modern and fully maintained manufacturing system, staffed with bright, energetic and alert managers, be prone to such decay? For a number of years the plant seems to serve the corporation well and then, sometimes overnight, becomes a problem child. Why is it that a plant, set up and tooled, staffed, and organized for efficiency and effective competition seems to deteriorate somehow over a period of time?

What happens? It does not seem to be a matter of obsolescent equipment or the running down of physical facilities. It does seem to have something to do with the way in which the facility is managed.

CAUSES OF DECLINE

While there are many ways in which companies get into trouble in manufacturing, they may be grouped into four principal categories:

1. Mismatch of manufacturing structure and manufacturing task.
2. Multi-product, do-all general purpose plant.
3. Simplistic performance evaluation.
4. Inconsistent elements in the manufacturing structure.

Mismatch of structure and task

Manufacturing structure—like the structure of a building—consists of features that frame its operation. Manufacturing is structured by the following decisions:

- Location of a plant.
- Size of a plant.
- Equipment and processes.
- Manufacturing organization.
- The key central approaches to production control, quality control, and inventory management.
- The key central approaches to the management of the work force, including the basic approach to job design and job content, wage system, and the amount and kind of supervision.

The *manufacturing task* may be defined as the unique manufacturing competence demanded by the combination of the firm's corporate strategy, its marketing policies, and any constraints imposed by the technology and financial resources.

The manufacturing task is clearly defined at the start-up. Usually, it consists of making particular products with specific technology and marketing requirements. The plant equipment, policies and procedures are designed to meet this particular set of demands.

When the plant began production, the management, plant policies, and personnel were apt to be inexperienced relative to the operation. Bugs had to be worked out. Production control and work force management approaches were developed and improved to help the operation to perform its mission. Gradually the whole operation worked out its problems and became proficient.

Evolutionary Development

However difficult the start-up, given sufficient time, any reasonably diligent group of people develops experience and competence in performing the task. They work through many problems and crises and tend to get better at what they are doing. They have had team experiences which they share and discuss. Their ability to perform improves. Such experience breeds a high degree of competence over time. The subtle and intuitive reasoning that goes on, anticipating problems, predicting previously unexpected variations in the product, the market, the technology, and in operating the equipment and processes, dealing with particular workers—all of these subtle, basic elements become built into the total competence of a manufacturing management group over a period of time.

As these people become more experienced through successfully solving countless problems, they learn to anticipate and meet their problems with an even higher degree of intuitive intelligence. They tend to develop their own sense of what is "good manufacturing practice" in their business. They develop a body of "conventional wisdom" as to what works and what does not work. They say to themselves and to outsiders, "In our company we have developed an effective philosophy of manufacturing. We know the kinds of problems and difficulties that you can easily get into in this business and we have grown to be good at avoiding them."

What happens next in many instances is that the manufacturing task subtly changes. Market conditions change, and to be successful, a company may have to compete in quite different ways than in the past. It may be that the emphasis in the past had to be on quality and on-time delivery. Now as the market changes, the emphasis may have to be on lower costs or getting new products into production quickly. The corporation's position in the industry may have changed from being a number one to a number two, or the company has become an innovator instead of a high volume, low-cost producer. Or there may be changes in the technology which require new pieces of equipment, or considerable changes in the product design. Or finally, perhaps there have been considerable changes in the volume levels of production and a gradual shifting in the product mix.

How are these changes perceived by a strong, experienced, competent manufacturing team? Unfortunately, but not surprisingly, these changes are not always seen or their significance fully perceived. After all, such changes seldom take place dramatically. They take place gradually over a period of time. After a year or two, the task at which the plant must now excel may no longer be what it was. Most management groups naturally tend to continue to apply the successful "philosophy" and practices of manufacturing they have learned and proven over the past. The structure of the manufacturing operation tends to continue, with a kind of momentum of comfortable and satisfying familiarity with only relatively minor variations.

Limited Flexibility

To accomplish a new task would require changes in the manufacturing structure. But the elements of this are difficult, expensive, and time consuming to change. Once established, a given manufacturing structure limits the ability of a manufacturing system to be competent in other than a limited task pertaining to a limited product mix. A machine tool plant highly capable of turning out large volumes of standard milling machines at a relatively low cost would be incompetent to produce a wide variety and limited quantity each of centerless grinding machines unless its structure were rebuilt.

A manufacturing structure not only limits the degree of product flexibility of a plant but also limits its flexibility to handle major changes in volume. A plant of a certain size and setup, with a certain type of equipment, may be economic at its planned operating level but quite uneconomic and inefficient at a 30% lower level of output. A given production team and its facility may be highly competent at producing a limited product mix but entirely incompetent to produce much shorter runs of a more complex product mix due to the problems of setups and changeovers on its equipment. Further, a given plant and its structure may be capable at producing with a two-month lead time, but if the market changes to allow only six weeks lead time, considerable changes in equipment and process technology as well as production control and inventory policies may be necessary. Finally, a given work force with certain skills, habits, attitudes, and concepts of what is "quality production" may be unable to change its mentality quickly and produce economically and efficiently at much different quality levels, either higher of lower.

The most important element of manufacturing structure is its equipment and process technology. The element of structure is usually the most difficult and the most expensive and requires the most time to change. Hence the importance of having "the right" equipment and process technology and hence, too, the difficulty of keeping the "right" equipment and process technology as products, markets, technology, and corporate strategy change.

Multi-Product, Do-All General Purpose Plant

A second typical process by which companies grow weak in manufacturing is the tendency to keep on adding additional products into one existing plant. The adding of products often makes it necessary to handle new technologies. It simultaneously adds a necessity for dealing with new and different market requirements.

In product A the emphasis may have to be on quality, in product B it may be on very short deliveries, and in product C it may be on very low costs. All three products are made in the same plant, with the same facilities, the same work force management policies, the same production planning and control policies, the same cost control system, the same accounting system, the same inventory management system, all typically under one manufacturing organization structure. The tendency is for the production control system to be well designed for product B, the wage and work force management system to be well set up for product C, while the equipment and processes are designed for product A. The result of adding products in the same plant is that manufacturing is unable to perform effectively for any single product group.

The consequences are even more serious. The manufacturing personnel must be able to deal with an increasing variety of market requirements, presumably different strategic approaches for success in each product, and a different equipment and process technology as well. Since experience breeds competence, competence is diluted and delayed because of the necessity for spreading a given amount of experience over a wider variety of products.

Substantive Differences

Let me emphasize that I am not considering modest product changes or additions in the product mix, which do not involve products with different strategic or marketing requirements or considerably different equipment and process technologies. My reference is to products with substantially different requirements in terms of strategies, markets, volumes, and technologies.

A good example is a plant where an electronic fuel gauge and an electronic auto pilot were made together. The company was unable to make money on the electronic aircraft fuel gauge and after many years of experimentation and improvement finally decided to go out of the business. At the last moment the plant manager proposed building a wall around the fuel gauge operation. From that time forth no employees worked on both the fuel gauge and the auto pilot products. There was a separate production control system, somewhat separate work force management policies and supervisory approaches, separate cost controls, separate equipment and process technology, a separate layout, a separate inventory and scheduling system. The fuel gauge business became profitable within approximately four months.

When high quality levels, high precision, tight specification products are mixed with those of less stringent requirements, the effects on both products are usually adverse. The high quality product is usually made with less quality than it needs and the low quality product is usually made more expensively. In the fuel gauge example the auto pilot gyroscope parts were nearly always carried around in special lined and padded boxes and the tendency was for the fuel gauge parts to be handled in the same way, adding totally unnecessary costs.

The mixing of quality levels within one plant is much more easily understood than other more subtle combinations which are forced together by adding to the product mix. For example, a production control system may be excellent for products that require short delivery time but would be inadequate for products in which market the company had a low profit but needed a good return on investment and therefore was required to keep inventories at an absolute minimum. In each of these two product sets the successful "name of the game" would be quite different.

White Elephants

Why do companies tend to continue to add a more complex mixture of products into an existing plant? What typically happens is that the plant is designed for a limited range of products. Over a period of years some of those products approach the end of their normal life cycle and other products take their place. A trend in many industries is to offer more specialized products in an effort to compete, resulting in shorter runs and a more complex product mix. Hence, as these products are added to an existing plant, the result is to force the plant management to attempt to mix a variety of technology and market requirements.

This problem is difficult to prevent. When a plant has built a trained labor force and a proven set of processes and equipment, there are strong economic reasons for using these facilities and not shutting them down simply because the products for which they were set up are no longer selling well. Nevertheless, there are better ways of handling these kinds of problems than simply lumping more products into the same factory which will eventually turn that factory into a "white elephant."

Over the last several years I have had a number of opportunities to study plants that had become white elephants. In most cases the plant was unusually big and complex and handled an enormous variety of products. The products had been added into an existing mix one by one. In most cases costs were high. Delivery performance was low. Inventories were large, lead times were long. In total, the plant was satisfying no one market or executive either in production or in the various product or sales groups handling the mixture of products.

Most companies attempt to overcome these problems by adding people and staff groups. Clearly, it takes more planning, more control and more people to try to handle a wide, rich variety of products in one plant. It takes more effort in terms of inventory control, more personnel, labor specialists, more accountants and cost controllers and a great deal more paperwork of all sorts to manage the large and complex multi-product, multi-market plant.

The temptation seldom denied is to add on to the existing facility and assign the new product to the existing organization. The theory is that by adding the additional volume onto the same plant structure the net result will be "savings in overheads."

The fact that this is seldom true may at first seem paradoxical. What happens is that the increasing complexity ultimately requires overhead out of proportion to the additional volume, making the overhead and cost control problem even worse. As the organization deals with more products and technologies, it becomes more complex in its purposes and faces more varied marketing and competitive pressures. The usual response is to try to surround the problem with more staff; more expeditors; more analysts; more people to plan, schedule, and control. The net result is additional confusion which compounds the situation. In contrast, as a general rule, plants that have the best competitive market performance nearly always have a restricted and manageable scope of products, equipment, technologies, and marketing tasks.

A final reason for the general tendency to keep adding new products is the pressure to minimize capital expenditures for buildings and equipment. But, it is often a false economy and a misguided philosophy to attempt to minimize capital expenditures while forcing manufacturing management to attempt to load more products with conflicting strategic and technical requirements into one plant. The frequent result of frugality in investment policy is an effort to make one plant and its equipment and process technology serve too many masters.

Simplistic Performance Evaluation

A third major cause of companies getting into trouble in manufacturing is the tendency for many managements to accept simplistic notions in evaluating the performance of their manufacturing facilities. By this I am referring to the general tendency in most companies to evaluate manufacturing primarily on the basis of cost and efficiency. There are many more criteria by which to judge performance than cost and efficiency. For example:

- Quality.
- Customer lead times.
- Reliability of promise dates given.
- Return on investment.
- Flexibility to introduce new products.
- Flexibility to handle substantial volume changes.
- Appropriate social criteria.

Companies get into trouble because of simplistic concepts for measuring performance by attempting to focus results on maintaining or improving cost and efficiency when other criteria are in fact more critical. In accepting the usual norms of achieving maximum productivity, management effort is typically focused first on minimizing direct labor costs and, second, other costs. Sometimes, however, it may be much more important for a company to spend a few cents more on a product and improve its quality. Or it may be important to run a product in a smaller lot size, which might increase its cost, but could improve its flexibility for meeting customer demands. Similarly, if the emphasis is on low cost, very high investment in inventories may be required in order to result in maximum machine utilization and minimum direct labor through longer runs. Thus other potential critical performance criteria suffer, usually inadvertently, when cost and efficiency are given top attention.

Simplistic criteria cause further problems when a set of criteria which has been valid for judging plant performance for several years becomes invalid under new conditions of technology, market, or corporate strategy. Executives of companies that appear to make these kinds of mistakes usually do not appear to understand the inexorable trade-offs that take place in choosing one criterion over another. It is seldom possible to maximize the plant's performance in accomplishing more than one or two of these criteria at the same time. Something else must give.

Inconsistent Elements

A fourth common cause of companies slipping into trouble in manufacturing is the frequent gradual growth of incongruent infrastructures within the plant. I use the word *incongruent* to indicate that the focus and objective of each of the elements of infrastructure should be directed toward the same goal. If they are not, they are incongruent.

Let me illustrate an incongruent infrastructure with an example:

A large machinery and equipment manufacturer, Company C, found its sales of new machines dropping steadily while its sales of spare parts and replacement items gradually climbed. An analysis of C's basic elements of manufacturing policy indicated that the work force management policies and production, planning and control systems were designed for the requirements of the original equipment business. In the original equipment business quality and reliable delivery promises were particularly important, much more so than cost. The company seldom had any complaints over the performance of equipment, and it had not missed a delivery date of a new machine for over 10 years.

The replacement parts business, however, was entirely different. In the spare parts business the element of handling an extremely complex mix of parts with very short lead time became vital for corporate success because the company's service reputation was dependent upon its keeping old machines in the industry running. When a machine broke down, early delivery of that replacement part was absolutely critical. In addition, handling an ever-increasing complexity of parts over the years became a major cost problem as machine models proliferated and more and more part numbers were active. Yet the production control system was set up to handle long runs of original new products rather than a fierce variety of short runs of special replacement parts.

Similar conflicts on internal systems occurred throughout the plant. The cost control system was not adequate for controlling costs of the large number of short run replacement parts. The production control system proved inadequate for handling the large numbers of short runs. The work force management approach featured incentive wages that rewarded the workers with long runs of parts of the new pieces of equipment and penalized those who were making short runs of replacement parts. In fact, quite different skills were needed, and an examination of the equipment and process technology indicated that the machines that were capable of general purpose work on short runs were needed in higher proportion relative to the special purpose, long run machine tools that had been used when the business was primarily one of producing original equipment. Thus the wage system, the recruiting approaches, and the allocation of job content to different workers were quite different for the two forms of business, and resulting head-on confrontations hurt performance on both ends of the business.

These incongruencies in internal manufacturing policy are not unusual. They are caused by the addition of products into a given plant and simplistic criteria for judging performance.

MANUFACTURING AUDIT

Companies need a regular audit of manufacturing policies, manufacturing tasks, and manufacturing structure. It is seldom realized that when there is a change in a company's strategy or technology, the company's manufacturing setup also needs an entirely different approach. These external changes are occurring ever more rapidly. Product life cycles are shorter; we are being bombarded with more and more technology changes; there are more choices of new tools and equipment and processes and products than ever before; competition seems to move on and off the scene with ever more determination. All of this means that manufacturing policies and manufacturing structures must be examined much more frequently.

A manufacturing audit can follow the form of asking and carefully answering, usually on paper, questions from the president to the manufacturing vice president *and* vice versa.

Questions the president should regularly be asking the manufacturing vice president:

1. What is your understanding of our manufacturing task?
2. What is *our* manufacturing setup especially *good* at?
3. How is manufacturing a competitive weapon for our company?
4. How often do we reexamine our manufacturing task?
5. What positions have we taken on key trade-offs in structuring our manufacturing?
6. What criteria do you use to evaluate manufacturing performance?
7. What alternate equipment and process technology (EPT) are available?
8. How does our EPT serve our manufacturing task?
9. Our work force policies?
10. Our production control policies?
11. Our control procedures?
12. Your use of your time?
13. Are you "boxed in" by our present manufacturing structures? What do you need? What would it cost? What would it do for us? At what risks?
14. What changes are occurring that may make our manufacturing task and structure obsolete?

Questions the manufacturing vice president should ask the president:

1. What is our competitive strategy?
2. How is (or is not) manufacturing now a competetive weapon?
3. What is your understanding of our manufacturing task?
4. What criteria will manufacturing be evaluated on over the next 12 to 18 months?
5. Do you concur with my general pattern for my use of my time?
6. Do you fully understand the positions we have taken on the various trade-offs in structuring our manufacturing? What are we giving up to gain what?

Wrestling with these kinds of questions on a regular basis can be the beginning of building a new approach toward manufacturing management. This is a top-down manufacturing approach. It originates in a company's strategy and marketing problems. It focuses at the plant manager's level but does not get involved with operational details.

OPERATIONALIZING MANUFACTURING STRATEGY CONCEPTS

The five chapters in this part deal with the "how to" of following the basic ideas of early chapters. Chapter 6 introduces the idea of "focus" for a factory, discusses its many advantages, and offers some ideas for accomplishing focus. Chapter 7 makes the point that managers today cannot afford to be "technology aversive" and suggests some basic, simple, effective ways for any manager to gain a vital managerial understanding of any technology. Chapter 8 is a "nuts-and-bolts" kind of chapter which goes into some depth on the difficult and demanding yet absolutely essential job of clearly and precisely defining the manufacturing task. Chapter 9 offers two checklists for analyzing and subsequently synthesizing changes in the various elements of the production system. Chapter 10, "The Accomplishing Manager," deals with a critical question: Why do some managers accomplish so much more than others?

CHAPTER 6

The
Focused
Factory

M any years of taking our industry health and leadership for granted abruptly ended in the 1970s when our declining position in world markets weakened the dollar and became a national issue.

In the popular press and at the policy level in government the issue has been seen as a "productivity crisis." The National Commission on Productivity was established in 1971. The concern with productivity has appealed to many managers who have firsthand experience with our problems of high costs and low efficiency.

Pessimism pervades the outlook of many managers and analysts of the American manufacturing scene. The recurring theme of this gloomy view is that (a) labor is too expensive, (b) productivity has been growing at a slower rate than that of most of our competitors, and therefore (c) our industries sicken one by one as imports mushroom and unemployment becomes chronic in our industrial population centers.

In this chapter, I offer a more optimistic view of the productivity dilemma, suggesting that we have the opportunity to effect basic changes in the management of manufacturing, which could shift the competitive balance in our favor in many industries. What are these basic changes? I can identify four:

This is an analysis based on my cases written in the electronics, plastics, textile, steel, and industrial equipment industries, supplemented by project research in the furniture industry. Financial support for this work provided by the Harvard Business School Division of Research and course development funds is gratefully acknowledged.

1. Seeing the problem not as "How can we increase productivity?" but as "How can we compete?"
2. Seeing the problem as encompassing the efficiency of the *entire* manufacturing organization, not only the efficiency of the direct labor and the work force. (In most plants, direct labor and the work force represent only a small percentage of total costs.)
3. Learning to focus each plant on a limited, concise, manageable set of products, technologies, volumes, and markets.
4. Learning to structure basic manufacturing policies and supporting services so that they focus on one explicit manufacturing task instead of on many inconsistent, conflicting, implicit tasks.

A factory that focuses on a narrow product mix for a particular market niche will outperform the conventional plant, which attempts a broader mission. Because its equipment, supporting systems, and procedures can concentrate on a limited task for one set of customers, its costs and especially its overheads are likely to be lower than those of the conventional plant. But, more important, such a plant can become a competitive weapon because its entire apparatus is focused to accomplish the particular manufacturing task demanded by the company's overall strategy and marketing objective.

My research indicates that in spite of their advantages, focused manufacturing plants are surprisingly rare. Instead, the conventional factory produces many products for numerous customers in a variety of markets, thereby demanding the performance of a multiplicity of manufacturing tasks all at once from one set of assets and people. Its rationale is "economy of scale" and lower capital investment.

However, the result more often than not is a hodgepodge of compromises, a high overhead, and a manufacturing organization that is constantly in hot water with top management, marketing management, the controller, and customers.

My purpose in this chapter is to set forth the advantages of focused manufacturing. I begin with the characteristics of the focused factory, then follow with an analysis of the productivity phenomenon which tends to prevent the adoption of the focused plant concept. Finally, I offer some specific steps for managing manufacturing to accomplish and take advantage of focus.

BASIC CHARACTERISTICS

Focused manufacturing is based on the concept that simplicity, repetition, experience, and homogeneity of tasks breed competence. Furthermore, each key functional area in manufacturing must have the same objective, derived from corporate strategy. Such congruence of tasks can produce a manufacturing system that does limited things very well. Within the factory, managers can make the manufacturing function a competitive weapon by outstanding accomplishment of one or more of the yardsticks of manufacturing performance. But managers need to know: "What must we be especially good at? Cost, quality, lead times, reliability, changing schedules, new-product introduction, or low investment?"

Focused manufacturing must be derived from an explicitly defined corporate strategy that has its roots in a corporate marketing plan. Therefore, the choice of focus cannot be made independently by production people. It has to be a result of a comprehensive analysis of the company's resources, strengths and weaknesses, position in the industry, assessment of competitors' moves, and forecast of future customer motives and behavior.

Conversely, the choice of focus cannot be made without considering the existing factory, because a given set of facilities, systems, and people skills can do only certain things well within a given time period.

Five key characteristics of the focused factory are:

1. *Process technologies.* Typically, unproven and uncertain technologies are limited to one per factory. Proven, mature technologies are limited to what their managers can easily handle, typically two or three (e.g., a foundry, metal working, and metal finishing).

2. *Market demands.* These consist of a set of demands including quality, price, lead times, and reliability specifications. A given plant can usually only do a superb job on one or two demands at any given period of time.

3. *Product volumes.* Generally, these are of comparable levels, such that tooling, order quantities, materials handling techniques, and job contents can be approached with a consistent philosophy. But what about the inevitable short runs, customer specials, and one-of-a-kind orders that every factory must handle? The answer is usually to segregate them, which I discuss later.

4. *Quality levels.* These employ a common attitude and set of approaches so as to neither overspecify nor overcontrol quality and specifications. One frame of mind and set of mental assumptions suffice for equipment, tooling, inspection, training, supervision, job content, materials handling.

5. *Manufacturing tasks.* These are limited to only one (or two at the most) at any given time. The task at which the plant must excel in order to be competitive focuses on one set of internally consistent, doable, noncompromised criteria for success.

My research evidence makes it clear that the focused factory will outproduce, undersell, and quickly gain competitive advantage over the complex factory. The focused factory does a better job because repetition and concentration in one area allow its work force and managers to become effective and experienced in the task required for success. The focused factory is manageable and controllable. Its problems are demanding, but limited in scope.

PRODUCTIVITY PHENOMENON

The conventional wisdom of manufacturing management continues to be that the measure of success is productivity. Now that American companies in many industries are getting beaten hands down by overseas competitors with lower unit costs, we mistakenly cling to the old notion that "a good plant is a low-cost plant." This is simply not so. A low-cost plant may be a disaster if the company has sacrificed too much in the way of quality, delivery, flexibility, and so forth, to get its costs down.

Too many companies attempt to do too many things with one plant and one organization. In the name of low investment in facilities and spreading tneir overheads, they add products, markets, technologies, processes, quality levels, and supporting services that conflict and compete with each other and compound expense. They then hire more staff to regulate and control the unmanageable mixture of problems. In desperation, many companies are now "banging away" at anything to reduce the resulting high costs. But we can only regain competitive strength by stopping this process of increasing complexity and overstaffing.

This behavior is so illogical that the phenomenon needs further explanation. Our plants are generally managed by extremely able people; yet the failure to focus manufacturing on a limited objective is a common managerial blind spot. What happens to produce this defect in competent managers? Engineers know what can and cannot be designed into planes, boats, and building structures. Engineers accept design objectives that will accomplish a specific set of tasks that are possible, although difficult.

In contrast, most of the manufacturing plants in my study attempted a complex, heterogeneous mixture of general and special-purpose equipment, long- and short-run operations, high and low tolerances, new and old products, off-the-shelf items and customer specials, stable and changing designs, markets with reliable forecasts and unpredictable ones, seasonal and nonseasonal sales, short and long lead times, and high and low skills.

Lack of Consistent Policies

That each of the contrasting features generally demands conflicting manufacturing tasks and hence different manufacturing policies is not understood. The particular mix of these features should determine the elements of manufacturing policy.

Instead of designing elements of manufacturing policy around one manufacturing task, what usually happens? Consider, for example, that the wage system may be set up to emphasize high productivity, production control to maximize short lead times, inventory to minimize stock levels, order quantities to minimize setup times, plant layout to minimize materials handling costs, and process design to maximize quality.

While each of these decisions probably looks sensible to professional specialists in their fields, the conventional factory consists of six or more inconsistent elements of manufacturing structure, each of which is designed to achieve a different implicit objective. Such inconsistency usually results in high costs. One or another element may be excessively staffed or operated inefficiently because its task is being exaggerated or misdirected. Or several functions may require excess staff in order to control or manage a plant that is unduly complex.

But often the result is even more serious. My study shows that the chief negative effect is not on productivity but on ability to compete. The plant's manufacturing policies are not designed, tuned, and focused as a whole on that one key strategic manufacturing task essential to the company's success in its industry.

Reasons for Inconsistency

Noncongruent manufacturing structures appear to be common in industry. In fact, my research reveals that a fully consistent set of manufacturing policies resulting in a congruent system is rare. Why does this situation occur so often? In the cases I studied, it seemed to come about essentially for one or more of these reasons:

- Professionals in each field attempted to achieve goals that, although valid and traditional in their fields, were not congruent with goals of other areas.
- The manufacturing task for the plant subtly changed while most operating and service departments kept on the same course as before.
- The manufacturing task was never made explicit.
- The inconsistencies were never recognized.
- More and more products were piled into existing plants, resulting in an often futile attempt to meet the manufacturing tasks of a variety of markets, technologies, and competitive strategies.

Let me elaborate on the first and last set of causes we have just noted.

'Professionalism' in the Plant

Production system elements are not set up or managed by professionals in their respective fields, such as quality control, personnel, labor relations, engineering, inventory management, materials handling, systems design, and so forth.

These professionals, quite naturally, seek to maximize their contributions and justify their positions. They have conventional views of success in each of their particular fields. Of course, these objectives are generally in conflict. I say "of course" not to be cynical. These fields of specialty have come into existence for many different reasons—some to reduce costs, others to save time, others to minimize capital investments, still others to promote human cooperation and happiness, and so on. So it is perfectly normal for them to pull in different directions, which is exactly what happens in many plants. This problem is not totally new. But it is changing because professionalism is increasing; we have more and more experts at work in different parts of the factory. So it is a growing problem.

Product Proliferation

The combination of increasing foreign and domestic competition plus an accelerating rate of technological innovation has resulted in product proliferation in many factories. Shorter product life, more new products, shorter runs, lower unit volumes, and more customer specials are becoming increasingly common. The same factory that five years ago produced 25 products may today be producing 50 to 100.

The inconsistent production system grows up, not simply because there are more products to make—which is of course likely to increase direct and indirect costs and add complexity and confusion—but also because new products often call for different manufacturing tasks. To succeed in some tasks may require superb technological competence and focus; others may demand extremely short delivery; and still others, extremely low costs. Yet, almost always, new products are added into the existing mix in the same plant, even though some new equipment may be necessary. The rationale for this decision is usually that the plant is operating at less than full capacity. Thus the logic is, "If we put the new products into the present plant, we can save capital investment and avoid duplicating overheads."

The result is complexity, confusion, and worst of all a production organization which, because it is spun out in all directions by a kind of centrifugal force, lacks focus and a doable manufacturing task. The factory is asked to perform a mission for product A which conflicts with that of product B. Thus the result is a hodgepodge of compromises.

When we may have, in fact, four tasks and four markets, we make the mistake of trying to force them into one plant, one set of equipment, one factory organization, one set of manufacturing policies, and so on. We try to cram into one operating system the ability to compete in an impossible mix of demands. Each element of the system attempts to adjust to these demands with variation, special sections, complex procedures, more people, and added paperwork. This syndrome, starting with added market demands and ending with incongruent internal structures, to a large extent accounts for the human frustrations, high costs, and low competitive abilities we see so much of in industry today.

Who gets the blame? Manufacturing executives, of course, get it from corporate headquarters for high costs, poor productivity, low quality and reliability, and missed deliveries. In turn they tend to blame the situation on anything that makes sense, such as poor market forecasts, subpar labor, unconcern over quality, inept engineering designs, faulty equipment, and so forth.

Experience accomplishes wonders, but a diffused organization with conflicting structural elements and competing manufacturing tasks accumulates experience and specialized competence very slowly.

TOWARD MANUFACTURING FOCUS

A new management approach is needed in industries where diverse products and markets require companies to manufacture a broad mix of items, volumes, specifications, and customer demand patterns. Its emphasis must be on building competitive strength. One way to compete is to focus the entire manufacturing system on a limited task precisely defined by the company's competitive strategy and the realities of its technology and economics. A common objective produces synergistic effects rather than internal power struggles between professionalized departments. This approach can be assisted by these guiding rules:

- Centralize the factory's focus on relative competitive ability.
- Avoid the common tendency to add staff and overhead in order to save on direct labor and capital investment.
- Let each manufacturing unit work on a limited task instead of the usual complex mix of conflicting objectives, products, and technologies.

In my experience, manufacturing managers are generally astounded at the internal inconsistencies and compromises they discover once they put the concept of focused manufacturing to work in analyzing their own plants.

Then, when they begin to discern what the company strategy and market situation are implicitly demanding and to compare these implicit demands with what they have been trying to achieve, many submerged conflicts surface. Finally, when they ask themselves what a certain element of the structure or of the manufacturing policy was designed to maximize, the built-in cross-purposes become apparent.

At the risk of seeming to take a cookbook approach to an inevitably complex set of issues, let me offer a four-step recipe for the focused factory based on an actual but disguised example of an industrial manufacturing company, a producer of mechanical equipment, which attempted to adapt its operations to this concept.

1. *Develop an explicit, brief statement of corporate objectives and strategy.* The statement should cover the next three to five years, and it should have the substantial involvement of top management, including marketing, finance, and control executives.

In its statement, the top management of the company agreed to the following:

Our corporate objective is directed toward increasing market share during the next five years via a strategy of (1) tailoring our product to individual customer needs, (2) offering advanced and special product features at a modest price increment, and (3) gaining competitive advantage via rapid product development and service orientation to customers of all sizes.

2. *Translate the objectives-and-strategy statement into what this means to manufacturing.* What must the factory do especially well in order to carry out and support this corporate strategy? What is going to be the most difficult task it will face? If the manufacturing function is not sharp and capable, where is the company most likely to fail? It may fail in any one of the elements of the production structure, but it will probably do so in a combination of some of them.

To carry on with the mechanical equipment company example, such a manufacturing task might be defined explicitly as follows:

Our manufacturing task for the next three years will be to introduce specialized, customer-tailored new products into production, with lead times that are substantially less than those of our competitors. Since the technology in our industry is changing rapidly, and since product reliability can be extremely serious for customers, our most difficult problems will be to control the new-product introduction process, so as to solve technical problems promptly and to maintain reliability amid rapid changes in the product itself.

3. *Make a careful examination of each element of the production system.* How is it now set up, organized, focused, and manned? What is it now especially good at? How must it be changed to implement the key manufacturing task?

4. *Reorganize the elements of structure to produce a congruent focus.* This reorganization focuses on the ability to do those limited things well which are of utmost importance to the accomplishment of the manufacturing task.

To complete the example of the mechanical equipment company, *Exhibit 6.1* lists each major element of the manufacturing system of the company; describes its present focus in terms of that task for which it was implicitly or inadvertently aimed, and lists a new approach designed to bring consistency, focus, and power to its manufacturing arm.

What stands out most in this exhibit is the number of substantial changes in manufacturing policies required to bring the production system into a total consistency. The exhibit also features the implicit conflicts between many manufacturing tasks in the present approach, which are the result of the failure to define one task for the whole plant.

The reader may perceive a disturbing implication of the focused plant concept—it seems to call for major investments in new plants, new equipment, and new tooling, in order to break down the present complexity. For example, if the company is currently involved in five different products, technologies, markets, or volumes, does it need five plants, five sets of equipment, five processes, five technologies, and five organizational structures? The answer is probably *yes*. But the practical solution need not involve selling the big multipurpose facility and decentralizing into five small facilities. In fact, the few companies that have adopted the focused plant concept have approached the solution quite differently. There is no need to build five plants, which would involve unnecessary investment and overhead expenses.

The more practical approach is the "plant within a plant" (PWP) notion in which the existing facility is divided both organizationally and physically into, in this case, five PWPs. Each PWP has its own facilities in which it can concentrate on its particular manufacturing task, using its own workforce management approaches, production control, organization structure, and so forth. Quality and volume levels are not mixed; worker training and incentives have a clear focus; and engineering of processes, equipment, and materials handling are specialized as needed.

Each PWP gains experience readily by focusing and concentrating every element of its work on those limited essential objectives which constitute its

Exhibit 6.1 Conflicting Manufacturing Tasks Implied by Incongruent Elements of the Present Production System

Production System Elements	Present Approach (conventional factory)	Implicit Manufacturing Tasks of Present Approach	Changed Approach (focused factory)
Equipment and process policies	One large plant; special purpose equipment; high-volume tooling; balanced capacity with functional layout.	Low manufacturing costs on steady runs of a few large products with minimal investment.	Separate old, standardized products and new customized products into two plants within a plant (PWP). For each new PWP, provide general purpose equipment, temporary tooling, and modest excess capacity with product-oriented layout.
Work force management policies	Specialized jobs with narrow job content; incentive wages; few supervisors; focus on volume of production per hour.	Low costs and efficiency.	Create fewer jobs with more versatility. Pay for breadth of skills and ability to perform a variety of jobs. Provide more foremen for solving technical problems at workplace.

Production scheduling and control	Detailed, frequent sales forecasts; produce for inventory economic lot sizes of finished goods; small, decentralized production scheduling group.	Short delivery lead times.	Produce to order special parts and stock of common parts based on semi-annual forecast. Staff production control to closely schedule and centralize parts movements.
Quality control	Control engineers and large inspection groups in each department.	Extremely reliable quality.	No change.
Organizational structure	Functional; production control under superintendents of each area; inspection reports to top.	Top performance of the objectives of each functional department (i.e., many tasks).	Organize each PWP by program and project in order to focus organizational effort on bringing new products into production smoothly and on time.

manufacturing task. Since a manufacturing task is an offspring of a corporate strategy and marketing program, it is susceptible to either gradual or sweeping change. The PWP approach makes it easier to perform realignment of essential operations and system elements over time as the task changes.

CONCLUSION

While the economy has moved toward an era of more advanced technologies and shorter product lives, we have not readjusted our concepts of production to keep up with these changes. Instead, with the mistaken rationale that the keys to success are limited investment, economies of scale, and full utilization of existing plant resources to achieve low costs, we keep adding new products to plants that were once focused, manageable, and competitive.

Reversing the process, however, is not impossible. In most of the cases I have studied, capital investment in facilities is not difficult to justify when payoffs that will result from organizational simplicity are taken into account. Resources for simplifying the focus of a manufacturing complex are not hard to acquire when the expected payoff is the ability to compete successfully, using manufacturing as a competitive weapon. Moreover, better customer service and competitive position typically support higher margins to cover capital investments. And when studied carefully, the economies of scale and the effects of less than full utilization of plant equipment are seldom found to be as critical to productivity and efficiency as classical economic approaches often predict.

The problem of productivity in the United States is real indeed. But seeing the problem as one of "how to compete" can broaden management's horizon. The focused factory approach offers the opportunity to stop compromising each element of the production system in the typical general-purpose, do-all plant which satisfies no strategy, no market, and no task.

Not only does focus provide punch and power; it also provides clear goals that can be readily understood and assimilated by members of an organization. It provides, too, a mechanism for reappraising what is needed for success, and for readjusting and shaking up old, tired manufacturing organizations with welcome change and a clear sense of direction.

In many sectors of American industry such change and such a new sense of direction are needed to shift the competitive balance in our favor.

CHAPTER 7

Technology
and
the
Manager

A persistent pattern seen in the autopsies of the major operating crises of large corporations and of the final failures of many small companies is the inability of one or more key managers to understand and to manage the technological component of their businesses. Analysis of the careers of executives who topped off their advancement in lower positions than their education and basic abilities should have allowed often reveals a similar pattern: lack of knowledge, skills, or personal confidence in their competence to deal with and manage the technology of their firms.

In an age that is dominated in so many ways by technology[1] and technological change, these patterns are perhaps to be expected: Technology is moving fast and its demands on managers are substantial and growing. But if this is true, why are so many managers either negative, reluctant, or simply untrained in their attitudes regarding the very technologies on which their businesses are based? And why do so many managers seem willing to work toward acquiring basic skills and techniques in finance, marketing, control, human relations, and even the sciences of probability and statistics while openly expressing their lack of interest or confidence in attacking and building strength in the technology relevant to their work?

---

[1] In this chapter *technology* is used to denote the set of physical processes, methods, techniques, tools, and equipment by which products are made or services rendered.

The importance of technology to corporations is evident. Corporations producing products or services must make decisions on their technology when they design products; plan services; choose equipment and processes; and devise operating facilities, distribution, and information systems. Because these decisions involve large commitments of funds and, often more important, large blocks of irreplaceable time, they are some of the most vital and critical decisions a top management makes. Once made, their reversal or even a major shift is apt to be difficult or even impossible. Unwise decisions on technological issues are frequently fatal in small business.

In many industries product and process technologies are changing so fast that technological forecasting is a key skill. Entire industries are vulnerable to almost overnight technological revolution. And for American industry as a whole, forced to compete against low foreign labor costs with strategies frequently based on product superiority and constant new product and process development, it appears that management of operations, manufacturing, and engineering—and hence, technology—is growing more critical.

Again, we must ask: If the importance of technology to the manager is so obvious and so clearly increasing as the rate of technological change continues to accelerate, why do so many corporations and most graduate schools of business administration allow managers' growth in competence in understanding and managing technology either to be a semi-accidental by-product or else not to happen?

Undoubtedly there are many reasons that contribute to individual and institutional aversion to technology. Without attempting to indicate an order of importance, there seem to be at least five factors or influences in this direction.

1. It is generally assumed that technological decisions can best be delegated to technical experts, such as engineers. "That is, after all, what they are paid for."
2. It is generally believed that many years of training are required to become competent in a technology.
3. It is generally believed that only engineers and scientists can cope with technologically based decisions.
4. Most managers who are neither engineers nor scientists feel personally inadequate or unconfident in matters of technology: They naturally fear making themselves look stupid or foolish before men "who know"; they stay away from things they know they don't understand; they defer to "experts"; they don't try to educate themselves in the technology

because others are too far ahead to catch up with; or "it would take too much of my time to keep up."

5. Conventional wisdom about managing worships the delegator, the man who never gets caught up in details. Executives of this type who are progressing normally are understandably reluctant to engage in learning and coping with technology that could become a bottomless pit, in which one could lose one's sense of perspective.

While these reasons for a tendency to be averse to technology are entirely understandable and human, technology-aversive behavior results in the kinds of serious business problems and risks of personal obsolescence referred to earlier. Such behavior unfortunately compounds itself as lack of knowledge creates lack of confidence.

The worst outcome of this syndrome is that technology-aversive managers are unable accurately to conceptualize technology-dependent issues because the process of concept formation requires some reasonably precise physical analogies that are simply not available to those who have not studied their technology. Such inaccurate conceptualization is all too likely to lead to the personal failures, deaths of small companies, and major corporate disasters that sometimes ensue.

Technology-averse managers face a dilemma: In these times most executives must be increasingly competent, confident, or involved with technology. They cannot escape it. They can seldom delegate choice of technology decisions to lower levels or to technical specialists because such decisions are so all-pervasive in their effects on product, markets, finance, ability to compete, and corporate strategy that people below the level of top management simply do not have the breadth of facts and skills necessary for wise decisions.

Individual executives who are technology aversive are dangerous to themselves and to their employers. As small company owners they could be tagged as suicide prone without much exaggeration. Yet competence in understanding and handling technology appears difficult to acquire, risking exposure of ones perspective to the bottomless pit of seductive specific knowledge. What to do?

The thesis of this chapter is that industrious managers can learn to understand and to deal effectively with the technology of their industry and that this process is by no means difficult, endless or distracting when approached from a managerial viewpoint. Experience shows that essential skills can in fact be readily developed. What is usually sufficient is a framework consisting of a few basic concepts and a set of questions that lead to the acquisition of that knowledge and those insights needed by a manager.

The balance of this chapter is devoted to the development of such a framework which a manager might use as a start in understanding and dealing with the equipment process and technology in his or her industry. For most managers, the best approach is to use such a framework only as a takeoff point for developing their own.

MANAGERIAL APPROACH

How can a manager master a technology to which engineers and scientists devote their professional lives? The answer is that a manager's mastery consists of certain basic understandings that are far less detailed and are different from those required by engineers and scientists. Managers need to know the answers to certain limited questions about a given set of equipment or a process technology. These questions can be identified and placed in a useful conceptual framework. It is widely understood and accepted that a manager needs some basic economics, basic mathematics, and basic psychology. A parallel need is for basic technology.

The manager needs to acquire and use three concepts or ideas or understandings about equipment and process technology.

1. *The pervasive influence of a technology.*   Because a given equipment and process technology (EPT) creates demands and requirements on all other elements of an operating system, all parts of the system must be designed and managed so as to be congruent and compatible with the chosen EPT. The choice of EPT is, therefore, the primary determinant of every operating system.

2. *A manager's understanding of technology.*   For the purpose of management decision making, any EPT can be described in terms of four basic parameters: (*a*) What it costs. (*b*) What it will do. (*c*) What it requires. (*d*) The degree of certainty of the above information.

3. *Technology, Economics, and Operations Management.*   A given EPT largely determines the economics and limitations of an operating system, which in combination with the competetitive strategy of the firm, determine the few particularly difficult factors or problems that are keys to success or failure of the operating system.

These three ideas may form the basis for an effective managerial understanding of equipment and process technology. Let's look at each of these three ideas in further detail.

Pervasive Influence

Most products can be manufactured in more than one way. Choices generally exist in the selection of the equipment and the process. One alternative or set of alternatives must be chosen from a variety of possibilities.

An ordinary flashlight casing, for example, may be machined out of a metal bar, formed from sheet metal and soldered to form a tube, deep drawn on a press using a die, die cast with a light metal and a mold, poured into a mold in a foundry and subsequently machined, cut out from brass, steel, aluminum or copper tubing, blow-molded in polyethylene, or injection-molded in a variety of plastic materials. It is plain to see that a company in the flashlight business has many choices and that, once chosen, the EPT has a massive influence on the entire manufacturing system. The most obvious difference, of course, is in the production equipment itself, but that is only the beginning. Compare a deep drawing EPT with injection molding EPT: Both use a form of metal dies but there are few other similarities, as Exhibit 7.1 shows.

This comparison of EPTs suggests how different would be the skills, the management systems, and the problems involved in a metal flashlight casing operation as compared to a plastic based one.

Two features are particularly striking. The first is that the scheduling and inventory system is vastly more complex in the metalworking plant where several operations must be performed on the same part. Paperwork must be provided to take care of moves from machine to machine and capacity must be planned and scheduled. In plastics—one operation.

The second major contrast is in the whole area of the work force, skills training, and supervision. The lighter, cleaner, more automated work in the plastics plant will allow for a lower skilled, male or female, lower wage rate job structure, with key technical and personnel administration skills lodged in a relatively few more highly paid employees.

At this point it may be clear how a given EPT choice spreads its effects from the workplace to the entire operating system and, finally, to the ability of the system to perform in a competitive environment. The necessity for all parts of the system—the system infrastructure—to be congruent and mutually consistent follows.

While this sounds obvious and indeed elementary, in actual practice perfect internal consistency is difficult to achieve. There are many ambiguities and real administrative difficulties in achieving a total operating infrastructure that is wholly consistent with the EPT employed. Two examples may illustrate the problem.

Exhibit 7.1   Equipment and Process Technology (EPT) for Metal Drawing and Plastic Molding

	Metal Drawing	Plastic Molding
Equipment	Massive press	Press size depends on capacity
Raw materials	Metal sheets	Many plastics
Tools	Die set—male or female	Split halves
Building	Heavy foundations to handle weight and impact	Ordinary floor
Engineering manufacturing	Mechanical, metal expertise	Plastics, hydraulics expertise
Maintenance	Mechanical	Mechanical, hydraulic
Operator	Heavier work, higher skill	Lighter work, relatively lower skill
Supervisory skills	Managing male work force	Mixed work force and machine troubleshooting
Inventory	Sheet metal and in-process	Plastic powder and parts
Operations	May require several plus finishing	One
Scheduling	Potentially complex	Simple
Safety	Dangerous	Safer
Quality/precision	Depends on die and machine physical setup	Depends on die and machine timing and cycle
Costs	Depends especially on die condition and setup	Depends especially on short cycle and changeovers
Flexibility		
Product change	Die change necessary	Die change necessary
Volume change	Add dies, machines, shifts or move to higher speed equipment	Add dies, machines, shifts; cycle limited
Potential for automation	Combine operations with transfer gear, install part location sensors, etc. Can be largely automatic.	Largely automatic

In the first example, the management of a plant that produced medium-priced pine and birch furniture, decided to change its EPT from individual assembly and finishing of each piece of furniture to conveyorized assembly and finishing.

When the process technology was changed, the wage system based on individual incentives was no longer appropriate because the conveyorized system paced the worker and one stoppage or problem slowed down the entire group. Lower skill levels were required because the individual jobs became narrower in content and more specialized. Demands on the supervisors shifted from scheduling and production record checking to providing supplies, handling technical problems that slowed the line, and quality control.

Thus work force management, cost and quality controls, scheduling and inventory control system requirements changed overnight with the adoption of the conveyor. The production management group had to recognize the need for and carry out all these system changes simultaneously.

In practice this proved difficult—difficult to foresee which old systems would be inappropriate and difficult to make many changes all at once. The net result was that almost two years of less than fully satisfactory operations ensued and the new conveyor was considered something of a failure during that time because each one of the incongruent systems individually made the new operating system less than fully effective.

The second example is of a plant that changed its product mix, but not its EPT. The old product mix consisted of low volumes of many different types of electronic transistors; the new product mix combined higher volumes of fewer transistors with the old product mix. The EPT of general purpose equipment with functional plant layout (equipment located by groups of similar functions—e.g., all grinders in one location) remained the same.

The general purpose equipment and processes were very flexible (i.e., changing from one product to another was quick and easy). But no economies of scale were possible. For example, holes were drilled individually rather than punched en masse with a die, and wires were soldered by hand instead of by a programmed wire wrapper. The result was high costs, long cycle times, long queues at operations that were bottlenecked by large orders, and late deliveries. Not only were separate EPTs called for for low and high volumes, but also different wage systems, supervisory skills, and production and planning systems. But the management was reluctant to tamper with the system because it was uncertain about the content of the future mix of business. It also feared that setting up two separate systems would cause worker discontent and perhaps interfere with deliveries in both kinds of business as well as require a major investment.

Thus far our emphasis has been that EPT is important and its choice is generally critical. Now we need to develop some basic questions that managers might ask to understand an EPT and make a wise choice among alternatives.

Understanding EPT

Consider a simple example of equipment technology, a process for cutting grass, a lawn mower.

A lawn mower could be described to a prospective purchaser as follows: "It costs $128. It has a gasoline engine and cuts a 24-inch wide swath of grass and is well made by a well-known manufacturer."

A technology aversive prospective buyer might say, "I'll take it," only to get home to the eight-inch-high grass that has grown up during his annual vacation and find that

- The cutting technology was based on a reel moving past a cutting bar. It could not handle grass much higher than one-half the reel diameter. It simply pushed forward and down his eight-inch crop.
- It was self-propelled but had no effective free-wheeling device, so that he could not work close to and around his wife's formal flower garden.
- It took 30 minutes to change the cutting height so that he could not leave his hillside grass longer (to cut down on erosion) and cut his garden grass shorter without taking half an hour to adjust it.
- It was not powerful enough to cut wet, thick grass going uphill.
- A reel type will not mulch leaves, desirable in the fall when he hated to rake.
- The mower had a two-cycle engine which meant that he had to mix oil with his gasoline each time he filled the little tank.

In short, he should have purchased an extra powerful, rotary blade, four-cycle, self-propelled mower with easy handling for tight maneuvering, built with a simple height adjustment mechanism.

To understand the equipment and process technology of lawn mowing to make a wise purchase of machinery would have required that the owner-manager develop an accurate mental concept or picture of the process of cutting grass with the machine operating on his hillside and in his garden, under a variety of physical conditions, including after a rain and after his annual vacation, with consideration for the availability of his own time, money, and skills. His most crucial mistake, of course, was in his choice of a reel-type technology rather than a rotary cutting blade. But if he lived in a house with low, big glass windows and with close neighbors' houses that were similarly constructed, he would have also needed to consider the danger from flying rocks and pebbles propelled by the rotary-type mower. In either case, a reasonably good conceptual approximation of the actual grass-cutting action would have provided him with the sense (common sense—once again proving to be not always common) to ask enough of the right questions to lead him to other useful questions. Choosing EPTs in manufacturing or service industry operations has many parallels to the lawn mower problem.

What are the basic choices in EPTs? What are the basic dimensions or factors involved? They are relatively few. The EPT decision must deal with four characteristics:

1. *Size and capacity.* Do we want one big machine or three smaller ones? Do we want extra capacity for contingency and growth and flexibility?

2. *General purpose versus special purpose.* A general purpose technology will handle a broader range of products or materials with a simpler change-over from one to another. A special purpose technology will do one product or operation very well, but it is limited in its flexibility—for example, an automatic screw machine versus a simple engine lathe.

3. *Precision and reliability.* We must determine the degree of precision of product specification the technology must produce and know the probabilities with which the technology will meet those specifications.

4. *Degree of mechanization.* In general, the more mechanized and automatic an EPT, the more its original cost, with less dependence on operator energies, skill, and judgment and more dependence on maintenance, engineering, and supervision for its care, adjustment, and repair.

These four characteristics require trade-offs between operating costs and different performance capabilities. They also imply trade-offs and frequently difficult decisions about the choice of the entire operating system infrastructure. Consider, for example, the amount of labor and the skill requirements attendant on each of the four characteristics above. Recognizing that the numbers and skills of production workers in turn have major implications on the wage system, labor agreements, recruiting, selection, supervision, and so forth, the vast and all-pervasive effects of EPT decisions start to emerge.

The same range of effects and trade-offs would occur for cost controls, production planning and scheduling and quality controls, plant engineering, and every other ingredient in a factory system. The complexity of the prob-

lem of choosing an EPT or operating with a given EPT is further compounded by the fact that the four characteristics often place conflicting
demands on various elements of the operating infrastructure that may be
difficult or impossible to overcome. So where do we start in making EPT
decisions? First, a manager needs a visualization of the EPT.

The place to start is with the actual physical process that takes place in
the technology. What actually happens to the raw material? How does it
happen? How does it work? What does the operator do? The executive must
be able to draw or graphically describe for others what goes on in the equipment or process. What are the machine's motions and actions?

If the manager's equipment is a machine tool, he or she must acquire the
concept of the moving tool, the machine-held work-piece, the chip-making
action, and so on. If the business involves an electronic black box, often
some hydraulic or physical analogies will do: "This box regulates the
electrical pressure that it sends out, smoothing its variations into an even
flow." In chemistry a visualization of molecular particles combining or
breaking apart under conditions of temperature or pressure can lead to sufficient understanding accurately to sense the kind of things that might go
wrong or must be carefully controlled. The concept, for example, of a
plastic resin being formed by molecules joining together in chains, with a
variety of chain lengths being formed, leads to an understanding of the
polymerization process and its demands on the operator for precise, "sixth-
sense" skillful control of the reaction.

To summarize, the first step is the acquisition of a fairly accurate mental
analogy or visualization of the actual physical process taking place. Until
the manager has this sense of what happens to the material in the EPT, he
will normally lack confidence in his perception and grasp of the EPT. A
homely or familiar analogy is usually sufficient. The formerly technology-
aversive executive begins to lose his or her fear of the unknown. He can
then explain in diagram form or state a familiar physical analogy to answer
the questions, What happens to the material during the process? How is it
changed? What motions and actions take place in the equipment? What
does the operator do? What must be done before the EPT can function?
What must be done after the EPT operation? What can go wrong? What is
most apt to go wrong?

Four Basic Parameters

Armed with a conceptual image of what happens in and around that black
box or noisy machine, a manager is prepared to work his way with questions into a useful knowledge of the EPT. Very briefly, he needs to know

what it costs, what it will do, what it requires, and the certainty of these three things.

Every machine (or EPT) can be described within these four general parameters. Each may be elaborated somewhat but the notion is simple. Taking each element in turn:

1. *What it costs.* An EPT's costs consist generally of initial investment costs; installation; de-bugging; and operating and continuing labor, material, maintenance, utilities, and other overhead costs. The economic life of the EPT may be used to annualize the initial investment costs, or they may be handled in a more sophisticated manner. All of this is simple and straightforward, and most executives are used to thinking in terms of costs and investments.

2. *What it will do.* This may be more difficult to determine, but not necessarily so. A given EPT will perform certain physical activities that can be predicted and measured. They can be described in terms of the materials it will handle, the production output per hour (capacity), the range of product variations that can be produced, and the qualities of the product produced (e.g., specification, performance characteristics, tolerances, reliability).

3. *What it requires.* Every machine (or EPT) must be operated, started, stopped, loaded, unloaded, changed over from one product to another, maintained, repaired, speeded up or slowed down as volume requirements change; and its waste products must be disposed of. These are operating requirements. Every machine or EPT also creates a set of "people requirements," consisting of human skills, which are largely determined by its technology. The numbers of operators, setup men, maintenance mechanics, or engineers are basically a function of the technology. And of course any EPT has other basic requirements in space, utilities, and raw materials, needs which may often be routine but are sometimes critical to its performance.

4. *Certainty/uncertainty.* Old, proven EPT's generally have relatively few uncertainties regarding their costs, performance, and requirements, but the opposite can be true of newer ones, particularly those that are crowding the state of the art.

Critical uncertainties may be involved in the following factors:

TIME How long will this technology be superior to competitive EPT's?

How long will this EPT last before it wears out or needs major maintenance?

RELIABILITY   How often will the EPT produce the desired product quality:

How often will the EPT produce at its expected capacity?

INFORMATION   How sure are we about all the pieces of knowledge we have about the EPT?

These are sometimes the most difficult questions a manager must face in deciding about a new EPT. And they are by no means uncommon questions, for "newness" is a normal part of the problem: Do we or do we not adopt this new EPT, buy this new machine? If it is new to the company, it immediately introduces uncertainties in the form of a learning period for company personnel to master its idiosyncracies. If it is new to industry, there are apt to be many engineering and scientific imponderables to which time, effort, and expense are the only answers. In either case, a debugging process for working out the uncertainties and overcoming the problems as they emerge is a critical element in planning and organizing for a change in EPT.

Seasoned top managers responsible for operations management acquire an understanding that any intelligent and energetic management team can master an EPT over a period of time. Smooth-running facilities probably have had ample time to debug, improve, and systematize their operations. But look out for change in an EPT! Established understandings, operations, and systems are apt to be immediately undone; production is interrupted, costs skyrocket, quality runs berserk. Abilities to predict, organize for, and handle these disruptions separate the few fully successful managers from many others.

What particular skills and techniques are useful for the manager in dealing with the uncertainties of new or changed EPTs? Is scientific or engineering training, after all, essential to the manager because of these uncertainties? Is technology aversion perhaps the better part of wisdom when the uncertainty level creeps up?

No. In many respects the professionally trained manager is at his best and dealing with his best weapons in coping with the uncertainties in EPT's. This is so because management training deals directly with uncertainties, applying useful techniques such as PERT, CPM, decision trees, sensitivity analysis, simulation, and the various varieties of probabilities and statistics. Most uncertainties can be quantified, their outcomes evaluated, and not only the risks (the "what ifs") but the organizational mechanisms to minimize risks come clearly into focus. Further, managers are in a position to demand and insist on the best technical and economic information available and to be more impartial and objective about it than involved scientists and engineers.

Exhibit 7.2 is a summary of the foregoing ideas about how a manager can learn to understand and work with the EPT.

Technology, Economics, and Operations

A given EPT largely determines the economics and limitations of an operating system that, in combination with the competitive strategy of the firm, determine the few factors or problems that are keys to success or failure of the operating system.

What is the effect of these constraints or inflexibilities on the firm and the operation? Essentially, they place limitations and they create organizational or system demands such as a particularly strong scheduling and inventory control system, or maintenance system, or quality control system. Take, for example, a new, highly automated auto engine block machining center.

Basically a general purpose machine, it could produce only a few ranges of engines without extensive changeover, had high setup and changeover costs, and was expensive to buy, but required only a small labor force of highly skilled technicians to operate. This EPT brought with it certain "musts" for the operating system. There must be good forecasting, scheduling, and inventory control systems to minimize changeovers. There must also be well-trained technicians available to minimize downtime. And there must be a steady, dependable flow of uniformly high quality castings to assure high volume operations.

This EPT also created a set of economics with high fixed costs, low variable costs, considerable savings with high volume, a high break-even point, high costs for product changes, and a good cash-flow payback if volume stayed high and product changes were kept low.

The result of these constraints and economics defined the key difficulties, focal manufacturing problems, and "the name of the game" (what the management had to be good at to succeed with this technology—i.e., the set of activities centering around production planning, forecasting, scheduling, and inventory control). But since the firm's competitive strategy was to offer a broad, flexible, wide product line of engine options, it meant that product changes had to be handled quickly and efficiently. Success depended on it once it adopted that EPT. Its engine plant organization reflected the requirements for good scheduling and inventory control plus special task force teams set up to minimize downtime in product changeovers. One might ask whether this EPT was consistent with the firm's strategy.

Exhibit 7.2   A Manager's Understanding of Equipment and Process Technology

Step 1   Explain, diagram, analogize the physical operation.

Why is the process necessary?
What happens to the material during the process?
What motions and actions take place in the equipment?
What does the operator do?
What must be done (load, make ready) before the EPT can function?
What must be done (unload, clean up) after the EPT operation?
What can go wrong?
What is most apt to go wrong?

Step 2   Identify precisely available knowledge concerning.

What the EPT Costs	*What the EPT Will Do*	*What the EPT Requires*
Original cost	Output/time	Materials
Economic life	(cycle, capacity)	
Direct operating costs	Range of products	Labor $\Big\langle$ skills, numbers $\Big\rangle$ set up, operate, load, unload
Indirect support costs	(specs, quality)	
		Supervision
		Technicians
		Maintenance
		Space $\Big\langle$ equipment, inventory
		Utilities $\Big\langle$ power, etc., waste, effluent disposal

Step 3   Identify the degree of certainty/uncertainty of the knowledge in Step 2.

What is known for sure? How do you know?
What is the range of possible outcomes?
What would be the effect of each?
What is the best estimate of the probabilities of each?
Use managerial techniques for dealing with uncertainties and linked effects,
   such as

PERT/CPM/ network techniques
decision trees
simulation
linear programming
sensitivity analysis
probabilities/statistics

to quantify effects of alternate decisions.

One other example shows how technology in combination with competitive conditions determines the name of the game in an industry.

The steel industry is characterized by high capital costs, relatively low variable costs, few pieces of equipment (vs. many, as in a machine shop), high transportation costs, lots of "art" as opposed to science in the EPT, and high volumes of tonnages. The fact that there are relatively few pieces of equipment implies greater operational risks, including long and difficult startups. Management must place an overriding emphasis on balance and integration between these pieces of equipment, and it is dependent on the skills of the direct labor force. There are also severe limitations on the product mixes that can be efficiently produced by any one plant and manufacturing team.

These characteristics make the following elements of steel manufacturing critical:

- Choices of equipment and processes with particular regard to sizing-capacity-product capability.
- Plant location.
- Number and size of plants.
- Balance of equipment.
- Timing of choosing a new technology and handling the uncertainty that goes with it.

One particularly difficult problem in the industry has concerned that of internal balance. There is the problem of maintaining balance at one integrated facility between blast furnace, steelmaking, and finishing capacity while technology has steadily offered significant improvements in each stage, changes in product mix are being demanded by the markets, and market demands are changing over geographical areas, especially considering the fact that equipment changes are extremely expensive, risky, and time-consuming.

There is the further problem of changes in cost and product flexibility over the span of four stages: raw material, blast furnace, steelmaking, and steel finishing. By and large, the process is less flexible for cost and volume and mix, and more flexible for product flexibility in the early stages and conversely in the later stages. A given plant can only handle certain products and certain volumes economically.

Exhibit 7.3 summarizes in diagram form some of these relationships between technology, economics, constraints, and managerial problems.

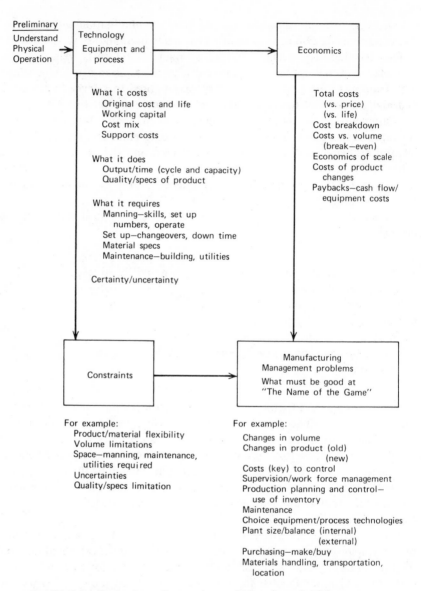

Exhibit 7.3   Technology, Economics, and Manufacturing Management

CONCLUSION

In these times of rapid technological change a manager cannot afford to be technology aversive. Technologies can be analyzed and characterized systematically by the nonengineer/scientist. Analogies can be worked out to develop conceptual understandings. The relationships between an EPT and its resulting economics and constraints are generally straightforward, as is the understanding that these three factors will highlight the especially difficult aspects of managing any operations, allowing the manager to focus his or her attention.

The end of technology aversion is a new set of skills and understandings that, like those in finance and marketing, can be developed with practice and coaching, once the reluctance to tackle a set of problems too often left to the technologist is finally overcome. My prediction is that the next generation of managers, by necessity and training, will handle these kinds of problems naturally and fluently as a normal part of being a manager.

CHAPTER 8

Defining
the
Manufacturing Task

When a manufacturing facility is focused on a limited task, top management can concentrate its attention on that task and thereby acquire a means or concept for managing a function that has been dominated by technically sophisticated people.

My purpose in this chapter is to illustrate the importance of the process of defining the task by offering a set of specific "how to's," based on work I and three colleagues did in a high technology company that makes chemical processing equipment. The concept is effective, for it relates manufacturing to the corporate strategy and forms manufacturing into a competitive weapon. My experience suggests that without exception the process of defining the manufacturing task is always difficult. It is easy to define *a* manufacturing task but hard to define it in sufficient depth and understanding that it becomes a powerful, mobilizing force that produces a set of integrated and consistent actions and structure.

In working with managers, consultants, professors, and students and in attempting to learn the art myself, I have observed five impediments to the development of focused manufacturing policies.

1. The importance of the manufacturing task is not understood, and the process of defining it is therefore given short shrift. The result is an academic statement rather than an effective, pervasive philosophy of manufacturing.
2. Corporate strategy, marketing, industry technology, or industry economics are not fully studied, thought through, and incorporated into the thinking of the manufacturing team and the task statement.

98

3. The statement of manufacturing task fails to go beyond a mere ranking of the criteria (see Chapter 3) for judging manufacturing performance into a set of priorities. For example, "the highest priority is reduced lead times; second is costs; third is quality . . ."
4. The manufacturing task is excessively general. That is, it does not include specific objectives or standards, and it does not identify which of these are going to be most difficult to attain.
5. The manufacturing task does not clearly state its implications and its disclaimers (e.g., what we will *not* do).

Executives must develop a clear and explicit concept of what the manufacturing function must accomplish. The manufacturing task, in short, is a statement of manufacturing philosophy in the sense that "philosophy" relates ends and means and links them together conceptually with a total plan and its rationale.

If it does not include these elements, the manufacturing task has not been thought through nor will it be effective as an end product. And most important, the process itself will not have been vital and effective as it must be. As the case I discuss below shows, the length and complexity of the process illustrates both the difficulty and the power of developing a manufacturing strategy. An important product is the impact the process has on the firm's manufacturing management team and its subsequent behavior.

MAINSTREAM TECHNOLOGY COMPANY

Recently I and three of my colleagues at Harvard Business School helped the "Mainstream Technology Company" to define its manufacturing task. MTC was a company on the sophisticated, high-technology end of chemical processing equipment with a five year history of rapid growth at the time of our study. Its rapid growth was based on a technical breakthrough achieved in 1970, a breakthrough that gave the company a major competitive advantage that was expected to continue for at least the next five years. Sales were approximately $150 million.

THE ORIGINAL PROBLEMS

Our work began with a meeting with the vice president of manufacturing. He told us that while manufacturing had been generally successful in coping with the challenges of rapid and massive growth, overhead costs and inventories had been rising to a level he now considered unsatisfactory. Further, having made continual annual additions to production capacity spread over a complex multiplant network, he was concerned about a possible lack of focusing, plant by plant, on a manageable span of products, market demand, technologies, and tasks.

OBJECTIVES

We agreed to hold a set of meetings to clarify MTC's manufacturing task in order to examine and possibly restructure the company's manufacturing policies and structure. The goal for the manufacturing team was to develop a structure and rationale about which products should be produced where. Such a focus would assist MTC in articulating its manufacturing task and improving performance on overhead costs and inventory investment. Our role as consultants was to stimulate, question, interpret, challenge, and ultimately summarize the thinking and conclusions of the manufacturing team.

ACCOMPLISHMENTS

The accomplishments of the six days of discussion may at first seem modest. The experiences and changes in understanding for each person could be reported only individually. However, the group as a whole made concrete progress in defining the manufacturing task on which structural decisions must hinge. The result was a product-process-plant matrix to be in place by 1980. This matrix structure not only differed from the company's 1975 set-up, but more important, it appeared to be promising for improving the focus on its manufacturing task ahead and reducing overhead costs and inventory investment. We also observed significant progress toward three key conceptual goals:

1. *The assimilation of a nonconventional approach to manufacturing management.* Instead of attempting to optimize along all the usual performance parameters (cost, quality, delivery, investment, etc.), which are inevitably in conflict and susceptible to continual external criticism, the proper task of manufacturing is derived from corporate strategic and marketing factors in conjunction with the constraints of the technology and economics of the industry. Manufacturing policy must then align the physical setup and organizational infrastructure to focus on the central manufacturing task. The MTC group wrestled and experimented with this concept enough to become capable of applying it to production management.

2. *The understanding that many (rather than few) alternatives exist.* This seems to be obvious. However, inevitably managers establish an experience-restricted radius to their purview of the range of options open to them. This limits their sense of the span of available alternatives for choosing equipment and process technology; the number, size, and location of plants; groupings of products by plants; organization structure; work force management; production planning and scheduling; and management controls. We saw considerable progress toward the goal of opening up the range of structural choices available and thus exposing the present structure to challenge.

3. *An evolution in thinking about the manufacturing task.* The evolution was absolutely critical, not only to the understanding but the use of the concept of manufacturing task as a top management approach to production management.

The struggles over what the manufacturing task means started with case discussions of how other companies had made decisions that involved a manufacturing task. We then proceeded with lengthy debates over MTC's task, a debate that ebbed and flowed intermittently over all six days. The discussion went through four distinct phases (Exhibit 8.1), back and forth to be sure, but gradually evolving as follows:

At stage 1 the task was seen as a set of objectives—for example, "we've got to grow at 30 to 40% and double our ROI, develop integratable products, deal with separated businesses, reduce cost on A items, and improve response time and flexibility on B and C items."

The problem with stage 1 is that this kind of definition is merely a collection of goals. It lacks ranking by priorities as a minimum conceptual step for answering the question: How do we *manage* manufacturing for the next four to five years?

As discussion proceeded, we arrived at a more advanced stage. Stage 2 was better than stage 1 because we recognized conflict and the need for priorities by deciding on ratings for the objectives. We began to develop a sense of strategy for being successful. That is, we suggested some decision rules that would provide some consistency. But stage 2 still was not very useful because (a) we had not suggested a rationale for *how* manufacturing was to be successful, and (b) explicit recognition, or even an inference, of what goals would be particularly difficult to achieve in the next few years was left out.

At stage 3, the definition began to include some specific tasks that were going to be particularly difficult to undertake but if well handled would lead to success. The task at this stage was again a collection of "musts," but

Exhibit 8.1 Stages in the Development of a Statement of Manufacturing Task

Stage	Statement: "Our Manufacturing Task Is:"	Characteristic
1	Grow at 30% per year React to mix change of 30 to 40% React to volume changes of $+10\%$ Improve asset utilization (ROA) from 7.5% to 15% Improve productivity (output per person) 50% Move toward product specific manufacturing Make a functional organization work Product reliability and process control improvement $\times$ 3	A collection of goals
2	First of all, to be flexible and grow. But we've got to do it with a doubling of ROA. This requires improvements in both productivity and inventory.	Goals with priorities
3	To try to meet corporate demand by tracking the market. But we could sink the company if we can't meet the commitments we make on deliveries, ROA, costs, and inventory levels. So our task is to maximize growth while meeting marketing and financial commitments.	"Musts" with priorities related to the corporation's critical strategic needs for successfully competing in its industry and financing its growth
4	First and foremost, we must be predictable. Manufacturing's role is to be a predictable known who makes clear commitments (cost, budgets, quality, schedule, ROA, etc.) and then meets them. When we are predictable, the rest of the company won't have to spend time or effort figuring out what we're up to or reacting to our surprises. Next our task is to grow—but only from a controlled base and only after	The "name of the game" is made explicit

Exhibit 8.1   (Continued)

Stage	Statement: "Our Manufacturing Task Is:"	Characteristic
	we have met the minimum constraints below: a. Cost. Maintain competitive product costs +5% of those of our best competitors. b. Quality/reliability. Maintain quality at +5% of industry norms. c. Delivery performance. 95% on time. d. Asset utilization. We will construct budgets that meet our ROA goals. Company inventory turns will be at least 2.5%. e. Employee relations. Maintain so that our employees judge us to be among the top quartile of companies to work for. In summary, we must be predictable. We will sacrifice growth to become no worse than any of the minimums above.	

with some priorities and awareness of constraints imposed by financial resources, technology, and marketing strategy. It included tracking the market, meeting commitments made to the company but also keeping costs within 5% of industry costs, making deliveries reliable but with comparable lead times to those of competitors, and improving the sales-to-assets ratio.

Stage 3 was more specific and realistic than stage 2, but we still had not articulated a key task with a rationale that would pervade decision making and thereby ensure consistency. And the statement did not lead managers directly to action nor clearly infer essential decisions.

Stage 4 took these requirements into account. It included objectives, priorities, constraints, and identified which of these would be most difficult. The definition now encompassed and dealt with the corporate financial and marketing tasks and strategy. Most important, perhaps, it inferred a "how to" and led to action in a way that was so simply understood that it carried

Exhibit 8.2   The Message from Stage 4 Manufacturing Task

---

1. You *must* be in control. This means meeting all your goals (cost, schedule, quality, assets, and employee relations) against current budgets.
2. Different plants/operations have more or less ambitious goals for all five parameters (one focused on cost reduction, one on flexibility, etc.). But *all* plants/operations have *all* five goals that must *all* be met.
3. "Over success" on one goal that results in failure to meet another goal is unacceptable.
4. "Surprise" is unacceptable!

SOURCE: An MTC manager.

with it its own cardinal imperative, a kind of "name of the game" for making consistent structural and operating decisions. It conveyed real sense of manufacturing strategy. For instance, the message received by one manager is reproduced as Exhibit 8.2.

Its key inclusion of "being predictable," for example, derives from MTC's being a large corporation growing massively, which means that the financial demands of growth create a situation in which the risks of not growing or not producing the absolutely necessary cash flows, of misleading or failing top management would be disastrous.

Being predictable carries with it a clear lead into action that is an essential part of effective manufacturing at MTC, for being predictable in a time of massive growth both in physical volume and in new products means that *control* is the key management tool and the key state of mind. If control and predictability is paramount, it begins to say a lot about the 1980 product/process/plant matrix.

I emphasize this evolution because it was based on an essential development in thinking that should be noted and labeled indelibly. Because conventional approaches to manufacturing were "burned" into most of us on our early formative years, we easily slide back into them.

After all that went into this definition, can we improve upon it? To try to do so is probably as risky as making a modest touch-up to improve a Michelangelo. But brush in hand, here goes!

THE MANUFACTURING TASK—A STAGE 5 STATEMENT

The MTC team defined the manufacturing task with a variety of words, but since the words used in Exhibits 8.1 and 8.2 seem to capture the ideas on which the group concurred, I refer to those words in the following comments:

1. As a statement of manufacturing task, it is quite useful, especially because its acceptance carries with it a number of structural and operational implications. However, in the heat and time pressure of the group discussion, we made no disciplined effort together to tighten the statement.

2. It is less than perfect as it now stands because:
   It doesn't say why the task is what it says it is.
   It doesn't state explicitly what may be most difficult.
   It contains some conflicting goals that have to be traded off against each other and therefore should be ranked.
   It contains some possible internal inconsistencies.

Manufacturing Task—Revised

MTC's competitive strategy is to gain a commanding, preemptive market share by aggressive engineering, product development, and marketing in an industry that is growing rapidly while beginning to mature with price competition and the shake-out of marginal competitors. MTC's critical top management task is reaching this preemptive market position while financing the massive growth it requires. And MTC risks insufficient funds in the event of missing sales targets.

Manufacturing's dilemma is how to handle the corporate imperative of raw physical growth through rapid product and technology change while minimizing the funds it needs for assets and maximizing the funds provided by minimizing the cost of goods sold. The paradox is how to avoid disastrous falldowns in delivery or cost performance (which would cripple the entire corporation and its finances and strategic position) without the equally unsatisfactory outcome of playing a lower risk game of promising and delivering less on growth, new product introduction, and return on assets.

The key job of manufacturing therefore is to promise and deliver vital, difficult improvement in sales and return on assets while keeping the risks of failure at an acceptable level. The manufacturing task, simply stated, is to be able accurately to predict the accomplishment of acceptable but difficult goals. Basically, it is to manage the risk-commitment curve. Such a curve is shown on Exhibit 8.3. This is the "name of the game" for MTC manufacturing.

This task has at least four clear implications:

1. It requires high skills and judgment to relate commitments to risk (on Exhibit 8.3, to be able to draw this curve with specifics, relative to

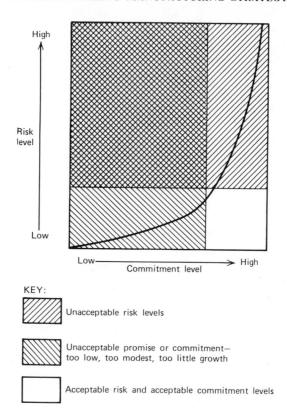

Exhibit 8.3   The Commitment Risk Curve SOURCE: HBS team.

various demands and needs—sales levels, new product introduction, CGS %, assets employed, ROA).

2. It requires obtaining and clarifying from corporate management the boundaries of what is acceptable and unacceptable (i.e., the shaded area on Exhibit 8.3).

3. It requires uniquely competent managers and management systems—information, control, communication—so as to deliver on the difficult commitments it makes.

4. It requires, in all probability, systemwide improvements so as to be able to move the Exhibit 8.3 curves down and to the right.

Just for fun, it is often useful to try to paraphrase the manufacturing task into a book title or a picture. One picture that tells the story pretty well is that of Babe Ruth, with two strikes showing on the scoreboard, pointing to the right field stands just before he hit the famous home run. Difficult but predictable and achievable, an acceptable risk for an acceptable payoff.

CONCLUSION

This work with MTC executives demonstrates that developing a manufacturing strategy is a process and that the process itself is as important as the product. If the specifications for the product—the statement of the manufacturing task—are demanding, and the product is inspected against those specifications, a valuable process experience can result.

In summary, these specifications for the manufacturing task are:

1. It must be written in sentences and paragraphs, not merely outlined.
2. It must explicitly state the demands and constraints on manufacturing derived from:
   The corporate strategy for competing successfully.
   Marketing policy.
   Financial policy.
   The technology of the industry and the firm.
   The economics of the industry and the firm.
3. It must state what manufacturing must accomplish to be a competitive weapon and, conversely, how performance can be judged.
4. It must identify what will be especially difficult ("the name of the game"). Its difficulty is forced by economic, human, competitive, or technological problems generally common to the industry. Therefore when the difficult task is accomplished, this will differentiate our company and its manufacturing policies and performance from others. The differences will result in successfully competing via the creation in manufacturing of a unique competitive advantage.
5. It must explicitly state priorities, including what may have to suffer.
6. It must explicitly state the inferences or impact of requirements on the manufacturing infrastructure[1], i.e., to accomplish this task we are going to have to improve, for example, production control by such and such policies or procedures or changes.

---

[1] By manufacturing infrastructure we mean the policies, procedures, and organization by which manufacturing accomplishes its work, specifically production and inventory control systems, cost and quality control systems, work force management policies, and organizational structure.

7. The communication of the manufacturing task may be facilitated by "boiling down" the task statement to a book title, a picture, cartoon, or slogan. This may seem breezy or "corny" but it has the result of bringing to larger numbers of managers what is key for the next period ahead. It puts a capstone on the process by permeating the organization with a functioning working understanding of the manufacturing task.

CHAPTER 9

Designing
the
Production System

Previous chapters have focused on why the manufacturing organization should explicitly identify its manufacturing task to be consistent with and supportive of the corporation's competitive strategy and then organize manufacturing structure to accomplish a sharp focus for that task. Our approach has been more on "why" than on "how." The question that remains to be discussed is, "What is the method by which manufacturing policies can be analyzed and changed or developed to meet the requirements of the manufacturing task?"

To move from analysis to synthesis the focus of this chapter is on designing the production system. The design process is necessary either to develop a totally new production system for a new plant or, as is more often the case, to determine useful changes for an existing system.

In designing a production system, what is being done essentially is to establish a set of manufacturing policies. Manufacturing policies are the means by which the basic structural elements of the system are made consistent and made to pull together. Manufacturing polices can be thought of in two parts.

The first part has to do with bricks and mortar and machinery. This is hardware or "fixed assets,"—the number, capacity, and location of plants and the equipment and process technology. The second part has to do with people and systems and procedures, or "infrastructure." In designing the infrastructure, decisions need to be made concerning the following manufacturing policy sectors:

1. What to make and what to buy.
2. Production planning, scheduling, and inventory control.

3. Work force management.
4. Quality control.
5. The formal organization.
6. Controls, reports, and information systems.
7. Purchasing.

The most typical serious condition in most manufacturing plants is that of inconsistencies existing within the infrastructure. Different sectors of manufacturing policy are implicitly set up to accomplish conflicting objectives. It is as if an automobile engine were designed for Indy racing, the transmission for fuel economy, the tires for comfort, the suspension for road race maneuverability, and the trunk space for camping.

The same phenomena exist in factories when there is no clear design objective or set of priorities. Further inconsistencies also come about either because of growth, product development, marketing pressures, management, organizational changes, or the influence of professionals in the organization who earnestly seek to optimize their own traditional professional goals which are normally in conflict. Frequently lacking is a concept, scheme, or broad outlook that binds together all of the elements of the infrastructure.

A *manufacturing audit* is an approach to take in examining the production system and the infrastructure. Exhibit 9.1 is a manufacturing audit checklist process that can be used in designing a production system or for analyzing an existing system to reveal inconsistencies and opportunities for improvements. Each element of the system must be examined from the standpoint of whether it is presently designed and operated to achieve the key manufacturing task. A useful procedure is to redesign each element of the system conceptually to provide focus on one task and then to compare the redesigned system with the present system.

A manufacturing audit can reveal which of eight "cardinal sins" may have been commited in the production organization. It can also suggest specifics for revised manufacturing policies and new procedures that would cleanse the organization from those sins. The sins are:

1. Manufacturing has a new manufacturing task but continues the old manufacturing policies and structure.
2. Managers in manufacturing have no clear, consistent definition or understanding of the manufacturing task facing the organization.
3. The manufacturing policies and the infrastructure being employed are inconsistent. Taken together, there is a distortion in coordination.
4. The organization lacks a focus. It is attempting to cover too many technologies or too many products and markets, too wide a range of volume, and more than one manufacturing task.

Exhibit 9.1 Manufacturing Audit Checklist Process

I. Make/Buy Choices
   A. Examine the gray areas of items that could feasibly be made or bought.
   B. What does present make or buy position imply about
      High make   High buy
      Impact on profitability
      Impact on cost structure (fixed vs. variable costs, investment level, break-even point)
      Impact on ability to ride economic cycles
      Impact on quality
      Impact on risk (assurance of supply, downside risk of excess capacity)
      Ability to meet the manufacturing task

II. Capacity Decision
   A. How does capacity compare with past, present, and future forecasted demand?
   B. Do we play capacity on the low side or high side? (Are we purposely low or do we try to be right on, or are we purposely careful always to have a bit extra?)
   C. What does this imply about
      Investment levels
      Costs, break-even point
      Service levels, response times
      Risks
      Work force management
      Quality.
      Ability to meet the manufacturing task

III. Plant Decisions
   A. Number of plants
      One
      Some
      Many
   B. Size of plants
      Large
      Medium
      Small
   C. Location of plants
      Near raw materials
      Near customers
      Other rationale for location _____
   D. Focus and organization of plants
      Work allocated by
         Products
         Process/technology
         Scale, volume
         Other _____

Exhibit 9.1 (Continued)

E. What does this imply about
Costs
Risks
Service levels
Organization
Control
Work force management
Production scheduling and inventory management
Ability to meet the manufacturing task

IV. Equipment and Process Technology
A. Relative to the industry and stages of existing technology describe the extent to which
We are mechanized
We are ahead or behind competitors in use of latest technology
We are sharp and agressive in
Tooling
Equipment
Process/manufacturing engineering
Industrial engineering
B. Describe key processes on dimensions of
Set-up and changeover requirements
General purpose versus special purpose capability
Process capability versus product performance and quality requirements
Mechanization-labor intensiveness
Skills required
Maintenance requirements, skills, and costs
Supervision needed
Flexibility for volume changes
Internal balance of capacities and bottlenecks
Maintenance requirements, skills, and costs
Supervision needed
Flexibility for volume changes
Internal balance of capacities and bottlenecks
Technology: mature, slow changing versus new, uncertain, fast changing
Cost of equipment and facilities in P & L (high or low) relative to other costs
C. What does above imply about
Competitive ability
Service levels
Investment levels
Production planning and scheduling-inventory management

Exhibit 9.1 (**Continued**)

Risks
Quality
Work force management
Organizational needs
Cost structure/break-even curve
Opportunities
Ability to meet the manufacturing task

V. Key Concept
  A. Key concept in the manufacturing audit is that the choices of make or buy levels; number, size, location, and capacity of plants; equipment and process levels determine, largely fix, or greatly influence nearly everything else. These are brick and mortar, structural, hardware, expensive, long lead-time, and difficult-to-change decisions. Once made, decisions on other elements of the infrastructure inevitably are restricted in range. By the same token, the decision process on the various elements of the infrastructure is made easier by the hardware group of decisions.

Turn now to the other elements.

VI. Production Planning and Control
  A. Describe the present systems for
      Forecasting and planning loads and capacities
      Establishing customer promises
      Ordering production/releasing work to the plant
      Order quantities
      Size and location of inventories
      Balancing inventories
      Coordination and timing/expediting/correcting falldowns
  B. What does each imply about the implicit manufacturing task?
  C. What alternatives would focus better on the actual manufacturing task?

VII. Work Force Management
  A. Describe the present systems and choices for
      Selection of employees
      Training
      Job content—big, rich jobs or narrow, specialized jobs
      Pay systems—how pay is determined
        What we are paying for
        Opportunity for upward mobility
        Pay ranges
        Safety, industrial health, housekeeping
        Supervision
        Communications with employees

Exhibit 9.1 (Continued)

    B. What does each imply about the implicit manufacturing task?

    C. What alternatives would focus better on the actual manufacturing task?

VIII. Quality Control

    A. Describe present systems and choices for

        Explicitly choosing quality levels

        Quality levels chosen

        Designing/engineering quality into product

        Process design and control

        Training and supervision for quality

        Monitoring

    B. What does each imply about the implicit manufacturing task?

    C. What alternatives would focus better on the actual manufacturing task?

IX. Manufacturing and Industrial Engineering and Maintenance

    A. Describe present systems and choices for

        Improving processes

        Improving equipment and tooling

        Keeping up with technological developments

        Level of effort

        Influencing product design engineering for producibility

    B. What does each imply about the implicit manufacturing task?

    C. What alternatives would focus better on the actual manufacturing task?

X. Cost and Information Systems

    A. Describe present system and choices for

        What is monitored

        What is budgeted, forecast

        Setting standards, goals

        Selecting who gets what information and when

        Taking action when standards are not met

    B. What does each imply about the implicit manufacturing task?

    C. What alternatives would focus better on the actual manufacturing task?

XI. Purchasing

    A. Describe present approaches to purchasing management

        Purchased part design/value analysis

        Use of competitive bids

        Vendor selection

        Vendor assistance/training/communications

        Manning, organizational emphasis

        Control systems

    B. What does each imply about the implicit manufacturing task?

    C. What alternatives would focus better on the actual manufacturing task?

Exhibit 9.1 (Continued)

XII. Formal Organization
  A. Describe the present formal organization
  B. Rank the functions in the order in which they are given organizational emphasis
    Manufacturing supervision
    Production planning, scheduling, inventory control
    Maintenance
    Manufacturing engineering
    Industrial engineering
    Quality control
    Purchasing
    Personnel, labor relations
    Cost control
    Product/program management
    Design engineering
  C. Describe the system for performance measurement and evaluation
  D. What does each imply about the implicit manufacturing task?
  E. What alternatives would focus better on the actual manufacturing task?

---

5. The organization has the wrong equipment and process technology for the present manufacturing task.
6. The organization uses only economic hurdles for capital investment instead of also considering what the manufacturing organization must do to become a competitive corporate weapon.
7. The organization's decision orientation is based too much on achieving economies of scale (i.e., low costs from high volume or large scale) instead of looking at total performance along the full range of criteria marking success.
8. Selection of products and processes for each plant in a multiplant setup results in mixing together, somewhat at random, a product organization, a process organization, and a volume-focused organization (or any two of the three) instead of focusing around one type of orgranization.

Each can have a disastrous effect on the manufacturing organization's ability to make manufacturing a strategic weapon.

The basic premise implicit in the manufacturing audit approach to designing the production system is that each part of the fixed asset structure and the infrastructure provides many options in design. There are many different ways, for example, to use inventories and to schedule production. The manager doing the audit or redesigning the production system may look at each option and make a choice among a variety of trade-offs. Each choice will have a different impact on the seven major criteria for production success. The objective in designing the production system is to design each element of the system so that each has a positive impact on the firm's ability to meet the manufacturing task.

An example may clarify this. A machine tool manufacturer made a strategic product decision to shift to a new line of modular machine tools, so that instead of providing conventional, standardized milling machine, the firm would be able to put together milling, drilling, turning, boring, and other machine capabilities in one machine tool in accordance with specific needs of customers. With that decision made in its basic product policy, a manufacturing audit would reveal the necessity of changes in much of its manufacturing structure. For example, the existing formal organizational chart of the plant showed a typical functional organization. But with the manufacturing task changing from producing a large volume of fairly standardized conventional machine tools to the new, modularized, customized product line in which most customers orders would be different, the organization would now have to be more effective at introducing new products and handling many customer specials. This placed a new emphasis on production planning, scheduling, and control. Emphasis on problem solving at relatively lower levels in the organization would be needed. For this reason, an increased emphasis was necessary both on production control and on establishing project management or product managers and giving them authority across the organization to get new products into production. Similarly, changes were necessary in the work force management, moving away from incentive wages and toward enlarged job content on a fixed wage or salary basis. Other changes were necessary in both production control and inventory management.

Another illustrative example concerns a cosmetics firm. Exhibit 9.2 is a one-page description of that company. The new owner's objective was to groom the company for sale by sprucing up the product line. The manufacturing task required rapid introduction of new products in a very seasonal business, demanding particularly effective production planning, scheduling, and control.

Strategically, at this point in company history, Deirdre Desiree required above all else low costs for a high earnings per share, heavy product development costs, and the preservation of the company's high quality image to enhance its value on the market. These objectives seem inconsistent, even impossible. The latter is accomplished at the expense of the former. How can both be done?

The economics of the industry indicate a cost structure in which materials and labor loom larger than plant, equipment, indirect labor, and

Exhibit 9.2   Deirdre Desiree*

Deirdre Desiree (DD) is well known for its broad line of high-priced women's cosmetics. DD had a slightly lower share of the market than its five or six main competitors and had been losing market share slightly for five years. Products were sold by exclusive sales to leading department stores and a few company retail stores. Advertising and reputation, effective retail salesmanship, and demonstration appeared to be critical. Business was highly seasonal with peaks at Christmas and Easter.

DD's strategy is to reverse market share trend by adding a new 10 to 15% of new products to its line of about 50 items while replacing about 10% of existing items and improving advertising effectiveness. Products consist of lotions, powders, lipsticks, and mascaras in equal proportions. Average unit price at factory is about $6, ranging from $2 to $12. Twenty percent of the products account for 50% of the dollar volume. Cost of direct labor averages $0.50, materials $2 of which $1 was for packages and boxes. Advertising represents about 25% of sales. Factory sales total about $72,000,000 per year.

The technology consisted of adding materials in bulk in large mixing kettles and drums and filling small-sized product containers (bottles, special packages, boxes) and then packaging. Automatic filling and packaging machines were available and generally economic at volumes exceeding 100 units per hour. Changing over an automatic line from one product to another required the line to be shut down for about five hours and a crew of five set-up men to do the work. Shelf life at the factory or in distribution channels generally caused no problems. FDA standards for cleanliness and bacteria counts were increasingly strict.

The location of DD's one manufacturing facility is in the New York City area at Long Island City.

Financially, DD is in a somewhat weak condition due to occasional unprofitable years over the past six years and large cash withdrawals by its recently deceased owner for her hobby of a stable of race horses. Ownership is presently in the hands of her estate, a large New York bank that had as its objectives eventual sale of DD as an acquisition target.

---

* This case was prepared as the basis for class discussion rather than to illustrate either effective or ineffective handling of an administrative situation.
Copyright © 1977 by the President and Fellows of Harvard College.

other overheads. Storage, inventory and handling costs are larger items. Costs are relatively flexible with volume. Transportation is not critical, but packaging and certain raw materials are substantial cost elements.

The technology of the industry is not complex. Compounding, blending, and mixing the parts are relatively simple batch processes requiring substantial precision and care for the most part only in the weighing out of ingredients. In contrast to many chemical and pharmaceutical processes, relatively little judgment and training is required of operators. Filling and packing can be substantially mechanized. Operations can be standardized, operators trained, methods engineered. Cleanliness and bacterial control are important but demand the mastery of no new technologies to handle adequately. Shelf life control requires good records in a simple system. Competent R&D work and packaging equipment are keys to success, but these functions are best handled outside the plant.

Perhaps the only difficult problem relative to many other industries is that of production planning, scheduling, and inventory management. Here the technology and the economics meet head on, for problems in bacteria control and shelf life collide with the economic advantages of long runs. And here, too, the problem of seasonality, forecasting consumer demand, new products, and changes in distribution policy meet the substantial costs of investing in and handling inventory. These problems are what require some management sophistication in the cosmetics industry.

Putting this all together requires an answer to the question, "What is necessary to be successful in manufacturing high quality cosmetics?" At Deirdre Desiree, our answer is, "A production system designed to achieve low losts and consistent quality and reliable delivery." This can be accomplished by:

1. A low cost location.
2. Inexpensive labor.
3. Thorough and competent, precise industrial engineering.
4. Careful and demanding training, especially in cleanliness and careful handling.
5. Development of reliable, well-accepted, and relatively tight (vs. loose) time standards.
6. Close, exacting supervision.
7. Alert, aggressive, hard-nosed, and sophisticated purchasing.
8. The maximum in mechanization via capital budgeting procedures designed to mechanize whenever possible (for low cost and high, consistent quality).
9. Skillful long-range sales forecasting.
10. Careful, top level, sophisticated aggregate scheduling and inventory costs.
11. Considerable economic analysis to minimize total set-up and inventory costs.
12. Cost controls that weekly identify key costs against control standards with clear accountability.

The plant organization in this industry has to be heavily "top down." The simplicity of the technology, the heavy labor, and materials, and inventory costs, and the problems of production scheduling require the key management skills to be in a small, closely knit, well-coordinated group at the top. The key thinking and all key decisions can be made by a handful of able, sophisticated managers at the top. (Contrast this with, for example, the electronics industry where judgment and technical skill is critical at nearly all levels or with the steel industry where the right equipment and capacity decisions make the difference.)

Each industry has its own "name of the game." In this industry it is *standardization, planning, and control* from the top down. Strength is developed in a few top people and in a rather formal system. This should be Deirdre Desiree's manufacturing philosophy; the manufacturing policies that can be keys to making manufacturing a competitive weapon at Deirdre Desiree are the 12 listed above.

If this seems obvious, or these manufacturing policies appear at first to be too general to be useful, let us emphasize the point by contrasting the present manufacturing policies observed in the Deirdre Desiree operations. These 12 are listed in the same order as those above.

1. Locate the plant convenient to Manhattan for close personal control.
2. Employ relatively experienced labor, with considerable longevity, and with a strong union.
3. Minimize costs of plant (industrial) engineering.
4. Place little emphasis on training; rely instead on experience and longevity.
5. Use time standards only for general estimating purposes.
6. Employ experienced supervisors, who know products and workers well, and leave them on their own to exercise considerable judgment.
7. In purchasing, place the emphasis on quality and vendor reliability. Foster long-standing vendor relationships.
8. Keep capital equipment costs low.
9. Emphasize manufacturing flexibility and ability to respond quickly to changes in sales demands.
10. Handle inventory planning and scheduling at a relatively low level in the organization with least expense. Keep it closer to the foremen so that it will be practical and feasible.
11. Handle length of runs and inventory decisions at a low level based on experience and convenience rather than economic analysis.
12. Have an ordinary standard cost system to develop annual cost data.

These manufacturing policies would be perfectly reasonable in some industries or at an earlier period in Deirdre Desiree history. But they are in sharp contrast to the first set of manufacturing policies that were developed from the economics and technology of the industry and Deirdre Desiree's current strategy and needs.

In contrast to our recommended manufacturing philosophy, the present one appears to be to keep operations flexible and versatile and make decisions as low as possible in the organization. This might be appropriate in high technology industries such as aerospace, electronics, or plastics polymerizing, but in cosmetics it causes high costs. Deirdre Desiree is in an industry where to achieve both low cost and high quality, centralized controls and standardized operations are necessary. Management strength and decisions must be concentrated at the top, where they can be closely coordinated with marketing, packaging, and sales.

Exhibit 9.3, Alternative Choices in Production System Design, is a further step in making a manufacturing audit. Exhibit 9.1 was largely an analytical process; where Exhibit 9.3 is a step-by-step approach for redesigning or synthesizing a production system. It takes the management through the criteria for judging manufacturing performance, the statement of the manufacturing task, and the desired economic structure by using a set of approximately 15 choices to make in designing the equipment and process technology and about 30 choices of manufacturing infrastructure. The list can be used first to indicate what ought to be and then the present manufacturing system can be compared against that list.

The manager should be constantly asking which criteria in overall success (see Chapter 3) will be maximized by each choice made. The production planning control system, for example, shows eight basic choices in the design of a production control system, and the system designer must make each choice with the objective of designing a production system that in total best meets the criteria in line with the key focus required by the manufacturing task. Similarly, in work force management, the analyst can ask the commonsensical question, "If our manufacturing task is, for example, to produce a customized set of low-volume customer specials in a high technology set of productions, what type of wages system makes sense?"

Subjecting the production system to this type of manufacturing audit uncovers inevitable inconsistencies and helps the manufacturing team to focus every element of the system on achieving the organization's current manufacturing task.

Exhibit 9.3 Alternative Choices in Production System Design

I. *Criteria for Judging Manufacturing Performance*

Cost/efficiency/productivity   ____

Quality/product reliability   ____

Short delivery cycle   ____

Dependable delivery cycle   ____   Rank in order of value to the

Return on investment   ____   company from the achievement of

Flexibility for volume changes   ____   exceptional performance under

Flexibility for product changes   ____   each criteria. (1–8)

Other (describe)   ____

II. *Statement of the Manufacturing Task*

A. At what must manufacturing be especially capable to satisfy strategic, financial, and marketing requirements over the next one to three years?

B. What will be most difficult—the particular challenge?

C. What, in the above, is changing from the past?

D. Product life cycle stage

Low volume, low standardization, one of a kind   ____   (Check one.)

Multiple products—many ECOs   ____

Multiple products—few ECOs   ____

A few major products   ____

High volume/standard/commodity products   ____

III. *Desired Economic Structure*

A. Cost of goods sold:

Labor   ____

Overhead   ____   (Fill in desired percentages.)

Depreciation   ____

Material   ____

    Total   100%

Exhibit 9.3 (Continued)

B. Fixed Costs—Variable Costs

| Low variable and High fixed | ←————————————————→ (Mark preferred point on spectrum.) | High variable and Low fixed |

IV. *Equipment and Process Technology (EPT)*
  A. Integration (make or buy)   Make little←——→Make much
    Forward (to end items)   Make little←——→Make much
    Backward (to suppliers)   Make little←——→Make much
  B. Number and size of plants: Few, big←——→Many, small
  C. Capacity versus market forecast
    Barely enough capacity←————→Comfortable capacity
  C. Location of Plants
    Locate near
      Raw materials/supplies   ——
      Customers/markets   ——
      Labor supply   ——
      Other (specify)   ——
  E. Focus of Plants
    Focus by
      Product   ——
      Process/technology/stage   ——
      Volume (long run vs. short run)   ——
  F. Degree of Mechanization
    Process stage

	High	Low
1	————	
2	————	
3	————	
etc.	————	

  G. Choice of equipment
    Degree of specialization   General purpose——————→Special
    Set-up/changeover time   Low←——————————→High
    Technological risk/uncertainty Low←——————————→High
    Flexibility to volume change Low←——————————→High
    Assignment of equipment   Pooled——————————→Dedicated
  H. Process Structure:
    Jumbled flow (flexible)   ——
    Disconnected line flow   ——
    Connected line flow   ——
    Continuous (systematic)   ——

Exhibit 9.3 (Continued)

V. *Manufacturing Infrastructure*

  A. Production Planning and Control   (Circle your choice.)

Investment in forecasting	Low		High
Produce	To order		To stock
Inventory			
RM's	Low	Medium	High
W in P-decoupling	Low	Medium	High
Finished goods	Low	Medium	High
Schedule	Chase	Smoothed	Level
Reorder via	Reorder point		MRP
Track/monitor/expedite	Low		High

  B. Subcontracting   Little   Much

  C. Purchasing—investment in aggressive, sophiscated purchasing   Low-High

  D. Quality Control   Low   High

Inspect at	Receiving	In process	Final
Inspection frequency	Infrequent	Sampling	100%

  E. Work force management   (Circle your choice)

Worker discretion	Low	Average	High	
Wages versus community	Low	Average	High	
Incentive wages	None	Some	All	
Job content	Narrow		Broad	
Cycle time	Short		Long	
Pacing via	Supervision	Schedule	Standards	Machine
Training	Little		Much	Paced

  F. Controls/Reports   (Circle your choice)

Focus: Time Quality	Investment	Cost	
Investment ct in controls	High	Medium	Low

  G. Manufacturing Organization

      Organizational emphasis   (high/medium/low)

Operations	_____
Production control and planning	_____
Personnel (labor relations)	_____
Industrial/manufacturing engineering	_____
Maintenance	_____
Purchasing	_____
Quality control	_____
Control of costs/controller	_____

Functional organization versus project/product versus other		(Circle one.)
Centralized vs. decentralized control		(Circle one.)
Role of a central staff group	Small	Large
Coordination with		
Marketing:	Loose	Tight
Engineering:	Loose	Tight
Customers:	Infrequent	Continued

CHAPTER 10

The
Accomplishing
Manager

OPERATING SKILLS OF THE MANAGER

Why is it that after expending much managerial energy and time in discussion or planning, often nothing happens? Why do managers who may appear crisp, logical, and determined at the conference table frequently accomplish little or nothing when they return to their offices? Why do certain managers work effectively both within and outside their organizations and produce a string of significant accomplishments in a short time?

Thirty-one managers were studied as a basis for this chapter. These managers were typically working in manufacturing industries. Large and small firms and top, middle, and lower level managers were almost equally represented. While the sample is small, our analysis of the case histories involving the 31 managers suggests a possibly surprising conclusion: Managers who consistently accomplish are notably inconsistent in their manner of attacking problems. They constantly change their focus, their priorities, their behavior patterns with superiors and subordinates, and their own "executive styles."[1] Managers who consistently accomplish little are usually predictably constant in what they concentrate on and how they go at

---

[1] By *executive style* we mean the mix of relationships, approaches in giving orders, communications, follow-up, delegation, pace, and risktaking that characterizes an executive's mode of managing.

Written with W. Earl Sasser, my colleague at The Harvard Business School.

their work. Consistency, if our findings are correct, is the hobgoblin of small and inconsistent accomplishment.

In this chapter our subject is the operating skills of the manager, the process of getting work done, changes made, and implementing rather than formulating policy. Our concern is that at least as many management careers seem to be damaged by weak operating skills as by a lack of competence in the realm of strategy and policy making. Beginning with some fundamental causes for poor accomplishment which emerged from our analysis of the most frequent themes in failure observed in the managers studied, we then trace some of the key dilemmas involved in the operating side of managing and present some ideas for resolving these dilemmas. These ideas center on the development of a constantly shifting and adaptive personal approach to problems in operating management.

FREQUENT THEMES OF FAILURE OF LOW ACCOMPLISHERS

Inadequate Involvement at the Critical Level of Detail

Well-educated, younger managers more often failed to be adequately involved at the detail level than less educated, "self-made" managers. The cause may perhaps be the widespread acceptance of commonly accepted notions such as: "A manager must stay out of detail"; "a manager must learn to delegate"; and "a manager must never get involved in day-to-day, short-term firefighting." These deceptively simple notions hurt several careers in our study and even, in our observation, devastated several enterprises. In-depth knowledge at the critical level of detail provides the manager with the facts as well as the confidence to come to a correct decision, stick to it without compromise, and effectively achieve its implementation.

On the other hand, attention to details without a strategy or plan or direction led several of our subjects to a morass of floundering and a further struggle for a sense of control. When things are not going well and the "pressure is on," the operating manager is often afraid to delegate much, tends to draw problems into personal control, becomes increasingly engrossed, and may finally be overwhelmed by the workload generated. This vicious cycle is a common syndrome most readers have probably observed. It was especially prevalent among older managers who have worked themselves up through the organization. They were apparently comfortable with what they knew best and they stuck with it, investing themselves with energy into nearly every problem that entered their span of observation.

Losing the Handle on Priorities

With the telephone constantly ringing, a never-ending series of meetings and conferences, and the flurries of a constant exchange of memos and paperwork, the operating manager can easily work day after day at a feverish pace and feel a comforting sense of accomplishments. However, for quite a few of the managers studied, results of the past six months of the year revealed that nothing major had been accomplished, even in the face of looming or existing problems; in some instances the situation for which they were responsible had deteriorated.

Indecision

Determining when to take action can also be difficult. We studied one manager who took a year too long to get costs under control. Although his primary assignment was to "reduce costs," he spent most of that year asking his people to give him advice and attempting to gain their wholehearted participation and support in recommending changes. Because the time available for reducing costs was short, he simply could not afford to take a long time to pull the improvements up through his organization or to let his ideas "trickle down." His division lost the next big contract for cost reasons and had to be closed down.

Failure of Boldness, Nerve, and Self-Confidence

This failure was observed in a number of the case studies. The theme is illustrated by a situation in which a young MBA assigned to a decentralized division could see after several months that the reason the division was losing money was a poor labor contract which made the company noncompetitive with foreign imports. Because the union was unwilling to renegotiate the contract, only a bold move leading to a major confrontation could correct the situation. The MBA recognized rightly that his boss, a middle-aged plant manager, would probably never precipitate this move. Afterward, it seemed apparent that the young man had been placed there by the management in the hope that his trained analytical skills and personality would force the issue. When he failed to do this because he was unwilling to make that bold and personally risky move, he was ultimately sidelined.

Failure to Admonish or Replace Ineffective Subordinates

Some managers who considered themselves excellent at developing subordinates took pride in attempting to "turn around" people to change their behavior radically. They were also reluctant to fire or replace an individual, always hoping that performance would soon improve. Some offered mild hints and suggestions for improvement; others ignored a bad situation in the apparent hope that the individual would be able to learn on his own. We commonly observed beliefs that "the best managers are those whose people are happy" and "happiness" came from encouragement and praise, and consistent demands for better performance were "bad for morale." With this conventional "wisdom" often came the simultaneous toleration of ineffective subordinates.

Not Seeking Advice or Help

Several failures could be attributed to a kind of "managerial arrogance", the inability of the manager to recognize or admit that help was needed. A director of manufacturing kept insisting to his superior vice president that he and his group could and would soon straighten out a set of new product problems that were bottlenecking all output at 50% of plan. The vice president was held at arm's length from personal involvement in a situation in which he was eager to help. His participation would not only have been useful but would have secured his involvement and probably defused his subsequent attack on the director of manufacturing, which resulted in the latter's firing.

Similarly, we observed failures of managers who were unable to seek advice from knowledgeable, experienced subordinates. They seemed to feel that this might be an admission of weakness and that they must always show themselves to be equal to their own problems. The result was a waste of know-how and, perhaps worse, a negative and critical set of subordinates.

Failure to Analyze

Accepting established "rules of thumb" without question or analysis was surprisingly frequent, even among highly trained managers. In most organizations informal rules ease decision making, and guides such as "carry two weeks inventory," "no overtime," "promote from within," or "keep direct labor costs at 19¢" become conventional wisdom. Rules such as these may have made sense at some time but often no longer have economic or strategic rationale. Unquestioning adherence to exisiting ways of doing things was surprisingly prevalent even among managers formally trained to analyze. The common tendency observed was to do a great deal of analysis in the first few months of a new job but to "wing it" after that.

Managing One's Own Emotions, Pressures, and Needs

Some managers failed because they felt compelled to "take command," to make a showing with a decision, and to deal with situations that probably would have been better ignored or pushed "upstairs." Compulsive needs to be the boss and exert leadership through immediate action were not infrequent in our case studies. There were several situations in our cases when no decision and a delay would have been wiser than moving aggressively ahead.

Blind Spots

Blind spots were frequent among the executives studied. Some managers acted as if they were unaware of their own weaknesses. As they described experiences, they did not appear to realize that they lacked a certain skill or body of knowledge. For example, a manager in a hardware manufacturing firm did a fine job in improving the sales force and developing effective sales strategy. He was moved into marketing and obtained good results in introducing new products. He was promoted to executive vice president. There he failed. His failure can probably be traced to his lack of realization that he did not understand production and manufacturing operations well enough to manage his subordinates. They were able to mislead him.

His blind spot was a realization that implementation, follow-up, and close attention to detail are critical in manufacturing and that his executive style was to focus solely on strategy and conceptual matters.

CONCLUSIONS FROM PATTERNS OF LOW ACCOMPLISHERS

Themes in failure are so numerous and so contradictory that they may seem frightening. They are! They explain why so many managers fail in the operating sector of their jobs. Managers get involved in too much or too little detail. They are too cautious or too bold. They are too critical or too accepting. They are too tough or too supportive. They delegate too much or too infrequently. They plan and analyze and procrastinate, or they blindly plunge ahead day after day without arithmetic, "homework," analysis, or plan. They are excessively aware of their weaknesses and damaging compulsive tendencies or they have blind spots.

In fact, at any level in the organization, the operating sector of managing is enormously difficult. When analyzed, managing is downright "scary," and it is amazing that any mortal succeeds for long. No single approach to these trade-offs seems to work consistently. You are "damned if you do and damned if you don't." The best formula seems to be "it all depends!"

To find a more useful approach we found ourselves looking at these themes of failure quite differently. They appear at first to offer contradiction—for example, the level of detail versus the level of generalization. The managers studied got into trouble at both ends of this spectrum. But the key to the paradox is that no manager observed failed because of performing at the level of detail at the wrong time and at the level of generalization at another time when it was equally inappropriate. On the contrary, each manager who had a problem had it consistently at one end of the scale or the other, but never at both. Each manager tended to develop a set style or approach, and when that manager erred, it was always in the same particular direction.

What went wrong for the low accomplishers was that the situation changed and the manager did not. Most managers had developed a certain set of habits, premises, and behaviors such that their "executive style" had become repetitive and altogether predictable. Serious failure occurred when some major elements of the situation changed quickly and the managers charged on with their usual assumptions, behaviors, and styles.

The less dramatic, but more prevalent problems are those of the average or below-average accomplishers. Consistency is their downfall, for the case research shows a general consistency of executive style for each manager and a tendency to persist in using a set style and a limited number of tools, techniques, and approaches to perceiving problems based on a small assortment of managerial premises which they use over and over again.

Each outstanding implementor had a different executive style and was inconsistent in personal executive style. A successful executive style turned out to be a "nonstyle." Successful implementators have many styles. They are regularly inconsistent.

The paradox is revealing. The high accomplishers get into fine detail in one situation yet stay at the strategic level in another. They delegate a lot one time or a little the next time. They are close and supportive one day and remote and demanding another. They communicate verbally with some colleagues and in writing with others, varying this pattern as well. They analyze some problems in great depth for months while they move with seeming abruptness and intuition on others. They talk a great deal or suddenly are apt listeners.

For the low accomplishers, consistency was the shadow of their failures. Apparently as bright, energetic, and mature as the high accomplishers, they sounded analytical and persuasive, but their results were hollow. Meanwhile, their styles were persistent and predictable. The consistent manager had a consistent executive style, one set of practices and "rules of thumb" hard learned from experience, usually a "philosophy of management," and a group of personal central tendencies affecting his or her action as a manager. The consistent manager had one executive style.

The consistency, which causes managers to fail, is not so surprising, for one cardinal imperative of life as a manager is the necessity to perceive differences from one situation to another and between people, circumstances, physical/technological realities, motives, assumptions, and antecedents. The manager analyzes to discern differences that can entirely change a situation.

The problem is that situations change, but the ordinary executive often does not perceive it and fails to adopt a different approach. The approach that has worked out so well often will not work on what seems the same problem. Why? Because one or two critical ingredients changed. Meanwhile, the harried manager is under pressure to simplify the decision-making process by extracting from experience generalizations for the next time that kind of problem is faced. The more experienced the manager, the greater the likelihood that she or he will have adopted one, consistent approach to decision-making, delegation, communication, and relationships. The missing quality is being unable to detect an incorrect approach. The executive could not learn about his or her own style. The style a manager organizes to simplify life may keep that manager blind.

Our study suggests that consistency, which arises from habit, premises about technology and people or organizations, psychological pressures for simplicity and mental-emotional comfort, and the adoption of one executive style, tends to lead to mediocrity or failures in operating management. An apparently small difference in any one factor changes the requirement for success. When the requirement changes, so must executive style and the appropriateness of certain tools and techniques for management and implementation, priorities, and timing.

Basic elements of personal behavior are apparently rather well fixed from childhood. How a manager can modify his or her rather basic psychological "givens"—motives, self-concepts, and cognitive styles—is beyond the scope of this article, but the fact is that some managers are able to modify their styles and modes of managing better than others. Our observation of successful operating managers includes men and women who seem to have always been versatile—inconsistent—and others who have apparently learned from experience to loosen their prior rigidities and adopt a more situationally adjusted mode of managing. In the balance of this chapter we offer some prescriptive concepts learned from the managers whose accomplishments were well above average and in some cases outstanding.

THE HIGH ACCOMPLISHERS

The high accomplishers were consistent, but in a different way. They were persistent in analysis and self-discipline which permitted them to be inconsistent in their own executive styles. Consistency was no problem for these people. We observed the following approaches, concepts, or techniques that they used.

Analysis

The high accomplishers were, above all, analyzers. They analyzed each situation. The most common cause of operating failure among the low accomplishment managers was their unwillingness to do this. Careful analysis reveals the facts, cause-and-effect relationships, and strategic realities. Careful analysis leads to an approach in operating management that is freshly tuned to the situation. Managers do it in MBA and advanced management programs; it is done in management training courses and seminars; it is done under pressure when a superior demands it. Good analysis produces power and credibility which cannot be turned aside easily. It leads to practical, realistic solutions and most important, develops personal confidence in the manager that he or she knows what is going on.

Most operating managers "wing it" 99% of the time. There seems to be little time to think things through. We rely on the lessons of past success. Curiously, most of the failures we observed were those of previously successful managers. What had always worked before was precisely what caused the failure. A consistent approach is the recipe for disaster. Operating skills can never be considered set; they must always be renewed, reconsidered, developed.

"Analysis" benefits from concepts and frameworks. We observed the following practices and concepts of the high performers which seemed to be useful in their processes of performing a situational analysis of what to do and how to do it.

An Operating Strategy

A strategy is necessary for the operating manager to develop and hold a sense of direction, purpose, and objectives. But a strategy is more than a choice of objectives; it involves recognizing what will be difficult and making an asssessment of the favorable and unfavorable factors involved in the situation and of strengths and weaknesses.

An operating strategy can seldom be long lasting; it needs reanalysis every three to six months. It includes a way to deal with key elements of the situation such as determining the needs, wishes, and expectations of the boss and the boss's boss. It clearly establishes objectives and sets priorities. It includes development of policies and plans that marshall alternatives, opportunities, and resources.

Awareness of Classical Themes and Dilemmas

The high accomplishers appeared to be aware that their problems and dilemmas were not unique. Indeed, this research shows that certain situations repeat themselves and that nearly every operating manager faces at one time or another a common set of problems. Understanding that there are common themes and dilemmas is an insight shared by most high accomplishing managers. They seemed to develop competent judgment and an element of maturity that enabled them to lift themselves beyond the bounds of their habitual responses and handle each situation appropriately.

For example, the first four to eight weeks on a new job is a situation faced by every manager. This time period is both critical and hazardous. The manager must size up the situation and subordinates at the same time that the manager is being sized up by them. They are especially sensitive to every signal that may indicate what it is going to be like to work for this new boss. What is done in those first few days and weeks is multiplied in its significance by those watching, involved, and concerned, both "upstairs" and "downstairs."

The new operating manager faces a further dilemma in that whatever standards of performance are set or not set for subordinates at the start tend to become precedents for the future. It is more difficult to criticize a poor practice after seeming to tolerate it for a month or two. But early criticism or demands for change are risky at best, for the new manager could be wrong, make a mistake, be unaware of valid reasons for the superficially apparent poor practice. The problem faced is how to avoid establishing unfortunate relations and precedents, tolerating low standards, or making foolish moves in the beginning when in-depth understanding of the situation is low.

Another set of classical issues or dilemmas for operating managers at every organizational level centers around information needs. The operating manager needs, but is often cut off from information about objectives, strategies, and priorities held by superiors. The manager must know the superior's expectations for the manager's organization. The dilemma, however, is that frequently this information is not available at the lower level because it is not communicated from "upstairs" levels purposely or carelessly. Sometimes it is not available, of course, because the executives at high levels have no plans and have not made their expectations explicit. The operating manager is often "in the dark" about not only what is expected but also what should *not* be done. In these circumstances several of the managers studied made moves that to their surprise immediately brought down upon themselves the wrath of their superiors.

Other dilemmas of the operating manager are equally inevitable. The operating manager must often deal with difficult employees, employees whose values or motives differ from the manager, or who have serious problems in morale, hold negative reactions to the organization, or unrealistic expectations. Dealing upstairs may be equally difficult. The examples of one manager studied is typical.

How do I deal with a boss who, while brilliant and held in esteem at high levels in the industry, won't sit down long enough to plan objectives and strategy or even read his mail. He says, "Don't write it, tell it." But when you talk with him, he's easily distracted. When you're discussing one problem, his mind jumps to another and he usually doesn't listen well. When you are trying to reason with him, he extends your argument to an absurd extreme, argues rhetorically with unrealistic "what ifs" or makes totally unreasonable "principles" out of your points. He makes sudden, impulsive and sometimes angry decisions based on little data and mostly intuition. In making these hasty, long-postponed decisions, however, he often fails to consider their inevitable second-order implications. He doesn't keep me informed and seldom levels with me about what's on his mind or concerns him. We never set clear objectives or goals. He forgets from one time to the next what we've talked about or decided. Sometimes he tells me the same thing two or three times. We have few staff meetings when we can discuss our problems and plan together. When we do meet, we ramble around and reach few clear decisions unless he suddenly and sometimes angrily lays down the law. He is successful and technically competent, but as a boss he's a disaster. All I get is specific criticisms or vague praise. He has no idea really, in any depth, of what I do.

This operating manager cannot be content merely to "blow off steam" and criticize his boss. He must learn somehow to find out what the organization and the boss need from him; he must assist the boss in the boss's own way to do some planning; he must learn to get through to him. He cannot blame things on the "disastrous boss," for he will usually be the loser if the relationship is poor and he's kept in an information vacuum. He is the one who will be criticized when things aren't perfect, when expectations, which are vague, are not met. The management of the relationship upstairs if often a necessary responsibility incumbent upon the subordinate. "It's his neck;" he must make if work.

Other typical issues and dilemmas may also be listed:

- How to stir up a sleepy, frozen, stagnant organization.
- When and how to question higher-level policies; running "the system" versus changing it; fighting city hall.
- How to handle "no-win" situations.
- Whether to seek consensus, wait for it to emerge, or go ahead and make a decision.
- How to indentify, manage, and make use of power, "clout," pressure points in the organization.
- How to overcome bureaucratic resistance, red tape, and inertia.

Variety of Operating Tools and Techniques

Lower accomplishers seemed to be unaware of the enormous array of techniques available to managers for implementing policy and bringing about change. They used a few techniques repeatedly. The high accomplishers were frequently masterful in the introduction of techniques that proved effective.

The range of operating problems is so great that one habitual set of responses or choice of tools and alternatives is entirely inadequate. The understanding that there is a vast array of tools and alternatives and that discriminating choices must be made appeared to be another part of the development of judgment of high accomplishers.

Our cases of operating problems showed the list of tools and techniques to be impressively large. Exhibit 10.1 is a list of a 39-item arsenal of action-oriented tools and techniques from which the operating manager can choose to introduce change and bring about improvements.

In spite of the existence of this powerhouse of tools and techniques, it was surprising how many managers felt baffled and frustrated about how little they could do in a situation. "I feel boxed in and helpless," one said. "The people and procedures and precedents are so firmly set up and frozen in place. Change is resisted by everybody around here. I can't seem to get any change whatsoever accomplished."

The frequency of this response among low accomplishers in the face of the great number of open options needs explanation. Our interviews suggest some reasons for this operating myopia which reminds one of a machinist or carpenter with a wall full of mounted tools before his eyes but who, scratching his head in discouragement, mutters to himself, "I don't know how to go at this job." Some managers were unaware of the tools and approaches and unfamiliar with their usage. When managers were too close to their problems, they lost perspective and, mentally locking out positive

Exhibit 10.1   Some Action-Oriented Tools and Techniques Available to the Operating Manager

Structural

 1. Formal organization
 2. Change EPT methods, processes
 3. Physical moves, relocations
 4. Expand resources, invest
 5. Procedures, systems, routines
 6. Job content(s)
 7. Job assignments
 8. Lend, borrow, exchange personnel
 9. Project, task organization
10. Long-range planning exercises
11. Consultants, outside advisors

Employee Management and Development

 1. Reward system
 2. Training, courses, management development, coaching
 3. Performance evaluations
 4. Incentives
 5. Informal assignments
 6. Problem-solving meetings
 7. Short-range planning exercises
 8. Encourage/initiate competition
 9. Replace managers
10. Increase participation in decision making

Communication

 1. Short-range goals
 2. Clear change in tone, atmosphere, system, norms, direction
 3. Management by objectives: set objectives, get precise plan to achieve, set up precise measurement/controls
 4. Timing: postpone/delay/speed up
 5. Written announcements
 6. Meetings
 7. Ceremony, speeches
 8. Conflict resolution
 9. Get commitment

Controls

 1. Standards, norms, limits, specifications
 2. Due dates/schedules/timing
 3. Measurement system regarding output, individual performance, subordinates
 4. Regular reporting sessions
 5. Ask for report, plans, process, results

Evaluation, redesign

 1. Evaluation of performance of unit, individuals, systems
 2. Analysis of falldowns
 3. Redesign to overcome organizational weaknesses
 4. Redesign to buttress/support own personal weaknesses

and constructive possibilities, tended to become either conservative or unimaginative. The discouraged manager believed that nothing would work, anyway. Arrogant managers believed that the few techniques or tools they were using or had used in the past were the proper and best ones to use again. They used these familiar approaches whether or not analysis of the situation would have indicated that another approach would be better. At other times there was either a failure of energy or the situation had begun to tailspin to the point that the manager was unable to pull together the time and organization to mount a carefully planned attack on the problem. A manager may lack self-confidence, boldness, and nerve. A manager may be afraid to take the initiative and try some bold approach if visibility is high and failure would be costly.

Changes in Executive Style to Fit Operating Situtations

The dilemma of the operating managers studied was that each person tended toward the gradual adaption of one executive style (Exhibit 10.2), while different situations called for different managerial activities and tactics. Our research suggests that for each different situation there is a particular executive style that would be most effective.

This was an enigma for most of the managers. It is a curious yet reasonable fact that nearly all managers tend to settle into a fairly rigid or limited

Exhibit 10.2   Some Attributes of an Executive Style

Attributes	*Range/Continuum*	
Analytical patterns	Intuitive ⟵⟶	Analytical
Cognitive style	Inductive ⟵⟶	Deductive, use of generalizations
Decision making	Authoritative ⟵⟶	Consultative
Decsion-making speed	Fast, quick ⟵⟶	Studied, worried
Delegation	Little ⟵⟶	Much
Explicit "rules of thumb"	Few ⟵⟶	Many
Type of follow-up	Loose, little ⟵⟶	Much, rigorous
Communication	Informal, verbal ⟵⟶	Formal, written
Personal relationships	Supportive ⟵⟶	Demanding, challenging
Pressure, pace	Relaxed ⟵⟶	Rigorous, energetic
Availability	Easily available ⟵⟶	Remote
Boldness, audacity	Bold, risk taker ⟵⟶	Cautious, risk aversive
Focus on time dimension	Seldom ⟵⟶	Continuous
Openness to persuasion	Flexible ⟵⟶	Dogged, persistent, single-minded
Work with subordinates	One on one ⟵⟶	In a group
Work with superior	Wants support ⟵⟶	Works alone

executive style. Each low-accomplishment manager studied had a certain profile when his or her regular practices were marked on the range of the 16 attributes listed in Exhibit 10.2. Managers tend toward a "set," because each manager proceeds from a given set of mental and physical capacities, a given amount of technical/managerial/industry training from which he has absorbed a finite set of knowledge or understanding, a fairly well-fixed hierarchy of motives inherent in personality and personal history, an implicit set of premises about people, a particular habitual and usually comfortable mode of relating to others, and a set of beliefs and assumptions about managing and management built from personal experience, rewards and punishment, success and failure.

In contrast, the high accomplishers seemed to tune in to the fact that the demands upon a manager vary enormously from one situation and one period of time to another. The analogy of a college or university is relevant: In one period of time the institution may need a president who is strong in building a faculty. In another time the need may be for fund-raising, extending relationships with the legislature and student groups, supervising the construction of new facilities, or developing financial control. Similarly, in business the needs change from the management of growth, new products, cost control, improved lead times, mergers, cash management, and so on. Each focus cannot be equally important. At any given time there exists indirectly or explicitly a key *operating task* that must be a success, which requires focus and a top priority and demands a unique executive style.

Yet typically, over a period of months and years one manager must be competent at a variety of key operating tasks. In baseball, when a particular quality of pitching is called for, the manager brings in a certain relief pitcher. In business management this step is a last resort. In a number of the situations we studied the manager was finally replaced when his executive style finally proved to be inadequate for handling a certain kind of problem. In each case the manager did not realize the need for a change in style, or if he did realize it, he was unable to accomplish such a change. Considerable flexibility was a hallmark of the high accomplishers.

This is a big order. It says, "Be different. Don't always manage the same way." Yet only a few managers studied were able to accomplish this kind of self-control and discipline. Those who did acted intuitively for the most part and often prior experience influenced them to realize that different behavior was called for in a particular new situation: "I've got to be tougher, more decisive, faster paced, delegate more than usual." Successful retooling and refocus of executive style appeared to be the most important change that might have turned failures to successes in the situations we studied.

Why this step is seldom carried out is due perhaps in part to the prevailing attitudes, "You must be natural and do your thing in your own natural way. "A successful manager would be foolish to tinker with his or her style." "A good manager can manage anything and any situation." Our analysis suggests that these notions are largely myths and that careful, honest experimentation with executive style is a tool of vast potential, seldom used.

How can a manager evaluate whether his executive style is appropriate for a given situation? The checklist in Exhibit 10.2 can be used to yield both a profile of the pro-forma executive style for a specific situation and a profile of the manager's present executive style. Examining the differences between the pro-forma and actual profiles should suggest the appropriate changes in the executive's style.

Analysis, self-discipline, sensitivity, intellect, and physical stamina are well-known requirements of the expert manager. To this list of superhuman demands we now add personal liability for careful tuning of one's executive style. Constant reexamination of one's own habits and assumptions is perhaps one of the most difficult of all demands on the person who seeks to be a great manager.

The final concern that emerged from our studies of operating managers was the widespread tendency toward stagnation. The consistency of style and attack that led to inappropriate executive style factors and blinded, myopic selection of operating management tools and techniques was born out of stagnation.

A high percentage of our subjects, old and young, had slipped into a kind of lethargy where one day and one experience led to another; time slid smoothly by; they became mature and integrated, rigid in their styles, and slowly, seemly inexorably, had become a member of the grey army of low accomplishers. Their problems surfaced only in our studies. They showed no realization that they had ceased being diligent.

Many managers settle into executive life and immediately begin to stagnate in their habits. Faced with a dramatic new situation, they may do some analysis, but ordinarily they "wing it."

A pattern of stagnation among active executives is a striking phenomenon. The very reason for employing executives is to provide organizations with a mechanism for making changes as situations and circumstances change. Bombarded as managers are by a continuous flow of change by corporate and economic events, normal human indolence and mental lethargy represent not only a pragmatic paradox but even a moral one. One answer seems clear: The promise of personal reward is not enough to refuel this state of intellectual energy which we found frequently dissipated. Needed is a state of mind that nature itself does not seem to evolve or fortify. As in the law of entropy, things run downhill.

SUMMARY: LESSONS FROM THE HIGH-LEVEL ACCOMPLISHERS

The high level accomplishers were characterized by the following:

They employed the practice of analysis with great effect. They used analytical tools and practice with such discipline and consistency that their establishment of objectives, strategies, plans and priorities were sound and distinctly tuned to the situation. At the same time, they developed controls and information systems so that they had a flow of data that uncovered details and operational problems on which they should spend their time.

From regular analysis on both the strategic an tactical levels, they decided how to allocate their time and focus their energies. They used analysis to give their work direction and so avoided the common trap of being consistent—and consistently getting into too much or too little detail. They thoughtfully tuned their styles to be appropriate to each situation.

They succeeded in motivating subordinates and satisfying superiors. The words *motivating* and *satisfying* are critical. In examining all interactions between an executive and a subordinate—leading, instructing, coaching, communicating, listening, demanding, delegating, reporting, supporting, and motivating—the key to high operating accomplishment was shown to be motivated subordinates.

Similarly, the satisfaction of the manager's superior is vital to the manager's bottom line performance. How to be a good subordinate is a part of the operating art that was frequently neglected. Managing the relationship "upstairs" was as or more vital then managing "downstairs."

They managed themselves. They understood their internal pressures and needs and their central tendencies in executive style; they disciplined themselves to control and modify drives toward anger, action, delay, or domination which would have been counterproductive; they were able to modify their styles according to the needs of the situation; they were sufficiently disciplined to do the analysis necessary to provide long- and short-term directional guidance for themselves. They avoided stagnation in mental and physical diligence.

They focused on one most important task at a time. We call this concept "the operating task." It is the task that is especially difficult, but absolutely critical at a given time to the achievement of one's objectives. Among all the tasks that could be accomplished, there is usually one task that makes of breaks the situation in the short run, and it must precede all others. For example:

A new production manager found himself in charge of installing a new coveyor system for funiture finishing. The equipment had been approved by his boss and was scheduled to start up in 10 days. A quick assessment of the equipment, however, suggested that there were going to be many start-up problems, and he doubted whether the equipment would actually work out nearly as well as anticipated. The operating manager's industrial engineer was enthusiastic about the new equipment. However, the superintendent stated that it would not work.

If he backed off, the new manager faced a disappointed boss. If he went ahead, he would probably "be hung" with the inevitable high costs and low production ahead. What was the operating task he faced?

He decided to do nothing and let the chips fall where they may. When the equipment did not work out well, his next four months were nearly disastrous. He "caught hell" from all sides.

What was his operating task during the first weeks? It could be to get the organization together to make a decision and full plans for what to do about the new equipment. Without such an operating task to set focus, strategy, and priorities, the low-level accomplishers often milled about from problem to problem.

CONCLUSION

These four concepts are perhaps a startlingly simple approach to what it takes to be a successful operating manager. A formula becomes clear from the experiences of our research subjects: Analyze, motivate subordinates and mind the "upstairs" relationship, understand and discipline oneself to avoid consistency, and the result could be to become one of the rare managers who always accomplishes a great deal.

We step back from this work with a sense of wonder and admiration for that small fraction of managers—the high level accomplishers—whose persistence in analysis and self-discipline permits them to be inconsistent in their own executive styles. The great managers we studied were permanently turned on—sensitive diligent, analytical. The observer sees no stagnation, no lethargy, but a person excited by challenge. The life of the accomplishing manager is exciting. That persistent state of mind is a key description of the accomplishing manager.

MANUFACTURING STRATEGY CONCEPTS IN PRACTICE

The chapters in this part give the reader a chance to take the ideas and application developed in the first 10 chapters into real business situations and see how they apply.

The approach is identical in each case: The case itself is first, followed by a conventional manufacturing analysis in some depth. Then the case is analyzed, using the concepts and approaches suggested by the book.

CHAPTER 11

Zenith Radio Corporation

The Zenith Radio Corporation was one of the leading manufacturers of consumer electronic products in the United States in 1965. Sales had grown from $142 million in 1956 to $625 million in 1965. Profits after taxes increased from $6.2 million to $33.6 million during this same period. Television receivers accounted for approximately 75 to 85% of sales, the proportion rising with the surge in color television demand; other products included radios, phonographs, a limited amount of military gear, and certain specialty products such as hearing aids. In the summer of 1966 the company was faced with the problem of deciding where and how to expand manufacturing capacity for consumer products.

HISTORY (1918–1961)

R. H. G. Matthews and Karl Hassel in partnership founded the Chicago Radio Laboratory in 1919. One of their ventures was the construction of a longwave radio receiver for the *Chicago Tribune,* which was used to pick up news dispatches from the Versailles Peace Conference from a longwave station in France. This short circuiting of the congested trans-Atlantic cable enabled the *Tribune* to beat competition by 12 to 24 hours on conference stories.

Eugene F. McDonald, a former Lieutenant Commander in the Navy, joined the partnership in 1921 as general manager and provided funds badly needed for expansion. In 1923 he founded the Zenith Radio Corporation which he was to guide until his death in 1958. Originally the company was only a sales agent for the Chicago Radio Laboratory, but soon Zenith

---

This case was prepared as the basis for class discussion rather than to illustrate either effective or ineffective handling of an administrative situation.

absorbed the partnership and entered the manufacturing end of the business. The company prospered in the late 1920s, establishing the reputation as a high-quality, innovation-oriented manufacturer of radio receivers.

The early depression years brought severe retrenchment for Zenith; sales dropped as low as $2 million in the year ending April 30, 1933, and losses were incurred from 1930 through 1933. The company survived relatively unscathed, however, in part because of an extremely conservative financial posture; expansion in the 1920s had not required an infusion of long-term debt, and investment in inventories had been kept to a minimum. Furthermore, new low-priced table and portable radio receivers, the latter selling for as little as $19.95, were introduced to fit the tenor of the times. Black ink appeared again in 1934, and aside from a slight loss in 1946, the company did not experience another deficit.

As the 1930s wore on, the notion of television began to generate excitement in the industry. Although Zenith indulged in a certain amount of R&D in this area and even originated Chicago's first television station in 1939, no attempt was made to market a commercial television set. The company's attitude is typified by a comment from the 1938 Annual Report:

The management continues to believe that television is not yet ready for the public and refuses to be stampeded into the premature production of television receivers for sale to the public. We are manufacturing television receivers, which are being loaned to experienced observers, not sold. Any television receivers sold at this time may become obsolete shortly. Your company is ready, but television is not.

The management's definite stand on the matter of television has greatly increased the company's good will with radio dealers and the trade in general. The sales, even in the New York area, of television have been negligible. Television one day will be a great industry, but that day is not this year.

The economic problems of television are far greater than the technical problems. One of the most important economic problems resolved itself into a vicious triangle. First, no radio manufacturer or broadcasting organization can afford the expense of supplying adequate television programs for a sufficient lenth of time to obtain circulation. Second, the advertisers will not contribute to and pay for the programs until circulation is acquired. Third, the public, which is the circulation, will not buy television receivers until they are assured of satisfactory and continued programs.

Immediately following World War II, the supply of component parts for consumer products became a grave problem for all manufacturers in the industry. To relieve this situation, the company in 1945 formulated a large-scale expansion program to provide manufacturing facilities for components such as coils, loud speakers, and record changers.

Then in 1948 the company put its first line of television receivers on the market. During that same year, to assure a source of picture tubes, the

Rauland Corporation, a noted Chicago supplier, was acquired. Continued expansion of facilities, including a $4 million enlargement of assembly capacity in 1952, enabled Zenith to participate in the initial surge of demand for black and white television. (Exhibit 11.1)

Relying on high-quality black and white television sets and a capable distribution network, Zenith gradually increased its share of the monochrome television market to over 20%, becoming the leader in that segment of the industry. While extensive research effort was expended on color devices, no attempt was made to introduce such a line until late 1961, more than seven years after the first color sets became commercially available. The brief comments in the 1958 Annual Report are indicative of the position taken during this time.

The company had produced in its laboratories transistorized television receivers and in conjunction with the Rauland Corporation, is continuing research and development on color television receivers and tubes so that the company will be prepared to enter into the manufacture of these receivers and tubes when the time is appropriate.

Company president, Joseph S. Wright, looking back on these events, commented in 1967, "We have learned a great deal from the problems others have had with new products. On the other hand, we have pioneered numerous innovations ourselves, many of which have been highly successful in building Zenith's markets." Examples of Zenith "firsts" were the superior picture contrast provided by the 1949 "black tube" television sets, turret tuning for channel selection, and full transistorized hearing aids.

Expansion 1962–1965

In 1961 the company reported sales of $254 million and profits of $18 million. Capital expenditures in the period 1957–1961 had amounted to

Exhibit 11.1 Zenith Sales and Profits, 1949–1955 (millions of dollars)

Year	Sales	Profits
1949	77.0	2.7
1950	134.0	5.6
1951	110.0	5.3
1952	137.6	5.8
1953	166.7	5.6
1954	138.6	5.6
1955	152.9	8.0

$10.9 million, with net property, plant, and equipment of $14.6 million on the books in 1961. Manufacturing facilities at that time consisted of over two million square feet of research, engineering and manufacturing facilities in the following locations:

Plant 1:	6001 West Dickens St., Chicago. Approximately 850,000 square feet devoted to black and white television assembly and phonograph production.
Plant 2:	1500 North Kostner St., Chicago. 600,000 square feet. Components manufacture for radio, television, and phonograph sets; also radio assembly; 1960 addition of 115,000 square feet for components.
Plant 3:	5801 West Dickens St., Chicago. Parts and Service Division.
Plant 4:	3501 West Potomac St., Chicago. Warehouse.
Plant 5:	6501 West Brand St., Chicago. Financial offices, hearing aids, engineering, special products and military products.
Rauland Corporation:	(Wholly owned subdidiary.) 4245 North Knox St., Chicago. 380,000 square feet devoted to black and white picture tube research and production and special-purpose electronic tube research and production.
Wincharger Corporation:	(Wholly owned subdidiary.) Sioux City, Iowa. Power generators.
Central Electronics, Inc.:	(Wholly owned subdidiary.) Paris, Ill. 100,000 square feet constructed in 1961; manufacture of components for radio and television.
Zenith Radio Distributing Corporation:	(Wholly owned subdidiary.) 912 West Washington, Chicago.
Zenith Radio Research Corporation:	(Wholly owned subdidiary.) Menlo Park, Calif., 30,000 square feet constructed in 1960; research.

Sales forecasts in 1961 were optimistic for all consumer electronic products, and it became apparent that the day of color television had finally arrived. Accordingly, Zenith announced a major plant expansion totalling $20.5 million that was to add over 1 million square feet of engineering and production space during the next two years. Several facilities were involved in this program. The major one was the 730,000 square foot Plant 6, across the Milwaukee Railroad tracks from Plant 1. It contained 325,000 square feet of color television and stereo assembly space, 250,000 square feet for receiving, shipping and storage, and 155,000 square feet for new administrative quarters. Facilities at the Rauland Corporation were also expanded, and the first color television tube production was started on a pilot basis in late 1962. Annual capacity was to reach a rate of approximately 1.5 million black and white tubes and 1 million color tubes a year by late 1965.

A long-standing Zenith policy called for balanced picture tube and television set assembly capacity; however, substantial outside sales of tubes were encouraged countered by a comparable quantity of purchased tubes. According to Robert Alexander, vice president of manufacturing, this practice has given the company an excellent way of keeping a finger on industry quality standards. He felt that certain economies were also gained from larger production order quantities and concentration on a smaller number of sizes and styles. In 1965 the company announced a second major expansion of color picture tube capacity, a 700,000 square foot plant (including additions since purchase) in Melrose Park, Illinois, designed to produce 1 million color tubes a year beginning at the end of 1966.

Hand-wired chassis are a feature almost unique to Zenith television. Most of the other color set manufacturers employ printed circuit cards which permit automatic component insertion and soldering. Zenith has maintained and extensively advertised that their handcrafted sets are of superior quality, a claim that has been credited with providing at least some of the current market acceptance for Zenith television. In addition, Zenith executives believe that the company has gained the favor of many television supply and repair people because hand-wired circuits are more accessible and easier to service than printed circuits, and many repairers have not been trained on printed circuit units.

Model changes are introduced in May and December each year. The amount of operator retraining necessary is generally not extensive, however, because circuit modifications evolve gradually; entire new lines are added less frequently. Historically, retail television sales have had a pronounced seasonal pattern, peaking in the fourth quarter and lagging in the second quarter. The average factory price for Zenith color sets has been about $350 to $400; black and white sets average $80 to $100.

"We have been very successful in matching production with sales," commented Alexander. "The accurate analysis of the field situation has been one of Zenith's secret weapons. As a result, we are able to operate with a minimum of finished goods inventory and still meet our distributor's requirements. Other manufacturers produce for inventory in an attempt to smooth production but it doesn't seem to work for them. Styles change or something else happens and they find themselves with as great a peak load as ever. We haven't experienced much of a seasonal pattern so far with color though." Exhibit 11.2 shows a ten year financial review. Exhibits 11.3 and 11.4 show recent balance sheets and income statements.

PLANS FOR EXPANSION

The production division realized that with forecasted demands and management's aggressive marketing policies, additional capacity would be needed in the near future. In fact, Zenith could not make all the color television and stereo sets that could be sold in 1966. The relief anticipated by some industry observers in black and white television sales had not occurred for Zenith: Sales of these units in the first half of 1966 continued to exceed those of the previous year. Exhibit 11.5.

Alexander described the situation:

The sales forecasts made it clear to use in the spring of 1966 that more space would be needed almost immediately: A little bit here and there was simply not good enough. We have also found that a components plant is not always adaptable to the manufacture of larger assembled units. As a result, we decided that an integrated plan should be put together that would lay out our requirements through 1970, taking into account the latest estimates of demand.

In May 1966 Donald MacGregor, the retired vice president of manufacturing, was engaged as a consultant to perform a thorough survey of Zenith manufacturing and engineering requirements and present a report of his findings to top management. The study began in June and was completed August 1, 1966. A number of the manufacturing and engineering groups had developed proposals that had already been placed before management. MacGregor collected these and formulated others. His report indicated that the proposal for a 151,000 square foot addition to Plant 6 for color television manufacturers, costing an estimated $2,730,000, would be needed almost immediately. A new 400,000 square foot, $6,330,000 plant for either color or black and white television would be necessary within the next six months.

Those portions of the MacGregor report dealing with proposals for the production division are presented in Exhibits 11.6 and 11.7.

The location of new facilities was not a direct issue at this time. However, it was a vital concern to the Manufacturing Group for a number of reasons, including freight costs. Since purchased materials may represent 70% of the cost of goods sold and the end products are fragile, have a high value, and are often bulky, plants located at the center of the market or supplier area have an advantage in this regard.

MacGregor touched on another facet of the location problem:

Several proposals are for plants distant from the Chicago area. This is because of the labor scarcity here and the deteriorating quality of such job applicants when available. However, facility planning should be made with close attention to the advantages of centralization. For instance, Zenith and its subsidiaries have costly toolrooms and model shop equipment manned by highly paid and scarce tool and model makers located at Plants 1, 2, and 5; the Rauland Niles Plant; and the Melrose Plant.

With the MacGregor report in hand, Zenith management faced the task of deciding how to provide for the anticipated growth in demand for the company's products.

Exhibit 11.2 Zenith Radio Corporation and Subsidiaries: 10-Year Financial Review (Dollars in Thousands Except for Per Share Data)

	1965	1964	1963	1962	1961	1960	1959	1958	1957	1956
For the year										
Net sales*	$ 470,503	$ 362,314	$ 323,597	$ 289,804	$ 254,553	$ 235,772	$ 239,819	$ 180,634	$ 148,459	$ 131,570
Income before federal income taxes	54,453	48,383	43,228	40,937	38,355	32,476	35,430	25,741	17,341	13,299
Federal income taxes	30,900	24,100	22,375	21,300	20,340	17,250	18,800	13,625	9,175	7,120
Net income	33,553	24,283	20,853	19,637	18,015	15,226	16,630	12,116	8,166	6,179
Per Share†	3.59	2.61	2.27	2.16	1.99	1.70	1.88	1.37	.92	.70
As a percentage of sales	7.1%	6.7%	6.4%	6.8%	7.1%	6.5%	6.9%	6.7%	5.5%	4.7%
As a percentage of beginning stockholders' equity	25.5%	20.2%	19.2%	19.9%	20.4%	19.1%	23.5%	18.8%	16.6%	13.5%
Dividends paid	18,679	14,378	12,381	10,896	10,499	8,160	7,732	4,925	2,462	2,462
Per share†	2.00	1.55	1.35	1.20	1.167	.917	.872	.556	.278	.278
Expenditures for facilities	10,852	4,177	12,289	9,662	2,116	4,242	2,590	747	1,218	1,134
Provision for depreciation	5,087	5,045	3,804	2,232	1,804	1,651	1,344	1,269	1,284	1,495
Number of employees (average)	15,000	12,700	11,300	10,300	9,100	8,900	8,900	7,400	7,100	6,600

As of Year end

Current assets	$172,368	$142,445	$122,470	$108,300	$103,941	$97,365	$96,946	$80,844	$65,077	$57,986
Current liabilities	61,882	42,178	35,196	35,087	34,700	29,080	35,542	27,850	19,889	19,875
Working capital	110,486	100,267	87,274	73,213	69,241	68,285	61,404	52,994	45,188	38,111
Working capital ratio	2.8	3.4	3.5	3.1	3.0	3.3	2.7	2.9	3.3	2.9
Property, plants, and equipment, at cost	65,121	54,706	50,146	39,203	31,006	28,807	24,592	22,154	21,615	20,480
Reserves for depreciation and amortization	30,031	25,360	20,421	17,141	16,378	14,721	13,252	12,003	10,893	9,644
Net property, plants, and equipment	35,090	29,346	29,725	22,062	14,628	14,086	11,340	10,151	10,722	10,836
Stockholders' equity	147,972	131,768	120,122	108,524	98,641	88,179	79,604	70,656	64,450	49,318
Shares outstanding†	9,354,497	9,307,537	9,199,129	9,104,029	9,031,542	8,935,842	8,864,352	8,864,352	8,864,352	8,864,352

* Restated to exclude excise taxes.
† Adjusted to give effect to three-for-one stock split on November 3, 1961, three-for-one stock split on May 6, 1959, and two-for-one stock split on March 31, 1958.

151

Exhibit 11.3   Zenith Radio Corporation and Subsidiaries—Consolidated Balance Sheets, December 31, 1965 and 1964

Assets	1965	1964
Current assets		
Cash	$ 36,284,991	$ 31,812,647
U.S. Government securities, at cost	44,929,530	37,046,384
Receivables, less reserves of $2,800,000 in 1965 and $2,675,500 in 1964	36,809,402	35,009,503
Inventories, priced at lower of cost (first-in, first-out) or market, including finished goods of $7,685,890 in 1965 and $9,424,615 in 1964	54,344,303	38,576,480
	54,344,303	38,576,480
Total current assets	172,358,226	142,445,014
Other assets		
Receivable from settlement of litigation, less $1,000,000 in current receivables	—	1,000,000

Liabilities	1965	1964
Current liabilities		
Accounts payable and accrued liabilities	$ 39,149,346	$ 22,759,458
Salaries, wages and taxes	10,570,811	11,077,858
Contribution to Zenith Profit-Sharing Retirement Plan	12,107,345	8,324,130
Provision for Federal income taxes, less U.S. Government securities of $24,700,000 in 1965 and $19,300,000 in 1964	54,432	16,743
Total current liabilities	61,881,934	42,178,189
Capital and Retained Earnings		
Capital stock, $1 par value per share; authorized, 12,000,000 shares;	9,354,497	9,307,537

	1965	1964
Prepaid expenses and other assets	2,395,044	1,154,942
Total other assets	2,395,044	2,154,942
Property, plants, and equipment, at cost	65,121,293	54,706,313
Less—Reserves for depreciation and amortization	30,030,987	25,359,998
Net property, plants, and equipment	35,090,306	29,346,315
Broadcasting stations, patents, and trademarks At nominal value	1	1
	$209,853,577	$173,946,272

	1965	1964
outstanding, 1965, 9,354,497 shares, 1964, 9,307,537 shares		
Additional paid-in capital (increase in 1965 represents excess of proceeds over par value of stock sold under employee stock purchase plans)	5,617,197	4,334,780
Retained earnings per accompanying statement	132,999,949	118,125,766
Total capital and retained earnings	147,971,643	131,768,083
	$209,853,577	$173,946,272

Exhibit 11.4   Zenith Radio Corporation—Statement of Consolidated Income and Retained Earnings and Source and Use of Funds for the Years Ended December 31, 1965 and 1964

	1965	1964
A. Income and Retained Earnings		
Net sales	$470,503,343	$362,313,884
Costs and expenses		
Cost of sales	351,017,161	267,232,322
Selling, advertising, and administrative expenses	37,838,828	33,329,845
Contribution to Zenith Profit-Sharing Retirement Plan	12,107,345	8,324,130
Provision for depreciation	5,086,940	5,044,776
Total	406,050,274	313,931,073
Income before federal income taxes	64,453,069	48,328,811
Provision for federal income taxes	30,900,000	24,100,000
Net income for the year	33,553,069	24,282,811
Retained earnings		
Cash dividends paid (1965—$2 per share; 1964—$1.55 per share)	(18,678,886)	(14,377,873)
Balance, beginning of year	118,125,766	108,220,828
Balance, end of year	$132,999,949	$118,125,766
B. Source and Use of Funds		
Source of funds		
Net income for the year	$ 33,553,069	$ 24,282,811
Provision for depreciation	5,086,940	5,044,776
Sale of stock under employee stock purchase plans	1,329,377	1,740,997
	39,969,386	31,068,584
Use of funds		
Cash dividends paid	18,678,886	14,377,873
Expenditures for facilities	10,851,795	4,177,128
All other, net	219,238	(478,850)
	29,749,919	18,076,151
Increase in working capital	$ 10,219,467	$ 12,992,433
Working capital, end of period	$110,486,292	$100,266,825

Exhibit 11.5   Zenith Radio Corporation (A) *Production Data,*
1963–1966 (in thousands of units

A.   Industry

	Color	B/W	Total
1. Television			
1963	700	7,203	7,903
1964	1,366	7,685	9,051
1965	2,747	8,028	10,725
1966 E	4,700	7,800	12,500
2. Radio			
1963		9,975	
1964		10,771	
1965		13,282	
1966 E		15,600	

	Portable	Console	Total
3. Phonograph			
1963	3,405	1,624	4,029
1964	3,418	1,739	4,157
1965	4,046	1,709	4,755
1966 E	4,000	2,000	6,000
E = estimated			

B.   Zenith Production

1. 1963 annual report stated: Black and white television receiver production exceeded 1 million units for the fifth consecutive year.
2. 1964 annual report stated: Black and white and color receiver production exceeded 1,750,000 units, and black and white exceeded 1 million units.
3. 1965 annual report stated: Black and white and color receiver production was in excess of 2 million units, and black and white exceeded 1,500,000.

Exhibit 11.6   Zenith Radio Corporation (AR), Production Division,* Proposals for New Facilities

---

Color Television

Zenith produced 500,000 color TV sets last year—1965. Sales demand increased during the last half of the year, particularly in the last quarter, when the production capacity could not be increased to keep pace with the accelerating sales demand.

Early this year 1 million color TV sets were scheduled for 1966—a 100% increase over 1965 actual production. The schedule was more a reflection of estimated possible production than of sales potential. It was predicated on the anticipated availability of color tubes, night shifts, reduced assembly of black and white sets, and fewer hi-fi stereo consoles than needed for expected sales demand.

The daily rate of color TV production must be upped from the present 3500 to about 4500 sets. Using all facilities available, this will require more night shifts, overtime, higher efficiencies, fewer rejects, and availability of parts—especially color tubes. Another of the major requirements for increased output is additional experienced, well-trained supervisory and technical personnel. The 1,000,000 figure is still a goal to be fought for, but to reach it will require some "good breaks" as well as superior and continuous production skills.

Next year's color TV sales forecast calls for a 50% increase over this year—a total of 1,500,000 sets. Obviously, with present facilities taxed to the limit, including night shifts and overtime, the 1967 schedule could be accomplished only with an increase of plant facilities, for which there is but slight prospect because of the considerable time required to plan, build, and equip new plants. Likewise, the hiring and training of new supervisors and technical personnel, under present conditions, may prove to be as time consuming, and even more difficult, than the planning, building, and setting up of new plants.

Possibly one or more plants, suitably located for adequate labor supply, technical and managerial personnel, transportation, and other important operational factors, can be purchased ready for occupancy. If so, time could be saved, but even though such a plant or plants were purchased soon, several months would be required to adapt the facility to Zenith's production requirements, and then several additional months to train the production and technical workers. In total, 10 or 12 months, at best, would elapse from the time a plant is acquired to the beginning of production in significant volume.

If, on the other hand, a plant must be built, the time span would necessarily be longer before the start of volume production. However, some time could be saved by starting a pilot operation while the plant is under construction, as was done at Paris, Illinois, about seven years ago.

---

* Reprinted from the MacGregor Report submitted August 1, 1966. Certain passages of proprietary nature have been eliminated.

Exhibit 11.6 (*Continued*)

Proposal I: 151,000 Square Foot Addition Adjoining Plant #6 on the East

The purpose of this Plant #6 addition is to increase production of Plant #6 color TV sets, to minimize night shifts and overtime, to obtain better material handling, and to lower color TV assembly costs. This new facility, together with other changes named below, will increase color TV output of Plant #6 from a present estimated 3000 sets per day with maximum use of night shifts to 3700 sets per day with nominal use of night shifts. This figure assumes the use for color sets of Plant #6 space presently employed for assembly of console stereo. It is also predicated on the purchase of the railroad vacant east of the Austin Avenue underpass.

Until recently, Production Division Management had favored the building of a production and warehouse facility of 340,000 square feet adjoining Plant #6 to the east. This would have yielded about 5250 color sets per day at Plant #6. However, this plan was abandoned for the following reasons:

A. Heavy manpower requirements.
B. Transportation difficulties inherent in adding 1000 to 1500 employees to the Plants #1 and #6 total.
C. Uncertainty as to whether air rights could be secured for the Austin Avenue underpass, or the possibility of many months or years of delay in getting such rights.

Summary

1.1 Construction costs	
Building—150,750 @ $10.50 sq. ft.	$1,582,875
Other	300,135
Total	$1,883,010
1.2 Purchase cost of land	$ 404,560
Total	$2,287,570
2.1 Occupancy costs	
Facilities, equipment, and installation	$ 442,500
2.2 Product: Color TV only	
10 F.A. lines will produce 3500/day	
Total cost	$2,730,070

Proposal II

Stereo Plant—Record Players—350,000 square feet
1500 Stereo—2400/day record players—1800 people

1.1 Construction costs	
Building—350,000 square feet × $8	$2,800,000
Parking lot, drives, sidewalks	350,000
Total	$3,150,000

Exhibit 11.6 (*Continued*)

1.2 Purchase cost of land	
40 acres × 43,560 × $.53	$ 871,200
Total	$4,021,200
2.1 Occupancy costs	
Facilities, equipment, and installation	$ 911,500
Total	$4,932,700

Proposal III

Components Plant—211,000 square feet—1500 people

1.1 Construction Costs	
Building—211,000 × $8	$1,688,000
Parking lot, driveways, sidewalks	193,000
Total	$1,881,000
1.2 Purchase cost of land	
20 acres × 43,560 = 871,200 square feet × $.50 square foot	435,600
Total	$2,316,600
2.1 Occupancy Costs	
Facilities, equipment, and installation	$ 874,700
Total cost	$3,191,300

Proposal IV: 400,000 Square Foot Plant for the Manufacture and Assembly of Color (or B/W) TV

All present color TV facilities with maximum use of night shifts and overtime yield about 4500 sets per day. Proposal I, for an addition to Plant #6, increases the daily yield of Plant #6 to about 3700 sets, assuming nominal use of night shifts and minimum overtime. This also assumes the removal of console stereo from Plant #6 to a new plant (see Proposal II). With Plant #1 producing some 1500 color TV sets daily (with night shifts and overtime), the total daily output of present color facilities plus the 151,000 square foot Plant #6 addition (Proposal I) will be approximately 5200 sets. This falls considerably short of the average daily estimated sales requirements of 6500 color TV sets for 1967 and 8500 for 1968.

A new 400,000 square foot facility will produce about 2100 color TV sets daily, bringing the total to 7300.

	Color Sets Daily
Plant #1	1,500
Plant #6*	3,700
Proposal IV	2,100
Total	7,300

* Assuming approval of Proposal I (addition to Plant #6) and Proposal II (new 350,000 square foot console-stereo plant).

Exhibit 11.6 (*Continued*)

A daily output of 7300 color sets meets the forecast sales requirements for 1967, but falls 1200 short of the estimated 1968 demand. This shortage could possibly be met by maximum use of night shifts and overtime—a dangerous course to follow, especially in a tight labor market.

An additional 200,000 square feet would be required to build the indicated shortage of 1200 color TV sets—thus, for a daily total of 8500 sets, Proposal IV should provide for a 600,000 square foot plant instead of a 400,000 square foot plant. However, knowing that 1968 output per square foot of plant can only be an estimate subject to variations according to labor efficiencies, model mix, and design factors— also, that the 8,500 sets per day figure is likewise an estimate subject to future unknowns—the conservative plan would seem to favor a 400,000 square foot plant, so designed as to permit easy and economical expansion to 600,000 square feet. This, as a matter of fact, might be started before completion of the 400,000 square foot plant, assuming that during the intervening months conditions had developed to make obvious the need for the larger facility. Of course, the location of the plant should be such as to provide labor availability for 3000 to 3500 color TV sets daily, and acreage should be sufficient for the larger plant, plus ample parking facilities.

Consideration has been given to retaining all color TV set production at Plants #1 and #6. At present, all black and white sets are made at Plant #1. If these black and white sets were to be transferred to a new plant and were replaced with color sets, the total output of Plants #1 and #6 would be 7900 color sets daily. This figure might be increased, with maximum use of night shifts and overtime, to the indicated requirement of 8500 daily for 1968, but this volume is doubtful and, of course, involves considerable extra costs and difficulties in maintaining quality standards because of crowding and other factors—all of which are present in current operations.

Another factor to be reckoned with is that Plant #1 is not too well adapted to color set manufacture. This is especially true with reference to Building #8. Moreover, converting Plant #1 to an all-color plant would be a very costly operation. Weighing all factors, it seems preferable to set up a new 400,000 square foot plant for color, even though initially greater problems will be encountered in training supervisory and technical personnel.

For close liaison with Engineering headquarters, this plant should be located as near as possible to Chicago. In any event, it will require a small staff of engineers as part of its organizational structure. From a transportation standpoint, the plant would best be situated south, southeast, or east of Chicago. In the unlikely event that an adequate labor supply could be found in an otherwise satisfactory location, there would be several advantages in combining this plant with the console-stereo plant (see Proposal II).

Exhibit 11.6 (*Continued*)

Proposal IV:
Color TV Plant, 400,000 Square Foot
(2100 sets, 1850 employees)

Color TV Plant to Produce 2100 Color Sets
1.1 Construction costs

Building—400,000 square feet × $8	$3,200,000
Parking lot, drives, sidewalks	350,000
Total	$3,550,000

1.2 Purchase cost of land

40 acres × 43,560 square feet = 1,742,400 square feet × $.50 square foot	$ 871,200
Total	$4,421,200

2.1 Occupancy costs

Facilities, equipment, and installation	$1,909,600

2.2 Product: Color TV
6 F.A. lines will produce 2100/day
Personnel approximately 1850

Total cost	$6,330,800

Exhibit 11.7 Zenith Radio Corporation—Summary Chart: A Comparison of 1966 Production Capacities and Plant Areas by Product Classes with 1968 Forecast Sales Requirements and Estimated Plant Space Needs

Line	Subject	Television		Console Stereo	Portable Phonograph (D)	Multiband Radio	Components	Warehouse	Military	Total
		Black–White	Color							
1	1966 maximum unit daily output (A)	6,000	4,500	900	1,300	600				
2	1968 unit daily sales requirement (B)	5,700	8,500	1,200	2,300	690				
3	Percent increase, 1968	Decrease 5%	90%	33%	77%	15%				
4	1966 plant area (square feet) (A) (C)	790,000	930,000	130,000	33,000	60,000			(E) 70,000	2,013,000
5	1968 plant area required (B) (C)	759,000	1,957,000		290,000				(E) 200,000	3,206,000
6	Percent increase, 1968	Decrease 4%	90%		30%				185%	60%

Exhibit 11.7 (*Continued*)

Line	Subject	Television		Console Stereo	Portable Phonograph (D)	Multiband Radio	Components	Warehouse	Military	Total
		Black–White	Color							
	Estimated Costs for Additional Plant Areas to Meet 1968 Requirements		*Addition to Plant #6 (See Proposal I)*	*New Plant (See Proposal IV)*	*New Plant (See Proposal II)*		*New Plant (See Proposal III)*	*New Warehouse (See Proposal V)*		
7	Land		$ 405,000	$ 870,000	$ 871,000		$ 435,000	$ 545,000		
8	Building (cost)		1,885,000	3,550,000	3,150,000		1,880,000	2,050,000		
9	Machinery, moving, setup		440,000	1,910,000	911,000		875,000	95,000		
10	Total		$2,730,000	$6,330,000	$4,932,000		$3,190,000	$2,690,000		$19,872,000
11	Building area (square feet)		151,000	(F) 400,000	350,000		211,000	300,000		1,412,000

NOTES:

(A) Maximum posible use of night shifts and overtime.
(B) Moderate use of night shifts; minimum overtime.
(C) Including rented warehouse space.
(D) Zenith only.
(E) Includes administrative, sales, engineering and production.
(F) See comments, preceding pages, on lines 2 and 11.

ZENITH RADIO CORPORATION CASE ANALYSIS

Conventional Analysis

WHAT HAS BEEN ZENITH'S ROLE IN THE ELECTRONICS INDUSTRY?

Historically, Zenith has been very successful in a highly competitive segment of the industry. This may be seen by comparing them with other major consumer electronics firms on almost any financial measures.

Financial Comparisons 1965

	Zenith	Admiral	Motorola	Magnavox	RCA
Net profit/net sales	7.1%	2.1%	6.1%	6.9%	5.0%
Net profit/equity	22.7%	8.3%	19.2%	28.5%	17.0%
Sales/net plant and equipment	13.4%	11.1%	6.4%	9.5%	6.4%

The reasons for Zenith's success appear to be at least twofold:

1. Keen sense of timing in product development and introductions. With both black and white and color television, Zenith has matched its entry almost exactly to coincide with the rapid growth position of the product life cycle.
2. Market orientation. Zenith has paid very close attention to the needs and desires of their distribution system with regard to the availability of products, and design features which facilitate maintenance (e.g., hand-wired circuits).

Another way of viewing Zenith's approach to consumer electronics is to identify the areas of concentration along several dimensions:

	Timing	Degree of Involvement	Dollars Committed	Risk of Acting	Risk of Not Acting
R&D, technological concepts	Tend to wait until opportunities are well defined before committing resources.	Monitoring others	Minor	R&D risky market may not be ready	Inability to duplicate, no market jump
Product development		Product design and modification	Moderate	Relatively small	Damage dealer rapport, produce noncompetitive products
Marketing development		Dealer relations close monitoring of market	Substantial	Designs may become obsolete	Loss of dealer space, Loss of timing precision, inventory problems
Manufacturing capacity		Build to meet market needs	As much as needed	Relatively small	Loss of market share, loss of dealers, loss of profits

Still another way is to compare Zenith with other firms in a number of areas, such as:

	Zenith	RCA
R&D orientation	Low	Somewhat more
Attitude toward risk	Adverse	Less adverse, willing to spend money
New product early strategy	Wait and adapt	Leadership
Marketing orientation	High	No so adept

WHAT ARE THE IMPLICATIONS FOR THE MANUFACTURING VICE PRESIDENT OF ZENITH'S COMPETITIVE POSITION?

The implications for manufacturing of the Zenith operating pattern is to place considerable stress on:

1. Flexibility and quick alignments to market shifts.
2. Ability to engineer and develop the production capacity for new products quickly.
3. High-quality products.

Manufacturing has been placed in a position where it can absorb the blame for not having capacity available, missing schedule dates, or producing faulty goods, but can rarely take credit for Zenith's success. As we shall see later, the cost of excess capacity is probably far less than the cost of not having it; yet Zenith has been reluctant to put money into brick and mortar perhaps because (a) management focusses primarily on marketing, (b) the company had survived the depression very well because they had not overexpanded, and (c) the management is ever mindful of the sales pattern experienced with B/W television in the 1950s.

WHAT IS THE COMPETITIVE ENVIRONMENT? HOW CRITICAL IS A KNOWLEDGE OF THE INDUSTRY SITUATION?

The case indicates that 75 to 85% of Zenith sales are from television. Thus for 1965, with some assumptions about market price and volume that are probably somewhat conservative, this would indicate:

	Sets (000)	Average Price $	Total (000)
Black and white	1,500	105	157,500
Color	500	360	180,000
Total Television			337,500
Total Company			470,000
Percentage			72

Historically, Zenith has held a 20 to 25% market share in monochrome television; one may infer that this is a reasonable target for color as well. To assess the environment, which will be increasingly dominated by color TV, one might consider the history of black and white TV during the 1950s in terms of sets sold, and average price. It appears almost certain that history will be repeated for color TV *at some point* (e.g., volume will stabilize and prices will decline); the issues are when will it happen and at what volume level.

Zenith is caught in a dilemma. The environment is characterized by products whose markets mature quite rapidly; the large profits are made when margins are high in the early years of the boom before capacity exceeds demand and prices decline. Thus Zenith does not want to be caught with excess capacity when the market stabilized but does not want to miss out on the race to market saturation either.

Million Sets

	Market Estimates	Industry	Zenith Objective 22%	Needed* Capacity
1966	Low	4.60	1.05	0.05
	High	5.50	1.20	0.20
1967	Low	7.00	1.54	0.54
	High	10.00	2.20	1.20

* Assumes current color TV capacity at 1 million sets.

On the basis of current estimates, Zenith would lose between $195 and $430 million in sales at current prices in 1967 if capacity were not available. In addition, the relationship with dealers would certainly be strained or possibly broken.

If the market stabilizes at between 8 and 10 million sets and color completely surplants black and white, Zenith theoretically should be able to convert B/W capacity to color:

Million Sets

	Current Capacity	Conversion Factor	Equivalent Color Sets
B/W	1.50	325/600	.820
Color	1.00	1.0	1.000
Total color			1.820

	Market Estimate	Zenith Share	Deficiency
High 10.0		2.20	.38
Low 8.0		1.75	(0.07)

Thus, even assuming that the B/W capacity could be converted, which is probably only partly possible, Zenith would in the long run still be facing a deficiency in all but the worst case. This does not take into account the needs for stereo and components capacity.

HOW SHOULD ZENITH RESPOND IN ITS CAPITAL EXPANSION PROGRAM?

When analyzing alternatives, the student should have in mind a number of factors that influenced the decision, including:

1. The labor shortage, especially around Chicago.
2. The amount of overtime and weekends and shifts to be worked and the effects on production and work force.
3. The lead time necessary to start a plant from scratch (12 to 18 months).
4. The effort in terms of management time and energy to start a plant and train a work force.
5. The balance of assembly capacity with parts availability, especially tubes, cabinets, and components made or assembled by Zenith.
6. Zenith's competitive position in the marketplace.
7. Future seasonal trends: effect on production capacity, warehouse space, and working capital of various policies.

The student report reproduced later indicates a reasonable approach to the analysis of capacity requirements. Sales needs are translated into numbers of assembly lines, this is matched under the proposals offered in the McGregor report under various assumptions about overtime and shifts worked.

In broad terms the McGregor report indicates one way that the 8,500 color sets per day sales estimate for 1968 can be achieved:

	Current Capacity	Proposed	Possible	Total
Plant I	1,500			1,500
Plant 6	3,000	700		3,700
Proposal IV		2,100		2,100
Addition to Proposal IV			1,200	1,200
Total				8,500

The issues may be raised by asking:

1. Should the new plant, if desirable, be set up for color or black and white?
2. how can flexibility be maintained to expand or contract operations?
3. How can the 1967 sales target be achieved?

4. Should B/W set production be converted to color even at the expense of B/W set sales?
5. What posture should Zenith take in building a run with regard to product design changes, especially a possible conversion to printed circuits? What is the responsibility of the manufacturing vice president in this instance?
6. What problems may be encountered in running a geographically dispersed manufacturing operation?

There are many alternatives that might be considered. This point is underlined by the fact that Zenith eventually took an approach somewhat different from any noted in the (A) case.

From a return on investment standpoint, the investment in TV capacity is extremely high, assuming it can be marketed at reasonable prices. In fact, one wonders why capacity had not been added sooner "just in case." For instance, for Proposal IV:

Investment

Plant and equipment		$ 6.33 millions
Working capital:		
Accounts receivable at 7.5% of sales	$14.20	
(0.75 × 360 × 2,100 × 250)		
Inventory at 10% sales	18.90	
Current liabilities at 7.5%	(14.20)	18.90
		$ 25.23

Incremental Profits after Taxes

Sales: $360 × 2,100 sets/day × 250 days		$189 million
Gross margin (assuming *all* costs variable		
except depreciation)		13%
Profit on a conservative basis	$24.6 million	
Taxes	12.3	
Net Profit		$ 12.3

Payback: 25.23/12.3 = 2.04 years

WHAT DO YOU THINK OF ZENITH'S METHOD OF DEFINING AND ANALYZING THE PROBLEMS?

Two criticisms are frequently leveled at Zenith

1. *No market forecasting is available.* This is actually unfair at Zenith because market data including estimated total market and Zenith share was

compiled and included in the report, though for proprietary reasons it could not be duplicated in the case. Market data and the confidence management has in it was perhaps the key to the decision in this instance.

2. *No return on investment calculations was made.* The response to this criticism raises one of the critical points in consumer electronics: It is not capital intensive. For Zenith the asset turnover is quite high; return on investment considerations become far less important than an assessment of the risk that sales may not materialize.

Some basic questions might be asked, however, given the facts that Zenith is in a highly liquid position ($45 million in government notes), expensive equipment is typically not required to assemble consumer electronic goods, startup times are lengthy, and the market surges with new products:

(a) What attitude should be adopted with regard to new plant and equipment? What are the risks of having too little or too much? Should Zenith change its historic policy?

(b) What is the role of the manufacturing vice president in ensuring that his company is able to handle the dramatic swings in the industry?

Conclusions and Summary

The case is an excellent example of the usefulness of an understanding of "the economics of the industry." It breaks wide open when one realizes that the gains on the "up side" from adequate capacity far outweigh the losses on the "down side" if extra capacity is built and not used.

It is a rough business when the amplitudes of market swings and consumer sales forecast uncertainty are taken into account. Manufacturing management is in the unhappy position of easily being blamed for any falldowns and little to be praised for. TV assembly just isn't that hard, technically.

But the problems are there, nevertheless. Inventory control, procurement, methods and industrial engineering, and work force management all must be handled well, amidst wild fluctuations of volume. Zenith's dilemma is just this, for it must produce fast when the market calls or miss the market altogether, a fact made all the more important by the further fact that prices get cut during the low sales periods.

In the perspective of the electronics industry as a whole, we do not see the technological uncertainties and problems in the plant as in many of the earlier cases. The TV industry and indeed most of consumer electronics is mature in that the customer is offered a product that is bug-free in a technical state.

Nevertheless, new technical advances have characterized consumer electronics just as in other sectors of the industry. Their effect in manufacturing, however, is not so much in having to master a difficult technology as it is in having to have production facilities that are poised for a wild takeoff about every three to four years when a new technological breakthrough triggers off the market into a frenzy of buying. And in between? Be ready to go (with facilities, trained supervisors, vendors poised, methods and processes all worked out, employees waiting in the wings), but also keep costs low! No corner of electronics seems to offer the easy life.

STUDENT PAPER

Zenith has about 80% of its business in the sale of television receivers. In Exhibit 11.8 we see that 57% of total sales came from color TV in 1966.

Zenith is among the 12 largest electronics companies in the United States but is number two in the sales of color TV with a market share of 23% of receivers (Exhibit 11.9—second only to RCA which has a 35% market share. The company has achieved this position by very aggressive marketing, where they have stressed the superior quality of their products due to hand-wired chassis, and so on. The company did not start production of their own color picture tubes until 1965, and will produce fewer tubes than own requirements until the new, large Melrose plant comes on stream in the beginning of 1967.

In Exhibit 11.10 we have compared the different companies in the industry. We see that Zenith in 1965 was among the most profitable seen both in relation to sales and invested capital. However, Motorola spent twice as much on plant and equipment in 1965 as Zenith, so we may have to investigate more thoroughly Zenith's expansion policy.

In the summer of 1966 Zenith, faces a difficult decision. The company has seen the sales of color television in the United States double every year in the past four years. The industry is very uncertain about the 1967 sales—

Exhibit 11.8　Breakdown of Zenith Sales 1966

Black and white TV	$150 million	24%
Color TV	$360 million	57%
Other products	$120 million	19%
Total	$630 million	100

Approximate figures computed from production figures and average factory prices of b/w and color TV.

**Exhibit 11.9   Market Shares
of Color Receivers, 1966**

RCA	35%
Zenith	23%
Motorola	12%

estimates vary between 7 million and 10 million units—compared with an estimate of more than 5 million for 1966. The company has, however, a vivid memory of what happened in the mid-1950s, when capacity for monochrome TV outstripped demand and the dramatic profit squeeze that followed. Even if Zenith managed to get through this crisis as a winner, the company is probably worried about the possibility of large overcapacity.

Zenith is very proud of its ability to keep factory inventories low, because of an accurate analysis of the field situation. We therefore have to take the company's figures for demand in the future seriously, and at least think they are on the conservative side. With a production of 4500 finished color sets per day, the company has barely been able to match demand in 1966. This will be increasingly difficult in the fall of 1967 because of the buying surge in this past year. Daily sales requirement is expected to be an average of 6500 color sets in 1967 and 8500 for 1968.

In the summer of 1966 Zenith has a total capacity in its final assembly operations of 4500 sets per day with a maximum use of overtime and night shifts. Proposal I suggests an expansion of 700 finished color sets per day, and Proposal IV suggests additional 2100 sets per day (as a firm). Because of necessary construction time and required training period for the personnel, these plants will not produce at full capacity for about 18 months; this expansion would make possible a production of 8500 sets per day by the beginning of 1968. This is similar to the expected daily average sales requirement in that year.

The increase in sales from 470 million in 1965 to an expected 625 million in 1966 is because of Zenith's increase in color TV by about .5 million units. The increase in net profits over the same period was $10 million. The company was therefore making 5.6% net profit on incremental sales of TV color

Exhibit 11.10   Financial comparisons

1965 figures	Zenith	Admiral	Motorola	Magnavox	RCA
Net profit/net sales	7.1	2.1	6.1	6.9	5.0
Net profit/equity	22.7	8.3	19.2	28.5	17.0

receivers. This is $20 per additional set (since the factory price is about $360).

Proposal I will increase assembly capacity by 700 per day. This would give Zenith $14,000 incremental profits per day, or about $350,000 per month. With a total cost of $2,730,070, the facilities would be paid back in 8 months. Similarly, the increased assembly facilities proposed in plan IV, giving additional capacity of 2100 sets per day will have a payback period of six months. These investments, therefore, have extraordinary high return and should be done.

During 1967 the company will produce 2000 color TV sets per day less than estimated possible sales. This will be about 500,000 lost sales during the year and about $10 million in lost profits, if Zenith cannot sell the tubes alone at a profit. In any case the profits lost will be millions of dollars because of this lack of final assembly capacity. Zenith should therefore by all means try to rent extra space or buy facilities temporarily to make possible an increase in assembly capacity as early as possible.

The picture tube is the most complex of the components in the color TV receiver. The case gives data on Zenith's production capacity for only this component.

Zenith presently has color tube production of about 4000 units per day— somewhat less than what is needed in own receiver production. Exhibit 11.11 shows percent share of the market. The company is following the interesting policy of selling some receivers outside to maintain contact with customers in the case Zenith ever should have overcapacity. The company is also buying from the outside to keep friendly with suppliers. This policy is going to be useful when Zenith in the end of this year gets its Melrose plant on-stream and thereby increases capacity to 8000 units per day— substantially above present needs.

To produce color picture tubes at full capacity in 1967, Zenith will have to sell about 2500 tubes per day average in case it will not be able to increase capacity faster than estimated in the proposals. According to a *Wall Street Journal* article (November 21, 1966) 1967 tube production is expected to match demand quite well. In 1968 the company will have to use all its tube capacity to meet the total production of about 8500 per week

Exhibit 11.11 Shares of Color Tubes Production, 1966

RCA	40%
Zenith	20%
Sylvania	20%
National Video	20%

Exhibit 11.12   Breakdown of Console versus Table and Portable TV versus Radio Combination

	Table/Portable	Console	Radio Combination
Monochrome TV			
1965	82%	16%	1%
Color TV			
1964	10%	81%	8.6%
1965	12%	79%	9.0%

later in that year. Therefore, in about half a year or so Zenith should start thinking about new color tube capacity.

Sales of black and white televisions are not expected to grow in the near future; rather, a decline is predicted, so no additional capacity is needed.

Zenith is very optimistic about its line of console stereos. The company presently has unsufficient capacity in this line and expects that the proposed new 350,000 square foot plant might be used at 100% capacity immediately.

The production division also has wanted to produce more components to meet the rapid increase in demand that, with difficulty, can be met from outside suppliers.

The third and last proposed facility is additional warehouse space that presumably will be fully used immediately.

Although it was relatively easy to get a feel for the return on investment in assembly facilities, this was impossible in the case of the latter three investments because of lack of information. Zenith has, however, about $80 million in cash plus $37 million in receivables to meet $69 million current obligations. Keeping current ratio at 1, the company can therefore spend $50 million on investments out of present cash. In addition, the company will generate $25 million internally in the course of the year. The company does not have any long-term debt and would be able to raise substantial amounts this way. We can therefore conclude that it is probably safe to spend all the $19.7 million that is suggested. The company will then have plenty of money for later expansion in color TV or in other areas.

Exhibit 11.12 shows one comparison between black and white and color TV. One must expect that color TV will change away from console models toward more portable types in the future. GE and Sears have started a move in the direction of lower priced color TV. Zenith should therefore plan ahead and try to formulate a strategy on quality and features versus price in the future.

My main criticism of Zenith's present approach to manufacturing policy is a lack of planning ahead. The company should plan the company's sales requirements several years in the future and start the building of plants early enough to meet demand when required. The present strategy leads to a severe shortage of production in 1967, which is going to strain Zenith's dealer relations to such a point that the company must expect to lose a large number of dealers. This is again going to hurt the company very badly when its capacity again is matching demand in 1968, and the company will have to sell a much larger output. If the company cannot establish temporary production in 1967 to meet some of this demand, it will lose millions of dollars in lost sales and deteriorated dealer relationship.

Another criticism is the company's lack of cost data and revenue data when evaluating investments. The company does not seem to use return on investment or pay back period as a criterion when evaluating investments because of a lack of the relevant figures.

Recommendations

1. Zenith should start building all the facilities in proposals I through IV as soon as possible at the best possible places.
2. Zenith should try to rent or buy additional space for additional assembly capacity as soon as possible.
3. From now on Zenith should start planning several years ahead—with a breakdown of capacity needed for all components and assembly/subassemblies.
4. Zenith should be prepared to meet changes in the type of color TV being sold.
5. Zenith should introduce a better cost system so that the company can know where they are making money to permit them to evaluate new investments based on payback period, evaluate make-or-buy decisions, and so on.

ZENITH: CASE COMMENTS

Manufacturing Policy Analysis

The conventional analysis contained a great deal of useful analysis and commentary. The manufacturing policy approach I suggest simply builds on this analysis but adds a somewhat different point of view.

Zenith's Strategy

Zenith has had a superbly successful strategy in the competitive approach to this extremely cyclical and difficult industry. The industry is characterized by long-term secular growth with major increases in sales about every three to five years based on major technological breakthroughs and advances in the industry. These were characterized by increases in picture tube size as well as improvements in the technology that allowed for a better picture and eventually color television. The industry was immature in its technology and growing rapidly.

Zenith's approach is to be number 2 (an "Avis type" strategy) in its investment in research and basic development. They let RCA go ahead, spend the money, take the risks; and they focus their own R&D work strictly on development and manufacturing and process engineering. As a result, when RCA makes developments, Zenith moves its product development extremely rapidly to get its competitive product to the market shortly after RCA's.

Zenith's emphasis has been on marketing and on "being ready." Its manufacturing capacity and products are ready to go at the time of the major volume surges that have occurred historically in the televison industry about every four years. Zenith's strategy has been to have a superior product, but not to be the technical leader. The emphasis has been on a high-quality, low-maintenance television set and an extremely able and competent marketing and distribution network. As the case states, they have endeavored to keep close track of the market and have their manufacturing "chase" the market. There is no attempt to maintain level schedules; on the contrary, they want to be able to increase or decrease volume skillfully on very short notice.

Manufacturing Task

As a result of this overall corporate strategy, the manufacturing task is both very simple and very difficult. The task is to track sales increases, particularly in the high-volume years. This means to be ready with plant equipment, processes, and products when the demand is there. In times of high demand, the dealers and the company maintain the highest margins, and as a result of these margins, are able to be very profitable in the good years. The "name of the game," therefore, is similar to that of the United States marines, *semper paratus*—always be prepared.

Regarding the manufacturing policy concerning capacity and the report to be prepared by the retired executive, it would be natural for him to recommend the same conservative approach to capacity employed during his years as a manufacturing president. This is exactly what he did. If the manufacturing task is to be ready for the market surges and changes in product development, the basic manufacturing policy of Zenith should clearly be to play the capacity decision on the high side of the forecast. Any capacity decision is based on a forecast, and upper and lower boundaries can be placed on the forecast assigning different probabilities to the different boundaries. Then the manufacturing executive must decide whether to play the forecast on the high side or the low side. Clearly, if the emphasis is to "be prepared," Zenith should play the forecast on the high side.

As indicated in the conventional comments, the economics support this conclusion. In other words, when the plant capacity is ready and available for the market surges that occur in the industry, a new plant can be paid for in about two years. The payback is extremely rapid, and excess capacity that is not used is essentially very inexpensive. This follows from the obvious observation that the television industry, unlike oil refining or steel making, is not at all capital intensive. The depreciation charge on the Zenith profit and loss statement in 1965 is less than 1% of sales. This would contrast to 10 or 15 times that level for a capital-intensive industry. In other words, Zenith should have plenty of capacity available, capacity even greater than the most optimistic forecast should allow. It is cheap capacity, and the only thing that is expensive for this type of situation is not to have the capacity when it is needed.

Seen in this light, the decision becomes very simple. Indeed, it would seem that if this decision came before the board of directors, it would be disposed of very quickly and without the expense and time involved in a report like the MacGregor report. The directors would simply ask the president and manufacturing people for their forecast, the basic economics of the cost of space in this industry, and insist that a company with Zenith's competitive strategy play it on the high side.

There are other issues as well—whether production should be concentrated more, whether the plant should be consolidated more, and whether the location of the plant should be outside the Chicago area and in a better transportation location. As the industry has begun to mature and to face Japanese competition and more price pressure, the company has begun to centralize its manufacturing to place more of the emphasis on large plants capable of producing at especially low costs, and has built facilities outside of the Chicago area with a large television plant in Missouri. The manufacturing policy shifted because of the recognition that the industry, as it matured, would have to move toward a larger volume, more standardized, low cost type of manufacturing.

Therefore, the approach of manufacturing policy analysis to this company starts with the economics of the industry, the competitive strategy of the corporation relative to its competition, and the forecast of future trends in the industry to determine basic manufacturing policies for the company concerning capacity, the number of plants, and plant location. The simplicity and clarity of the manufacturing policy approach is especially well illustrated by this top-down approach to the decisions facing Zenith.

CHAPTER 12

American
Printed
Circuit

L ate in the afternoon of Saturday, December 3, 1966, Fred C. Graham,
President of American Printed Circuit Company sat down at his new
desk in a front corner office of the recently constructed building his company had moved into during that day. It was a moment of considerable
personal satisfaction to Graham, for the move into new and enlarged
quarters climaxed a 45-month effort on his part to build the company, a
manufacturer of printed circuits, from an annual sales rate of $90,000 in
1963 to sales of $660,000 in the most recent fiscal year.

The new building, located in an industrial park area outside Minneapolis,
Minnesota, offered the company more than twice the space it had previously occupied, along with vastly improved working conditions and an
attractive appearance. The walnut panelled walls, modern furniture, and
deep blue carpet in his new office was as sharp a contrast to the cramped,
bare, and spartan appearance of his former quarters as the change in the
company's production and sales volume.

As Graham began to unpack his personal files, he recalled that the decision to make the move into the new building had seemed quite difficult
when he had finally decided to go ahead with it last summer. The company
had been growing rapidly and there was no question that the physical conditions under which they were operating were marginal at best. There were 70
employees working in only 4200 square feet of space; ventilation and light-

ing were poor, and the walkout basement location, he felt, presented a mediocre company image at best.

His hesitation at making the move, as late as September 30, however, stemmed from the company's continuing tight financial condition (Exhibit 12.1), coupled with the cost of the move and the rent increase from $350 to

Exhibit 12.1   American Printed Circuit Company: Balance Sheets (thousands of dollars)

	November 30, 1966	April 30, 1966	April 30, 1965	April 30, 1964
Assets				
Cash	$ 9.0	$ 29.1	$ 21.0	$ 0.8
Accounts receivable	140.1	43.4	38.4	26.8
Inventories				
Materials and supplies	17.3	13.9	9.9	2.8
Work in process	17.6	9.9	8.5	6.5
Total inventories	$ 34.9	$ 23.8	$ 18.4	$ 9.3
Prepaid assets	6.6	5.4	5.8	5.6
Total current assets	$190.6	$101.7	$ 83.6	$ 42.5
Fixed assets	$ 77.1	$ 78.2	$ 57.0	$ 55.7
Less depreciation	(39.5)	(34.0)	(18.4)	(18.0)
Net fixed assets	$ 37.6	$ 44.2	$ 38.6	$ 37.7
Other assets	2.7	0.7	3.6	29.7*
Total assets	$230.9	$146.6	$125.8	$109.9
Liabilities				
Accounts payable	$101.3	$ 21.4	$ 24.9	$ 30.4
Notes payable	35.6	8.1	16.0	0.0
Accruals	27.3	16.2	8.2	6.0
Total current liabilities	$164.2	$ 45.7	$ 49.1	$ 36.4
Long-term debt	—	—	8.1	35.7
Stockholders' equity				
Capital stock	8.7	8.7	8.7	115.0
Paid-in surplus	106.3	106.3	106.3	—
Retained earnings	(14.3)	(46.5)	(68.1)	(25.7)
Profit year to date	(34.0)	32.4	21.7	(51.5)
Total	$ 66.7	$100.9	$ 68.6	$ 37.8
Total liabilities	$230.9	$146.6	$125.8	$109.9

* Includes $22,400 research and development and $7,300 leasehold improvement.
NOTE: Fiscal year ends April 30.

$1030 per month. Further, he was concerned about the immediate effect of the move on the company's production output and efficiency. Both the backlog of $265,000 and customer delinquency of $90,000 as of December 1 prompted these concerns, and operating results over recent months had not been satisfactory (Exhibit 12.2). He had, nevertheless, decided to go ahead with the move at that time because of the shortage of space and poor working conditions and need for increasing production capacity, combined with the need to sign a new lease if the company was to stay in the old building beyond June 1, 1967.[1]

The move into the new 9200 square foot building had been accomplished that Saturday without serious problems, and Graham expected production to resume on Monday. He was disappointed, however, over several aspects of the move. First, his former landlord had notified him during the past week that he intended to charge the company $4200 for repairs and modification to the building caused by the American Printed Circuit Company occupancy.

Second, the move itself and the outfitting of the new building were clearly running into a good deal more money than he had estimated would be required. The original plan had forecast a total of about $10,000 for the moving expenses, new partitions, plumbing, electrical, ventilation, and factory leasehold improvements. A total of $30,000 now looked more realistic, mostly due to additional construction expenses in the new location (e.g., electrical work was estimated at $16,000). Finally, the progress on the new building had been delayed by the contractor's work load, and much work remained to be done. Pipes and wires and lumber were strewn around, and this work might interfere with production over the next week or two.

COMPANY HISTORY

The American Printed Circuit Company (APC) had been organized in May 1962 by two partners in a successful Minneapolis printing firm. With the help of 12 friends they raised $112,000 and hired an experienced printed circuit engineer to manage the company. Sales of $11,000 during the first seven months were disappointing, however; and the company had lost $25,000 in that period.

At that time the firm began negotiations with Fred C. Graham, who was vice president of a competing firm located in St. Paul. This company was in the process of being acquired by a larger company, and he agreed to join APC as general manager at the time of the acquisition, March 1, 1963. The

---

[1] The former lease had an escape clause allowing the lessee to terminate the lease on 90 days notice.

Exhibit 12.2 American Printed Circuit Company: Profit and Loss statements (thousands of dollars)

	1966							Fiscal 1965	Fiscal 1964	Fiscal 1963*
	November	October	September	August	July	June	May			
Gross sales	$78.0	$59.2	$51.6	$65.0	$50.0	$44.3	$41.9	$660.5	$397.7	$315.4
Returns and allowances	(5.9)	(5.0)	(2.3)	(2.0)	(3.7)	(5.7)	(2.3)	(60.6)	(19.8)	(15.1)
Net sales	$72.0	$54.1	$49.2	$62.8	$46.3	$38.5	$39.5	$597.5	$377.9	$300.3
Labor and materials	$54.2	$38.2	$36.1	$40.0	$28.2	$28.0	$30.8	$347.8	$199.3	$223.9
Factory overhead	12.8	13.3	14.6	14.3	10.0	8.6	9.1	136.0	70.3	78.9
Cost of goods sold	$67.0	$51.5	$50.7	$54.3	$38.2	$36.6	$39.9	$483.8	$269.6	$302.8
Factory profit	$ 5.0	$ 2.6	$(1.5)	$ 8.5	$ 8.1	$ 1.9	$(0.4)	$113.7	$108.3	$ (2.5)
Selling, G&A	8.1	8.4	8.0	9.6	9.0	8.5	6.6	80.4	56.2	41.8
R&D	0.1	0.1	0.1	0.1	0.1	0.1	0.1	0.7	30.5	7.2
Other income	—	—	—	0.4	—	—	—	—	—	—
Net profit before tax	$(3.2)	$(5.9)	$(9.5)	$(0.7)	$(1.0)	$(6.6)	$(7.1)	$ 32.4	$ 21.7	$(51.5)
Factory wages	31.1	27.5	26.5	31.3	21.7	20.7	14.8	218.6	101.8	n.a.

* Fiscal year 1963 ended April 30, 1964.
NOTE: Some totals do not add due to rounding.

Exhibit 12.2A   Analysis of Factory Overhead, November 1966

Source of Overhead	November 1966	7 Months Ended November 1966
Fixed		
Rent	$ 350	$ 2,454
Electricity	467	2,922
Heat	96	214
Insurance	200	1,100
Water and sewer	18	1,224
Building maintenance	—	100
Cleaning and sanitation	162	914
Personal property tax	100	550
Depreciation—manufacturing equipment	950	6,650
Amortization, leasehold improvements	—	—
Total fixed	$2,343	$16,128
Variables		
KPR stripper	143	1,310
Precious metal plating supplies	546	3,418
Silk screen supplies	190	1,371
Photo resist supplies	(426)	3,093
Etching supplies	1,753	9,891
Scrubbing supplies	21	451
Solder plating supplies	383	5,319
Inspection supplies	—	523
Through hole plating supplies	853	7,549
Drilling supplies	3,348	11,016
Printing supplies	—	54
Fabrication supplies	113	460
Vapor degreaser supplies	668	4,276
Maintenance and repairs—dies	166	846
Maintenance and repairs—equipment	470	2,771
Equipment rental	—	—
Hand tools	69	169
Payroll taxes—factory	1,138	8,393
Stripping supplies	115	586
Fluborates	—	574
Routing supplies and bushings	562	2,396
Freight, insurance	196	993
Outside tests	113	1,068
Total variable	$10,421	$66,527
Total factory overhead	$12,764	$82,655

first fiscal year of APC, which ended two months later, showed sales of $40,000 and an operating loss of $40,000.

When Fred Graham assumed his new duties in March 1963, the former general manager concentrated his efforts on engineering, but after a number of months left the company to accept a position with a competitor. In August 1963, the board of directors elected Graham president.

Fred Graham was 36 when he became president of APC. He had graduated in 1951 from a well-known eastern business school with a master's degree and joined the Honeywell Corporation as a production coordinator in the Aeronautical Division. He stayed with Honeywell for nine years, working in production control and office automation areas. In 1960 he left Honeywell after persuading the proprietor of a small printed circuit shop to incorporate, to "go public," and to raise $250,000 in equity funds. After handling these financial arrangements with the underwriters, Mr. Graham became vice president and general manager of the firm. He left this firm to join APC.

The ownership of APC prior to Mr. Graham's arrival had been divided as follows: the two founders, 30,000 shares (15,000 each); 12 friends of the founders, 39,750 shares; Bill White,[2] 2,500; totalling 72,250 shares.

As a condition of joining the American Printed Circuit Co. Fred Graham purchased 15,000 previously unissued shares at 20¢ per share, bringing the total number of outstanding shares to 87,250 as of March 1, 1963. In 1965 Graham purchased 14,000 shares from one of the original founders, increasing his total of shares owned to 29,000.

In 1966 the company's board of directors consisted of one of the founders who had retained his stock; Graham; the company's attorney. John Mixon (company treasurer); and two of the 12 original investors. Fred Graham was given an entirely free hand in managing the company, and the board members and other stockholders were generally inactive between annual meetings.

Financial and operating results between 1963 and 1966 are detailed in Exhibits 12.1 and 12.2. During this period of time the company's line of business consisted of producing circuit boards on a customer-order basis for a broad variety of customers in the electronics industry. Although much of the business was concentrated in the midwest, customers were located as far east as Boston and as far west as Los Angeles.

MARKETING AND COMPETITION

One of Fred Graham's early moves was to set up an organization of independent manufacturer's representatives. By late 1966 the company had a

---

[2] Plant manager from 1962 to 1965.

"rep" who covered the area surrounding the following cities: Minneapolis, Chicago, St. Louis, Dayton, New York, Boston, Atlanta, Los Angeles.

The "reps" received a commission on net sales which ranged from 5 to 10%; depending on the particular arrangement each had negotiated with the company. Fred Graham felt that "reps are worthless for getting new customers:

They don't know the product and company well enough to impress engineers, and they don't sell aggressively. They're great for follow-up and servicing accounts, though. We need a sales manager to sign up and work with reps to get new customers, but we can't afford it now. I personally do most of the selling. In fact, during the past year we've really done no marketing. We wait for the orders to come to us. And they've been pouring in. The big problem this last year was what orders to accept and which to discourage or turn down. The backlog has just kept rising (Exhibit 12.3).

Graham felt that the total market for printed circuits had been growing at a rate of 15 to 20% per year, and he estimated that the total United States market was probably about $150 to 200 million per year, excluding about 150 captive processors who produced the equivalent of another $100 to 150 million.

Fred Graham felt that the market would continue to grow.

The application of printed circuits is expanding. As integrated circuits grow in use, printed circuits will be used to interconnect assemblies instead of just discrete components. Hence, I see the uses of printed circuits as broadening even though some applications may be diminishing. Multilayer circuits [where printed circuits are layered together to make a three-dimensional total circuit] are growing in use, and flexible circuits [which can be bent to follow a curved contour] are growing at a 50% annual rate now. We're not equipped for this work but hope to be next year.

Exhibit 12.3   American Printed Circuit: Order Backlog, End of Month

November 1966	$265,000
October	235,000
September	215,000
August	180,000
July	167,000
June	154,000
May	98,000
April	98,000
April 1965	70,000
April 1964	43,000

He stated that there were approximately 20 competitors in Minnesota alone and perhaps 500 competitors in the United States. Four companies had sales totalling $38 million: One company in Los Angeles had sales of $16 million; a Chicago firm, about $10 million; a New York firm, $7 million; and a Minneapolis firm, $5 million. Locally APC probably ranked fifth behind firms with sales of $5 million, $3 million, $2 million and $1.6 million respectively, according to Mr. Graham's estimates.

APC sold to approximately 40 customers. Its largest customer[3] took about 50% of the company's sales volume, and the next four together typically accounted for another 20% of sales. As of December, $265,000 in open orders were on the books, from 31 customers. About 75% of APC's business came from customers located within a 300-mile radius. No records were kept of sales by geographic area, but Graham estimated that the company's business was derived from the different areas approximated as follows:

	Total	By Reps
1. Minneapolis, St. Paul	50%	2%
2. Chicago	11	11
3. St. Louis	0	0
4. Dayton	3	3
5. New York	6	6
6. Boston	4	4
7. Atlanta	1	1
8. Los Angeles	0	0
9. Other	25	0
	100%	27%

Order quantities followed a wide dispersion. Fred Graham estimated that the quantity of circuit boards per order averaged about as follows:

	Quantity per Order					
	1–5	6–20	21–40	41–80	81–150	over 150
% of orders received	20	25	10	10	15	20

Typical prices and sales volume were as follows:

---

[3] Not the CAVU Corporation, a relatively new customer, whose recent order status is discussed on pages 198 and 200.

% of Sales Volume	Type of Circuit Board	Typical Size	Typical Unit Price for an Order of 25 Pieces
33	single sided[1]	4 × 5″	$3.50
33	double sided[2]	″	5.50
33	plated thru hole double sided[3]	″	9.50

[1] Circuit printed on one side of board only.
[2] Circuits printed on both sides of board.
[3] Circuits printed on both sides and holes through the board are plated with copper to give a front to back electrical connection.

Sizes ranged from ¼″ x ½″ boards to 12″ x 18″. Prices could run from 8¢ to $75 per board. Quantities ran as high as 30,000 boards per order. Approximately 250 orders were being received monthly in late 1966.

Pricing was done jointly by Fred Graham and the production control manager. They included factors such as:

1. Build up of estimates of times and cost for each operation.
2. Historical price in same or similar circuit boards.
3. The competitive situation.
4. An estimate of what the market will bear.
5. "Gut feel."

Although a short-lived effort had been made in 1964 to accumulate costs by order, it had been found expensive and impractical because so many orders were processed each month.

ORGANIZATION AND PERSONNEL

An organization chart is shown in Exhibit 12.4. In December 1966 the company employed 79 persons—70 in the factory and nine in the office. Exhibit 12.5 gives a detailed breakdown of the employees by each category.

In October APC's wage and benefit policies were revised. The letter announcing the new wages and benefit program is included as Exhibit 12.6. Essentially, wages were increased in October by about 15¢ per hour to meet local competitive conditions. Under the former wage plan, workers moved from their starting rate to a top rate in six months. Top rates had been 25¢ per hour above the starting rate.

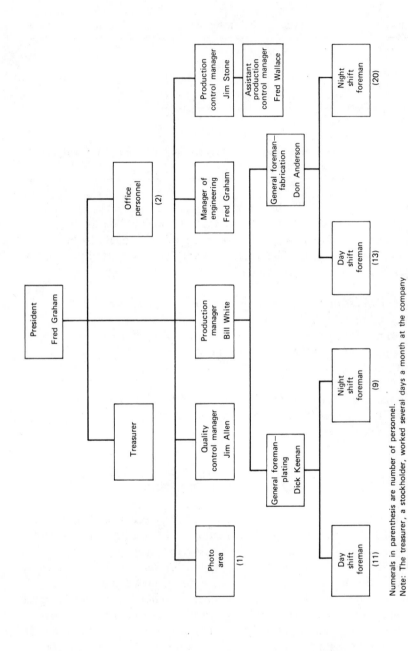

Numerals in parenthesis are number of personnel.
Note: The treasurer, a stockholder, worked several days a month at the company without compensation.

Exhibit 12.4 American Printed Circuit: Organization December 1, 1966

Exhibit 12.5 American Printed Circuit: List of Personnel

Salaried
President	Fred Graham
Treasurer	John Mixon
Production Manager	Bill White
Production Control Manager	Jim Stone
Assistant Production Control Manager	Fred Wallace
Quality Control Manager	Jim Allen
Office	Barbara Snyder, Susan Black
General Foreman, Plating	Dick Keenan
General Foreman, Fabrication	Don Anderson
Foremen	4

Hourly

	First Shift	Second Shift	Total
Photo area	1	—	1
Inspectors	7	5	12
Plating Area	11	9	20
Silk screen	1	—	1
Etch print, solder plate	5	7[1]	12
Spotting	2	2	4
Repair	1	—	1
Maintenance	1	—	1
Precious metals plating	1	—	1
Fabrication area	13	20	33
Stock preparation	—	1	1
Drill	9	17[2]	26
Routing	2	1	3
Punch press	2	1	3
Total hourly			66

[1] Includes 3 on third shift.
[2] Includes 6 on third shift.

Over the years since Fred Graham assumed the presidency there had been only two major changes in the organizational structure. Bill C. White, who had been production manager in March 1963 was replaced by Jack Day in August 1965. Mr. White, who was in his mid-fifties, had found the long hours to be a hardship. After August 1965 he concentrated on process engineering, working out the specific process to be used on each new order. Jack Day was 42. His previous position had been as production manager of

Exhibit 12.6   American Printed Circuit—Memo Covering Revision of Wage and Benefit Policies

---

October 21, 1966

To: All Employees
Subject: Revision of Wage and Benefit Policies

1. *New Wage Structure*
We are pleased to announce the following new wage structure, which is effective Monday, October 24, 1966.

Hourly Wage Rates

	Drill press operators, spotters	Etchers, platers	Photo technicians, senior etchers, senior platers
Starting Rate	$1.60	$1.80	$2.25
3 months	1.65	1.90	2.35
6 months	1.75	2.00	2.45
12 months	1.85	2.10	2.60
18 months	1.95	2.20	2.75
24 months	2.05	2.30	2.90
36 months	2.15	2.40	3.05

The rate for fully qualified inspectors is $.10 additional. This rate will be earned only after the individual has served as an inspector for a 30-day probationary period and has demonstrated his proficiency in inspection. Senior Etchers and Platers will normally have had a minimum of three years of plating experience and must demonstrate a high level of knowledge and proficiency in plating and/or etching activities. Lead personnel will receive $.15 additional. Shift differential is $.10 for second shift and $.15 for third shift.

Any adjustments necessary in individual pay rates as a result of this new wage schedule will be made on October 24, 1966, and your foreman will notify you of such adjustment.

The wage rate progression outlined above is not automatic in that these wage adjustments for individual employees will be based primarily on job performance, not on length of service alone. The step adjustments must be earned and will require the foreman's favorable recommendation that the production of the employee is continuing to improve in both quality and quantity.

It is our aim to have each employee look on wage adjustments as an incentive to do better work, with the realization that better work, or taking on work with more responsibility, will be rewarded by higher compensation.

Exhibit 12.6 (Continued)

2. *Merit Pay*
As a further incentive, we are continuing our plan of merit pay, which is an extra bonus in hourly rate awarded to those individuals who demonstrate truly outstanding and exceptional performance in quality and quantity over a period of time.

The overall wage structure will be reviewed once each year, and adjustments will be made when justified to maintain our compensation program in line with pay practices in the area for jobs requiring a comparable level of skill and responsibility.

3. *Overtime*
Time and one-half will be paid for all hours worked over 40 in any one week. Hours worked on Sunday and holidays are paid at double time.

4. *Paid Holidays*
We will observe 6 1/2 paid holidays each year: New Year's Day, Memorial Day, Fourth of July, Labor Day, Thanksgiving Day, one-half day before Christmas, and Christmas Day. Should any of the above holidays occur on Sunday, the following Monday will be observed as a holiday. If a holiday falls on Saturday, it will be observed either on the preceding Friday or the following Monday, based upon the community and school practice and the mutual interest of both the employees and the company. An employee will be eligible for holiday pay after 30 days of employment. To receive holiday pay, an employee must have been at work the work day preceding as well as the work day following the holiday.

5. *Paid Vacations*
Vacations with pay will be provided to all full-time regular employees on the following basis: one week after the completion of one full year of continuous employment; and two weeks after four years of continuous employment. An additional day of vacation will be allowed when a recognized holiday falls within your vacation period. In all cases, arrangements for vacations must be made at least two weeks in advance with your foreman. The foreman will exercise judgment in the granting of vacations, considering work load and department staffing, to make sure that the best interests of the company and our customers is recognized. Vacation pay is calculated by averaging the straight time rates during the preceding year. Vacation time cannot be accumulated from year to year. Vacation time must be taken unless production requirements are such that you are asked to forego the vacation and take pay instead, and you agree to do so. An employee who terminates his employment before completing at least one year of continuous service, or an employee who quits without giving at least one week's notice, will not be eligible for any vacation payment. The possibilities exist that in the future we will have a general plant shutdown for a vacation period, and if this becomes the case, this will be announced well in advance.

6. Hospitalization Plan

After one month of service, each employee is eligible to participate in the group insurance plan covering hospitalization, surgical, and major medical expenses. Benefits are $20 per day up to 70 days plus $400 of other hospital charges, $4 per doctor's in-hospital visits, $250 surgical expenses, and up to $5000 of major medical expense on an 80% co-insurance basis. The company pays somewhat over half of the employees cost, with the employee paying for the balance which amounts to $1.86 per week during the first month and $.93 per week thereafter. Benefits are also available for dependents, with the employee paying the entire cost of $2.48 per week additional. Costs are handled on a payroll deduction basis.

7. Other Benefits

All employees are covered by company-paid Workmen's Compensation Insurance, which protects you in the event of a job-connected injury or accident. In the case of layoff or future unemployment for other reasons, all employees are covered by company-paid Unemployment Compensation. Finally, each employee is in "covered employment" within the meaning of the Federal Social Security Act. Current deductions for Social Security are 4.2% of the first $6600 earned, and the company contributes a like amount to your social security account.

We appreciate and thank you for your contributions and help in bringing our company to this stage in our growth. It is a fine accomplishment to be able to look forward to moving into the new plant within the next month. As you can appreciate, it is going to require a lot of additional hard work and dedicated effort on the part of everybody in the company to achieve the future continued success we are all looking for, and to make the move as smoothly as possible.

Sincerely yours,
AMERICAN PRINTED CIRCUIT CO.

/s/ Fred C. Graham
President

FCG/scb

---

a medium-sized company that manufactured floor waxing machines. Day spent 15 months with APC, putting in long hours and introducing more systematized production procedures and operations. He was popular and well accepted, according to Fred Graham, but the company lost money during this period of time. After 15 months Fred Graham asked Jack Day to seek another position and Bill White reassumed direction of the production operation. Fred Graham determined the processing steps for each new order, taking over the work Bill White had been doing. Then on December 1 Bill White submitted his resignation, which was to become effective at the end of that month.

PRODUCTION PROCESSES

1. *Photo section.* When an order was received it was normally accompanied by an ink or tape tracing of the exact pattern of the circuit board, magnified several times. This drawing was photographed and reduced in the photo section to produce a master that was used in the process step of printing. The following steps were usually required, though often in different order, depending on the particular job.

2. *Preparation of material.* The base material, usually fiber glass laminated epoxy coated with a thin copper film, was cut to size and then scrubbed with cleanser to remove dirt, grease, and oxide.

3. *KPR coat.* The panel was dipped in a liquid solution of KPR (Kodak Photo Resist) dried and baked.

4. *Print.* The panel was exposed to a very bright light with the master preventing the exposure of those areas that were to be solder-plated later.

5. *Develop.* The panel was sprayed with hot trichloroethylene to remove the unexposed KPR.

6. *Dye.* The panel was dipped in a dye solution that adhered to the KPR.

7. *Spotting.* In this step the board was carefully examined, and any defects were touched up with resist ink.

8. *Solder-plate.* The board was immersed in an electrolytic solution, and solder was plated on the exposed copper surface. The purpose of the solder-plating was to improve the susceptibility of the board for soldering in the customer's plant.

9. *KPR strip.* The KPR was removed by dipping in a methylene chloride solution.

10. *Etch.* The copper, now exposed by removal of KPR in the above step, was etched off in an acid solution.

11. *Etch inspect.* An inspection operation to see that the board at this stage was satisfactory.

12. *Silk screen.* The printing of numbers and codes on the board by a silk screen process.

13. *Drill.*   An average of 100 holes were drilled in each board, using one or more of three methods:

(a) Eyeball—a small single spindle drill press.

(b) Excellon—a multiple spindle drill press.

(c) Nawide—a single spindle, upside-down drill press with a scope attachment.

14. *Drill inspect.*

15. *Shear.*   The board was cut to a final size on a large mechanical shear.

16. *Rout.*   This is the process of cutting irregularly shaped holes. A router is similar to a drill press but uses a tool that can cut horizontally as well as vertically.

17. *Slot.*   Similar to routing.

18. *Chamfer.*   Beveling the edges of holes and the periphery of the board itself was done with a conical shaped tool in a chamfering machine.

19. *Deburr.*   This process is done by hand.

20. *Final inspect.*

21. *Rescrub.*   A final cleaning is done to remove dirt, fingermarks, and other marks.

Exhibit 12.7 contains data relating to the process described above. Exhibit 12.8 lists the pieces of equipment used and their original cost. Exhibit 12.9 shown the layout of the new plant.

PRODUCTION PLANNING AND CONTROL

Jim Stone, 33, had been manager of production control since he joined APC in October 1966. He had studied mechanical and industrial engineering at Iowa and had eight years of prior industrial experience including seven with UNIVAC as an industrial engineer and production control supervisor.

Stone had the responsibility for scheduling each order, planning when it would start and the amount to produce each week. Graham consulted with him before setting a promise date on any new order. Stone also prepared special reports for Graham on the backlog, work loads, and delinquency, as requested. Stone's assistant, Fred Wallace, the production coordinator, started jobs in the shop. He conferred with the general foremen to make sure that all necessary materials and supplies were on hand and followed jobs in the shop when their due dates required expediting.

The production control group issued three reports on a regular basis. The weekly schedule showed the job number, part number, balance on order,

Exhibit 12.7   American Printed Circuit: Process Date

Process Step	Equipment	Range	Average	Set-up Time
		Minutes per Board		
Photo	Printing frame and developing trays	15.0–360.0	120.0[1]	20
Material preparation	Shear and drill press	.25–2.0	.3	5
KPR coat	Tank and oven	.5–1.5	.75	2
Print	Printer	1.5–3.0	1.0	1
Develop	Degreaser	.3–2.0	.5	2
Dye	Tank	1.5–3.0	1.5	0
Spot	—	1.0–30.0	15.0	0
Solder-plate	Tank	1.0–30.0	3.0	0
KPR strip	KPR strip tray	1.5–3.0	1.7	0
Etch	Etcher	.01–4.0	.5	5
Etch inspect	—	.25–30.0	5.0	0
Silk screen	Silk screen table	1.0–1.5	1.25	30
Drill	(a) Drill press	1.0–50.0	10.0	10
	(b) Excellon	1.0–120.0	10.0	20
Drill inspect	—	2.0–30.0	5.0	0
Shear	Shear	.1–1.0	.25	3
Rout	Router	.25–5.0	1.0	20
Slot	Router	.5–2.0	.6	20
Chamfer	Chamfer machine	.25–1.0	.5	5
Deburr	—	.5–3.0	1.0	—
Final inspection	—	1.0–40.0	5.0	—
Rescrub	Power brush and oven	.5–1.5	1.0	—

[1] All figures in this column are minutes per board except for "photo." Two hours are required for the photography work for the "master" for an average circuit board and the resulting "master" can be stored and used for that particular circuit board in the future.

total in work (started), and the customer promise date as shown on the purchase order. This report was essentially a recap of customer requirements for use by Graham and Stone.

The production schedule was also produced weekly. It listed by customer the job number, part number, balance on order, total in work, and the shipment schedule by weeks for eight weeks. Several typical pages are attached as Exhibit 12.10.

The third report was the backlog sheet. It showed billing by dollars and the total work on order by customer and when it was due. This report was

Exhibit 12.8   American Printed Circuit: Major Items of Equipment

Item	Original Cost
Router	$3,500
Punch press	2,000
Printer	2,000
Etcher	10,500
Excellon drills (2)	8,500 each
(1) used	5,000
Plating tanks (7)	1,000 each
Drill presses (10)	500 each
Vacuum frame	800
Oven	2,500
Nawide drill	3,200
Vapor degreaser	2,000

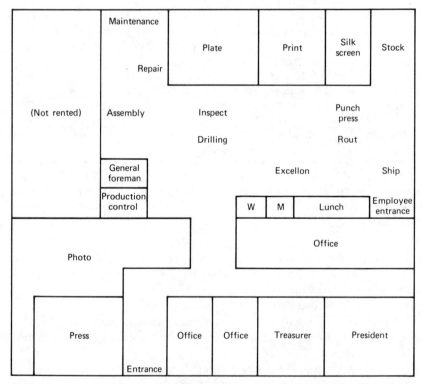

Exhibit 12.9   American Printed Circuit: Plant Layout

JOB NO.	PART NO.	BAL. ON ORDER	TOT. IN WORK	SCHEDULED AMT.	DATE	11/28	12/5	12/12	12/19	12/26	1/6	1/13	1/20	REMARKS
									SHIPMENT SCHEDULE WEEK BEGINNING					
	FABRI-TEK													
5291	130-261	93	80	80	11/21	58								12/5, 2/1 - 35
5375	130-6009	6		32	10/25	6								12/1
5567	130-6044D	146	36					20						12/21
5568	130-6086	276	30					16						12/21
5569	130-6030	165						10	10	10	10			12/23, 12/28, 1/6, 1/13
5570	130-6043	171												HOLD
5751	130-455	8	10			8+								9/26
5782	130-460	2	4			2+								10/10
5900	130-33	3				3+								10/10
5907	130-700	19	19	42	1/1	19								12/1
5911	130-4185C	3	6			3+								1/1
5916	1000-436	14		21	11/17	2/12								11/28, 11/30
5970	130-305	3	8	4	11/17	2/1								11/28, 12/2
5989	130-303	61	70	80	11/15	29/32								11/28, 12/1
5992	130-4305	1	4	4	10/27	1+								11/14
5996	130-4171	3	6			3+								10/21
5997	130-4181	17				44/13+								11/15, 11/28

Exhibit 12.10   American Printed Circuit: Production Schedule

JOB NO.	PART NO.	BAL. ON ORDER	TOT. IN WORK	SCHEDULED AMT.	DATE	SHIPMENT SCHEDULE WEEK BEGINNING								REMARKS
						11/28	12/5	12/12	12/19	12/26	1/6	1/13	1/20	
6015	130-387	72												HOLD
6033	130-6155	12	24			12+								1/8
6034	130-6000	53	63			42+ 11+								11/15, 11/21
6076	130-33	23				23+								11/9
6097	130-4160	2				2+								11/9
6159	1050-6033	102	114	120	11/21	57+ 20+								11/14, 11/25, 12/12
6178	130-4146	15	6			5+		10						11/22, 12/19
6179	130-4207	10	16	16	11/21	10								12/1
6201	1050-82	62	72	72	11/10	62+								11/25
6202	1000-135	1	2	2	11/21	1+								11/15
6205	130-4168	5	8			5+								11/25
6206	1000-218	3				3+								11/25
6207	1000-221	3	6	6	11/17	3								11/28
6214	130-6150	192				2	148 42							12/1, 12/6, 12/8
6215	130-6009	15					15							12/12
6218	130-54	655					100	300		255				12/6, 12/13, 12/28
6233	1000-402	2					2							12/12
6243	130-6114	60							60					12/20

Exhibit 12.11   American Printed Circuit: Backlog Report (thousands of dollars)

| | | On order | | Due in Week | | | | |
| | Number of | | Number of | | | | | |
As of (date)	Customers	$	Orders	1	2	3	4	5
December 31, 1965	24	$148	NA	$70	$ 4	$ 2	$ 2	$ 3
January 1, 1966	29	133	NA	63	2	2	0	3
February 7	27	134	NA	29	13	16	1	2
March 14	22	131	NA	34	11	13	3	4
April 14	22	99	NA	34	4	3	1	1
May 7	21	88	NA	14	5	2	3	4
June 6	22	101	NA	18	12	3	2	10
July 11	24	145	290	48	23	23	5	4
August 8	26	167	316	55	6	9	12	7
September 9	28	215	395	61	13	12	18	9
October 11	27	230	391	60	21	18	20	13
November 14	26	278	385	53	34	35	22	19

used for planning direct labor and for making customer promises. Totals on the backlog report for December 1 are shown on Exhibit 12.11.

QUALITY CONTROL

Quality control was under the direction of Jim Allen. Allen, 28, had three and a half years of college credits in anthropology and, more recently, in quality control management. He had had six years of QC work with Honeywell before two years in the army and one in the Peace Corps. He joined APC in July of 1966 after the quality control job had been unfilled for two months. He felt that the company had many quality problems that centered around:

1. "Insufficient time is allowed for our inspectors. We are always under pressure to ship.
2. "We have no formal receiving inspection system."

Allen indicated, "Now the general foremen are much more conscious of scrap than they used to be. We are developing a real team between the general foremen and myself. The new building should help. We still need several improvements, however, to get better quality control."

DAILY OPERATIONS

Daily operations were under the direction of the two general foremen, Dick Keenan and Don Anderson. Keenan, 30, was in charge of the plating department, which included all operations except stock preparation, drill, rout, punch press, assembly, and shipping, which were under Don Anderson. Keenan had a high school diploma and 10 years of experience in the graphic arts industry, mostly in printed circuit work. He had joined APC in 1964 and in January 1965 became a foreman. In March of 1965 he left the company to work for a competitor as a process engineer for eight months but rejoined APC in November 1965 after the competitor had financial problems.

Keenan felt that the new pay rates and range were well received by the operators.

Turnover is decreasing. I see no union pressure because basically our people are satisfied and see a future. For us in supervision this is a high pressure job. I've got to keep the work coming out of plate and etch to keep the rest of the plant busy. Over the long haul the move to the new plant will be good. Our working conditions were lousy, especially with the fumes. Our big quality problem is with etching rejects. Processing is the problem. Sometimes we use the wrong process or we miss certain steps.

Don Anderson, 33, general foreman of the fabrication section had the longest seniority of any employee in the company. He had had five years in the air force as a supply sergeant after high school. This was followed by two years of silk screen work with a printed circuit firm, and nearly two years in the same work at UNIVAC. He joined APC in November 1962 as a foreman and assumed his present responsibilities after Jack Day left APC.

Anderson and Keenan both expressed concern that they were being "swamped" by too much work in their departments. The order rate had been accelerating for seven months, and the general foreman felt that the combination of "hurry and rush and more orders" was causing rejects and leading to confusion in the plant. "Business is good, but the problems of hiring and training and limited equipment are keeping us working 60 hours or more."

CAVU ORDERS

One of the major factors in the pressure for more production was a large influx of orders from a relatively new customer, a major manufacturer of computers, the CAVU Corporation. These orders were mostly for one

Exhibit 12.12 American Printed Circuit: History and Status of C.A.V.U. Orders as of December 1, 1966

Orders Accepted in	Number of Circuit Boards Promised for Delivery During										
	June	July	August	September	October	November	December	January	February	March	April
May	945	—	—	—	—	—	—	—	—	—	—
June		45	555	260	—	85	1,000	315	—	—	—
July			1,095	10,780	5,516	230	22,835	5,675	2,200	—	—
August				2,595	16,720	16,215	10,300	4,800	1,200	500	—
September					—	470	—	9,000	6,500	2,000	300
October						—	—	—	—	—	—
November							—	—	—	—	—
Total promised	945	45	1,650	13,635	22,236	17,000	34,135	19,790	9,900	2,500	300
Total delivered	1,430	1,335	1,470	4,509	3,488	16,454[1]					
Later rejected (by 12/1/66)[1]	9	266	169	10	597						

[1] The company would usually not be notified of rejections until 30 to 60 days after the product had been shipped.

general series of designs for a circuit board. The average price was about $1.30 per board. It was not considered a difficult board compared to other jobs APC regularly handled. Nevertheless, with the pressure of other work, the company had fallen behind in deliveries against promises, and recently many boards had been rejected. Exhibit 12.12 shows the history and status of this work on December 1.

The recent CAVU rejections were a source of frustration and concern to Fred Graham and his management group because until recently the CAVU rejections had been quite low. For example, the major cause of rejects had been "Transistors do not seat properly," meaning that if the holes for the transistor leads were not spaced correctly, the transistor would not sit close enough to the board. But the specifications did not show a specific tolerance in the pattern so the precise accuracy required in the location of holes drilled was not clear. It appeared to Don Anderson that CAVU had simply been tightening their inspection procedures. There seemed to be little that APC could do at this point but accept the rejections.

Fred Graham was concerned too about whether CAVU might enforce a special purchase agreement clause which technically allowed CAVU to reduce the price by 5 to 10% (depending on the particular order) per week for each week of late delivery. In addition, a standard CAVU clause printed on the reverse of the purchase agreement stated that the vendor was liable for any "reprocurement charges." This meant that if CAVU cancelled an order because of missed deliveries or insufficient quality, they could hold APC liable for the additional costs of procuring the order from another vendor at a higher unit price.

Don Anderson was hopeful that the move into the new building would help to improve costs, delivery, and quality. The additional space and better working conditions could provide not only better visual control but improved employee morale. All but one employee had agreed to continue employment at the new plant.

AMERICAN PRINTED CIRCUIT: CONVENTIONAL CASE ANALYSIS

1. *Financial Situation*
   It is clearly urgent that something be done to stop losses.
   A. *From balance sheet*
      a. Cash is about two to three days' sales or one week payroll.
      b. A/R may not all be good.
      c. Inventory 17.3 for materials and supplies—1 month.
         17.6 for work in progress if 50% completed looks *low* versus that needed to meet customer commitments.

Raises question: *Can* production be built up in time? Where will working capital come from?

d. Cash flow depends almost entirely on profits.

e. To increase production as necessary, what will be required? Backlog and delinquency adds up to about $125,000 minimum per month or about an 80% increase.

$.8 \times (190.6 - 128.6) = $ approx. $50,000 additional working capital

f. Thus it can be seen that finances are very tight and will get tighter. Losses would be unfortunate, even disastrous. More working capital will be needed. Better start looking for it now.

B. *From P & L*

	1964	1965	1966 to Date
a. From Exhibit 12.2—Labor and materials	50%	53%	65% of gross sales
Labor	26	33	45
Materials	24	20	20
Overhead	18	21	20

∴:Present problems in CGS is due to labor.

b. 15¢ increase in late October is about 7 to 8% increase.

c. 66 workers $\times$ 176 hours $\times$ wage rate = $31.1 payroll monthly and wage rate is = $2.67 per hour if no overtime, but from case exhibits of workers and wages, total $/hr. is $123.55 for all of crew

$123.55 \times$ hrs./mo. = 31,100
hrs./mo. = 252 hours!

This can't be; it must be overtime, effect of premium

$(123.55) (176) + (123.55) (1.5) x = 31,100$
$x = 51$ hours overtime (for entire crew, on average)

Thus it looks like the factory works 11 hours per week overtime and 30% of DL cost is in overtime work, and 10% of DL cost is due to overtime premiums.

Since DL percentage has risen 15% versus sales, without overtime premium rise would be only 9% of sales, but problem is both in overtime premiums and reduced productivity.

Action: hire workers (possible in limited space), second shifts, analyze processes, supervision, training, methods, morale.

C. What about costs of rejects? Where do they show up?

2. Exhibit 12.7 Analysis

Set up totals 123 minutes versus 64.85 minutes to produce one board. Assuming one setup per order and average of 118 boards per order, setup time would be only $123/(7640 + 123) = 1.6\%$ of total labor time.

Equipment balance—no great problems.

Crew balance—Material preparation underloaded

Drill underloaded.

Print, KPR develop, dye underloaded.

"Spotting" looks like serious bottleneck.

(If overloaded, quality likely to suffer.)

Standards, *in total,* don't look bad. For 110 orders and 1300 boards, crew, with overtime, checks out fairly well.

3. *Order Pattern*   (assuming price for large and small orders is the same)

OQ	% of Orders	Avg. OQ	OQ × %	% of $ Sales
1–5	20	3	60	0.5
6–20	25	13	325	2.7
21–40	10	30	300	2.5
41–80	10	60	600	5.1
81–150	15	115	1,720	14.6
150	20	X	20X	74.6
	100		11,800	100.0

From Exhibit 12.11, average order is $725. With average board price of $6.17, average order quantity is $725/6.17 = 118$ boards and total weighted OQ × 100% is 11,800.

Solving for X, X = 440 $\dfrac{11,800 - 3,005}{20}$

Thus big orders are carrying the business in terms of sales, and 65% of the orders produce only 11% of sales. The old ABC problem—80% of the orders (and headaches and overhead) produce only 25% of the sales. Yet both must be handled, apparently, for the small experimental trial orders are necessary to capture bigger ones in the future. But should all orders, big and small, be handled in the same shop by the same people with the same processes?

4. *CAVU Situation*

A. $80,601 shipments necessary to get caught up, Exhibit 12.12 (62,001 boards).

B. Delinquency at end of November is skyrocketing.

C. Through November production was best yet.

D. The specs should be clarified—this could be tragic.

E. Rejections October 597 versus production August 1,470, or 41% rejections look very high and climbing. If 25% of November production were to be rejected, this would be 4113 boards!

F. Penalty clause for late deliveries is scary. This should be straightened out.

G. Ditto re reprocurement penalty.

H. CAVU pressure will hurt our performance for other customers.

I. Low December production would be disastrous.

5. *Overall Backlog Situation* (Exhibit 12.3)

Ratio of backlog to output has risen from 2 to 3. Success in industry depends on prompt delivery record. We must, therefore, increase production faster. Production must quickly get up to 100,000 to 125,000 per month.

6. *Graham as Administrator*

Apparently he can sell and can raise money. The record shows this. However, the losses since he took over the processing, his failure to build a strong production organization, his lack of ability to build technical high quality into his team and products, his loss of control over direct labor and total costs—all raise serious questions as to his results as a general manager.

It all adds up to a real crisis of too much business, with sales outrunning production's ability to deliver and keep up quality levels. But it is compounded by a financial crisis—an immediate need for working capital compounded by operating losses.

APC has a narrow line which makes it highly vulnerable to in-plant competition. Its reason for existence is overload work calling for ability to produce quickly and reliably. Price may be somewhat critical in the future as the shake-out in the P/C business takes place. A few companies are getting big; the small garage shops are less able to compete technologically. I/C's loom in the future. The components business in prebuilt circuits is changing to (a) more sophisticated technology, (b) higher volume of "standard circuits," and (c) lots of low quantities of specials, low production items, and experimental boards. APC is thus at a critical stage in terms of not only its present but its future.

But Fred Graham's hands were too full to do anything about the future. The present situation was explosive.

7. *Conclusions and Summary*
    1. Students must wrestle with this variety of problems:

        Operating losses.
        Finances.
        CAVU situation.
        Rising backlog and customer delinquencies.
        White's replacement.
        The strategic position of APC.
        Graham as a manager.

    2. Immediate and drastic action is necessary—yet extremely difficult to
        bring off.

        Increase crew.
        Eliminate spotting bottleneck.
        Tighten training, supervision, processes, quality control.
        Set up real standards and enforce.
        Concentrate on CAVU or renegotiate contract.
        Get in working capital.

    3. One possible approach that could be fruitful would be to reprocess
        the CAVU work, get it out of the present job shop mess and into a
        line flow arrangement with its own operators. An ABC type of
        processing/production setup in fact makes much sense. They are
        mixing all the work together, short- and long-run, high, medium, and
        lower specifications of quality and precision.

AMERICAN PRINTED CIRCUIT: CASE COMMENTS

Manufacturing Policy Approach

Much of the conventional approach to this case is useful, but putting it into
a manufacturing policy framework can be revealing.

Strategic Situation

The company has grown and has been profitable until the last six months by
the following strategic approaches: The growth has come from focusing on
an engineering type of printed circuit boards—that is, customer specials. In
these customer specials the emphasis has been on meeting individualized cus-

tomer specifications, producing in low quantities, having flexibility and organizational ability for making rapid changes and adjusting to customer demands, producing on a relatively short cycle, and being very reliable on deliveries. Financing has been by debt and by cash flows from profits. Cash has been very tight. The equipment and process technology has placed a major emphasis on the individual worker and the individual worker process, with relatively high skills demanded and excellent communications between workers and supervisors essential.

Manufacturing Task

What is difficult yet necessary for success in this kind of business is control. Schedules and loads must be controlled against capacity and processes, and the work done on individual PCBs must be controlled in terms of customer specifications. All of this must be done in the midst of a good rate of growth and very individualized equipment process technology. What is central, therefore, is keeping control and focus. The work pace must be managed in terms of what each worker does on the flexible and continuously changing processes and specifications. Further, loads must be measured constantly against capacity, and the promises that are made must be entirely realistic and feasible. Finally, worker training, morale, supervision, and communications with the workers are essential. The "name of the game" therefore is "focus," and the manufacturing task is to focus on achieving customer needs and demands—in other words, control.

In contrast to this manufacturing task, American Printed Circuit Company let themselves give up focus and control in nearly every respect. They took on too great a load. They set themselves up in a new plant at the very time they were extremely busy; they disrupted the ordinary flows and by getting new, excess floor space, allowed space for flows to become disrupted and become inventories of work in process. They took on the CAVU work which resulted in the plant being asked to meet an entirely different task. The CAVU task was low cost, high volume, and standardized production at an extremely low margin. It required, indeed allowed for, a production flow in which tools and equipment and routings could be entirely standardized and in which large volumes of repetitive operations could be set up for the first time.

But instead of setting this up separately, if indeed they should have taken it on at all, they mixed the work into the regular plant and totally confused the situation. The large CAVU order would completely disrupt the small individual customers specials and vice versa. The task for CAVU was almost a mirror image of the task for the customer specials. As a result, they lost the very focus and control that is the name of the game and the key manufacturing task. They lost it in terms of process, supervision, controls, and indeed management. They were unable to meet the cost requirement on the CAVU work, and the delivery and specifications became impossible to meet without setting that work aside in one corner of the new plant. Because of taking on this additional work and attempting to have one plant do a manageable job on one set of problems, they ended up with one plant attempting to meet the requirements of two entirely different businesses including market requirements, technical requirements, volume requirements, and engineering requirements. As a result of this lack of focus, the business went under.

What they might have done

What they should have done, according to the manufacturing policy approach, would have been to attempt to get rid of the CAVU contract immediately. If they had to continue it at all, they should have separated it and reprocessed it on a mass production basis. An analysis of the other loads should have been made and those loads rescheduled as necessary to become manageable. A new analysis then should have been made of the workers and the processes by which the workers were expected to do their work, including methods, communications, supervision, and the day-to-day management of jobs in process. Beginning on December 1, the case date, the effort should have been made to regain the focus and control the company had once possessed.

r

CHAPTER 13

Instrumentation
Laboratory

In mid-September 1966, Thomas Frost, the president of the Instrumentation Laboratory Corporation, and the members of his top management group were seriously concerned with their progress in producing the two most important products in the company's line. The company's backlog of orders had nearly tripled during the past year, and total production had increased by a factor of only 35%. On September 1 total backlog of equipment on order including supplies and accessories was approximately $1,760,000,[1] which represented about four months of current sales. Most serious, however, was the fact that on two of the company's main products the backlog had been increasing for nine months and production had remained nearly level until the last two months when it had actually declined.

Product 113, blood gas analyzer, was the company's original and most important product in terms of dollar volume and contribution to fixed costs. Its backlog of orders had risen from 210 in May to the present total of approximately 300, while production had dropped from 93 in May to 64 in June, 62 in July, 54 in August, and in September was expected to be no higher than 58. The second key product was product 143, a flame photometer. Its backlog had gradually climbed from 320 in April to the present total of 382, while production, which had been 85 in April, 94 in May, 138 in June, and 158 in July, dropped to 105 in August.

[1] Certain figures in this case are disguised.

Case material of the Harvard Graduate School of Business Administration is prepared as a basis for class discussion. Cases are not designed to present illustrations of either effective or ineffective handling of administrative problems.

One reason for the company's serious concern with the situation was the fact that working capital financing was based on the factoring of accounts receivable. The shipments were immediately (daily) borrowed against to finance production. If production output was low, the financing necessary to meet payrolls and accounts payable during the subsequent weeks was simply not available. Thus it was considered critical that production be increased in September and October.

COMPANY BACKGROUND

The Instrumentation Laboratory, Incorporated (ILI) was founded in 1958 by its president, Thomas Frost. During its first two years the company operated essentially as a marketing organization, selling a number of products manufactured by small companies in the field of medical electronics. In 1959 ILI began to design and manufacture medical instruments, systems, and accessories. Thomas Frost was joined in 1961 by David Sanderly who subsequently became vice president of engineering.

Exhibit 13.1   Instrumentation Laboratory, Inc.—Product Line

Model #	Name	Approximate Retail Price
105-S	Blood pH electrode assembly and stand	$360
107-S	Blood pH electrode assembly and stand	$300
113	Blood gas analyzer	$2400–$2500
119	Deluxe rolling console	$500
123	Blood gas analyzer	$1750–1850
125-A	Portable oxygen analyzer	$600
125-S	Oxygen analyzer system	$1150
127	Bath	$300–$1200
135-A	pH electrometer	$600
135-S	Blood pH analyzer system	$1100–$1200
143	Flame photometer	$2000
145	pH electrometer	$470
145-S	Blood pH analyzer system	$1000–$1050
165	pH electrometer	$300
175	Portable pH meter	$185
181	Pico-metric amplifier—field unit	$365
205	Digital pH meter	$600
225	Portable oxygen analyzer—field unit	Prices
245	pH meter	to be
265	pH meter	determined

The ILI product line began with the blood gas analyzer and a very sensitive pH meter, and new products were added each year. Exhibit 13.1 lists the products and their individual prices.

ILI was privately owned, with Frost in control of approximately 85% of the stock. Other members of the management held virtually all of the remaining shares of stock, having acquired them through stock options.

The organization and personnel in September of 1966 are shown in Exhibit 13.2, 13.3, and 13.4. The total number of employees at that time was approximately 384. The company was located in Watertown, Massachusetts, and occupied approximately 67,000 square feet of rented space spread over four floors in a 50-year-old building.

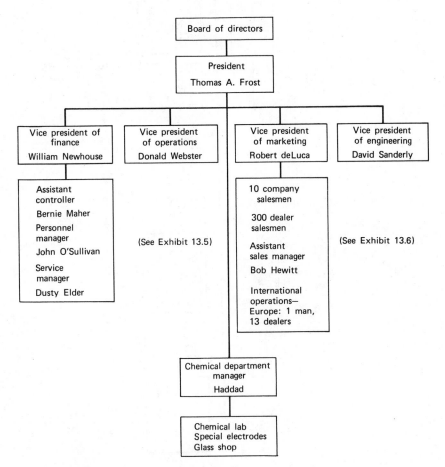

Exhibit 13.2   Instrumentation Laboratory, Inc.—Organization Chart

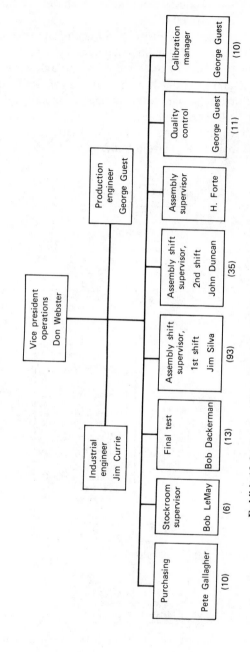

Exhibit 13.3 Instrumentation Laboratory, Inc.—Manufacturing Organization

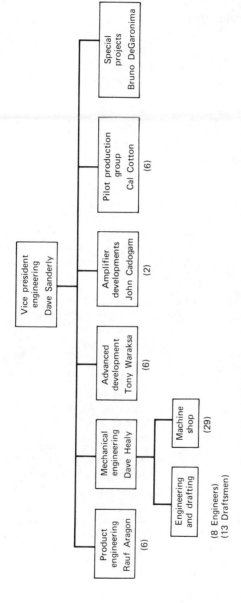

Exhibit 13.4   Instrumentation Laboratory, Inc.—Engineering Organization

Vice president engineering
Dave Sanderly

Product engineering
Rauf Aragon
(6)

Mechanical engineering
Dave Healy

Advanced development
Tony Waraksa
(6)

Amplifier developments
John Cadogam
(2)

Pilot production group
Cal Cotton
(6)

Special projects
Bruno DeGaronima

Engineering and drafting

Machine shop
(29)

(8 Engineers)
(13 Draftsmen)

Marketing

In early 1966 a Harvard Business School student made the following comments regarding the marketing function:

The marketing function is perhaps the strongest of ILI's operating areas in that it seems to have the least number of "loose ends" to tie up in the face of the tremendous growth now occurring. It is obvious to me that ILI really knows what it takes to sell medical electronic instruments and the fact that the company is well organized to sell them is evidenced by the terrific growth in sales being experienced.

ILI recognizes that its products are sold chiefly by demonstrating them. With this in mind, the marketing program puts great emphasis on the relationship with the distributor, particularly with regard to educating his salesmen in sales and service techniques. ILI sells through two national distributors, ALOE Scientific Division of Brunswick and Scientific Products Division of American Hospital Supply Corporation. The combination of these two distributors gives ILI a network of some 300 dealer salesmen throughout the United States. International sales are supervised by one man in Europe who has 13 dealers under him. The distributors are granted discounts ranging from 25% to 35%. Education of distributors is accomplished chiefly by ten ILI salesmen who are stationed throughout the United States, and who are paid on salary, expenses, and an annual bonus based on performance.

Advertising is done mostly through medical journals. In addition ILI exhibits its products in approximately 11 trade shows during the course of a year.[2]

The director of marketing, Mr. Robert deLuca, stated in September 1966:

I cannot push sales right now because we simply do not have the production. The blood gas analyzer is running five to six months behind compared to the 30-day delivery our competition is offering. The customers like our equipment, but how do I get my sales group excited when production is so slow?

These products really sell themselves, so we don't waste time with a customer unless the customer clearly can use the equipment. I have been simply amazed at the market. There are now 4000 instruments in the field, so it is a lot easier than it was at first. Some say the market is now saturated, but we are selling replacements in multiple units in hospitals, and of course, our equipment is getting better all the time. We have continually improved it. We have 10 regional managers and we sell through the two main distributors. We now have eight servicemen to cover all of the United States and provide service to customers in terms of repair and any maintenance problems.

---

[2] Quoted by permission from student report of John Ludutsky, 1966.

Exhibit 13.5 Instrumentation Laboratory, Inc.—Balance Sheets as of March 31, 1966 and August 31, 1966 (thousands of dollars)

	August 31, 1966	March 31, 1966
Assets		
Current Assets		
Cash	$(176)	$ 21
Accounts receivable	984	634
Inventory	774	717
Other	38	46
Total current assets	$1620	$1418
Fixed assets		
Gross fixed assets	$243	$218
Less accumulated depreciation	99	93
Net fixed assets	144	125
Other assets	2	1
Total assets	$1766	$1544
Liabilities		
Current liabilities		
Accounts payable	$ 408	$ 544
Notes payable	654	496
Accruals	186	168
Income tax liability	131	62
Total current liabilities	$1379	$1270
Long-term debt	54	66
Capital stock and surplus		
Common stock—no par value		
Authorized—10,000 shares		
Issued and outstanding—1143 shares	40	40
Earned surplus	203	168
Total capital stock and surplus	$ 333	$ 208
Total liabilities	$1766	$1544

Exhibit 13.6   Instrumentation Laboratory, Inc.—Income Statements, Years Ending
March 31, 1964 and 1965 and Five Months Ending August 31, 1966 (thousands of
dollars)

	1966 Five Months	1966	1965
Net sales	$2768	$3926	$2267
Cost of goods sold			
Direct labor	304	390	234
Materials	966	1507	923
Manufacturing overhead	299	408	206
Freight in	26	17	—
Work in process inventory increase	—	—	(115)
	$1595	$2322	$1248
Gross profit	1173	1605	1019
General and administrative	175	207	178
Marketing	371	642	445
Research and development	384	503	310
	$ 930	$1352	$ 933
Operating profit	243	252	86
Other income	21	5	3
Other expenses	31	75	27
Profit before taxes	$ 233	$ 182	$ 62
Provision for income taxes	108	88	18
Net profit	$ 125	$ 94	$ 44

Mr. deLuca had joined the company in 1961. Before this he had been an advertising manager for a medical company in New York, a managing editor for a medical journal; he came to Boston because he found the editorial work too quiet and lacked challenge. He had majored in public relations and was graduated from Boston University in 1956.

Balance sheets and income statements are included as Exhibits 13.5 and 13.6.

PRODUCTION PROBLEMS

The vice president of operations, Donald Webster, was particularly concerned and frustrated over the difficulties being experienced in the production operation. Sales in August had been $98,000 less than his last quarterly forecast. Over half of this falldown was centered in the model 113 blood gas analyzer.

Model 113

A sequence of serious problems had arisen, largely centering on subassemblies. One problem had been in a chopper[3] in which a great deal of time and effort had been invested, but as Webster put it:

Sometimes it works and sometimes it does not. It seems like black magic. Sometimes after potting (encapsulation in epoxy material), we do not have good insulation resistance and, obviously, if the chopper is no good after potting, we simply have to throw it away. The insulation on the leads is sometimes melted or damaged while we solder onto shielded wire. So we are trying out some Zofar wax instead of potting. We are also instituting a 100% preinspection procedure by the lead person who is inspecting all the subassemblies, so that when they leave subassembly before potting we can be pretty sure that they are good. Sometimes we find that we are nicking the wires when we strip them. This is just poor workmanship. But with all of the problems of getting people, this is very difficult to overcome. We have also discovered that we have been scratching the surface of the silicon oxide coating on a neon bulb involved when we are measuring the depth with a depth gauge. Now it turns out the depth is not really very important.

Model 143

The problems on the model 143 flame photometer were equally serious and of more recent origin. One cause had been a severe parts shortage on a plexiglass burner base. The base was cast in plexiglas and then machined by ILI. The mold for casting had been coated with Teflon to prevent sticking, which improved it for a while, but then it began to stick in spite of the Teflon. Webster then shifted to a new mold but found that the castings still stuck and the molds needed chrome plating. But in attempting to get new molds in a hurry, the company had run into a continual shortage of machinists in their own shop. Two of the four men in the shop were ill, one with diabetes and the other with a bad back, and they were attempting to set up a second shift and to get more people, but found these jobs hard to fill. After absences had hurt production for several weeks, they were attempting to do more subcontracting.

In late August a new drill jig was made for drilling critical holes in the part. The new jig held eight units, which seemed to offer improved production of this part. But Webster said, "ILI has a history of using cheap

[3] The chopper provides a means for determining the characteristics of an unknown signal.

'make-do' jigs which often get us into trouble; but cheap jigs really make sense in the long run because we have so many design changes." The new jig had been ordered by the group leader of the mechanical engineering group, Dave Healy, who reported to engineering. Webster said, "He makes good decisions and I don't get into these problems unless there is a fire to put out." The machine shop, in which much of this work was done was run by engineering. Typically over half of the work in the machine shop was for engineering projects.

Another problem on the flame photometer occurred in the servo assembly. The assembly included a motor, a gear train, a digital counter, and a feedback device. In July the motors were found to be failing in the field at a prodigious rate. When the motors began to fail, the company made an effort to find a substitute motor that would operate better and last longer and in the meantime had begun to replace the defective motors that were returned. New motors were modified by turning down the armature, covering the windings with milar sleeves, and epoxy. These were considered quite "tricky" problems. The motors were then shipped to a vendor who placed a pinion on the motor and assembled a gear train. But some of the shafts were found to have been buckled by forcing on the pinion. In these cases the gears had to be reworked. In recent months the field failures had suddenly increased from 10 to 30 per week. This phenomenon was using up the company's limited supply of motors and gear trains. For every 300 motors received, 100 were lost by failure, 100 were sent into the field for replacements, and 100 were going into new products. The net result was a serious shortage of motors and gear trains for new products.

Webster said:

This is a continual problem. It is one of uncertain usage. We just don't know how many parts of this sort to place on order. We have been on the low side all along. But sometimes new employees learn fast at a reworking job like this, and sometimes vendor problems clear up, so the bottleneck can be broken quickly. This motor was selected on the basis of cost and is being run at somewhat higher speeds than it was designed for. The engineering department has now slowed it down by 30% by different gearing, but this was four months ago, so we don't know yet whether it will decrease field failures.

Another problem on the photometer was also typical of problems on many ILI products. Six printed circuit boards were being used in the photometer, and problems were being experienced with these boards. They were especially difficult to test, requiring 75 minutes apiece, which was considered to cost too much. The lengthy test time was due to the complex circuitry involved. Subsequent field failures indicated the necessity of doing even more testing on these boards. To get around this, the engineering department worked out a new design that made the circuit on the circuit board less complex. These new circuits, however, made the device more temperature sensitive, which led to another series of design changes. It did cut the test time to 10 or 15 minutes. However, through the process of redesign for reduced temperature sensitivity, the test time had grown to about 30 minutes. According to Webster:

This is a very serious problem in an undermanned group. We simply can't hire people. We need people who understand transistors and circuits and how they work; in other words, technicians. But we can't get technicians. The test equipment could be improved so as to lower the skills required, but it would have to be designed by production engineering. And in production engineering we are completely overloaded. The production engineering group is doing a good job and working extremely hard, and their output is twice what it was a year ago, but still, because of all the problems they are trying to cope with, they are slow to respond and improve.

Since last March we have increased our quality and workmanship standards, especially in regard to soldering. But the reeducation process has been slow and painful, and it is still hurting. The result has been good and the salesmen like it, but sometimes a product that will pass inspection and work well in the shop will fail after the vibrations and jostling around it receives during shipment. Thus costs have been increasing in rework and longer lead times as we have been trying to get more inspection and better quality into our product. But we simply lack enough good inspectors.

Another problem typical of problems being experienced throughout the plant was rearing its head in the flame photometer. An air orifice was clogging up and causing a malfunction of the instrument. In its operation, air was blown across an aspirating table in order to draw up a sample to be tested. The sample was sloshed around the periphery of a container and evaporated and drawn into a flame by the air blowing through the orifice. When the sample vapor was burned, it gave the colors of various elements present. Lithium was used as a testing standard, and it was found that the lithium reading began to drift off due to flecks of dirt in the orifice. These flecks were too small to analyze, but when the small pipes were taken apart they were found to be clogging the orifice.

At first the problem was thought to be that the propane gas had dirt in it. Then it was recognized that the product had recently been moved to be manufactured in a newer part of the plant and that a previous operation of flushing the plumbing out with methanol was now being skipped because the new area of the plant had been considered cleaner than the former area. A regular flushing system with Freon gas was established and the problem was believed solved. However, after a week it was found that when testing the propane gas supply, the problems would reoccur in the final check. The plumbing was flushed out and again specks of dirt were found. They learned that it was necessary to blow out both sides of the plumbing with 80 pounds of air pressure for 20 minutes to get rid of the specks.

All members of the production operation including Webster came in on a Sunday to work on this problem in order to improve shipments. The instruments were cleaned out and they worked. They then went to test on Monday, and they did not work. After they were blown out again, they functioned again. Some dirt was found and it was felt that perhaps the specks were coming from the plumbing compound that was being used in assembling the copper tubing. (The air entering the orifice was heated in a copper tubing which was wrapped with a type of heating wire to which was applied 110 volts. Two holes were drilled in the copper tubing in order to set a pin in it to hold the windings in place.)

After the suspicion was raised that the specks in the orifice may have been coming from the plumbing compound, an empty tube was heated with the electrical winding for one hour. There was no compound used and no connections. At the end of an hour a substance that looked like coffee grounds was found growing on the ends of the tube. The tube was copper with cadmium plating. The cadmium plate had been introduced six weeks before because of corrosion problems on the unplated copper tubing which had occurred during some military high humidity testing of the product. It now seemed possible that the cadmium plate was breaking down from the heat in the heater and depositing the small specks. In late September an all-out effort was being made to expedite new tubes without cadmium plate to see if this would eliminate the problem.

Typical Problems

These problems were typical of those ILI was running into during the summer and early fall. As one problem was solved, another surfaced. Minor and routine changes made in an effort to solve one problem often seemed to cause others to appear. Each time a new problem was discovered that interfered with the functioning of an instrument, mounting special experiments and engineering changes were necessary. In some cases instruments had to be recalled from the field or at least those in stock had to be modified. This in turn caused problems in the parts supply of both manufactured and purchased parts. These problems were also interfering with the normal flow of production through the various groups and in final tests.

A problem affecting many products was that the period of unusually high economic activity being experienced throughout the country was causing a general shortage of electronic purchased parts of all kinds. Ordinary resistors and capacitors, for example, were suddenly requiring six- to nine-month deliveries. With the difficulties in forecasting sales and the rapid rise of orders, the company was finding it extremely difficult to obtain the necessary parts, even the most standard ones. Expediting was being done by long distance telephone; the engineering department was being asked to consider substitutes; and expensive or premium parts were being purchased wherever necessary to keep production going. Expeditors traveled about the country visiting vendors, surplus agencies, and doing anything possible to bring in the parts needed.

PRODUCTION ORGANIZATION

The manufacturing operation was headed by Donald Webster. He graduated from Rensselaer Polytechnic Institute with an electrical engineering degree in 1952 and spent six years in the Navy on destroyers and submarines. In 1958 he joined Grumman Aircraft as an electronics engineer and in 1961 received a Master's degree from Brooklyn Polytechnic Institute in electronics engineering. In the fall of 1961 he entered the Harvard Business School and received his MBA in June of 1963. For a year and a half after graduation he worked as an assistant to the treasurer of a small electronics company in Newton, Mass. This work included production scheduling. In December 1964 he joined ILI as treasurer and continued in that post until April of 1966 when he was made vice president of operations. Webster liked this job more than being treasurer because it offered more action.

My only complaint, he said, was that there is not enough time for thinking. We really need a production manager and should have one.

The former treasurer, who had left the company, returned to ILI as vice president of finance.

Production Planning and Control

Purchased parts and raw materials were ordered in advance, using a quarterly forecast made up by Webster after he conferred with deLuca. This forecast covered three months ahead on a firm basis and indicated the tentative schedule for another three months. The purchased parts and raw materials then were stocked on the basis of minimum balances determined by the stockroom based on usage, procurement time, and a safety stock.

Until August a two weeks safety stock was used, but to decrease stock-outs, a change was made in August to use a six weeks' safety stock.

A constant problem was that of uncertain yield. Because of rejections in both receiving inspection and final test, it was always difficult to know how many extra parts to order. Generally about 10% more than was actually required was ordered, but a good deal of judgment was permitted in this stockroom decision.

Robert Dackerman, who was in charge of final test and shipping, had the responsibility for making promises to customers:

It is up to me to see that the promises are met. We are now way behind schedule on many items. As the due dates get closer, I notify the customer if we are not going to make the promise. I usually do this a few days before or just after we have missed the date. I act as a central control for dealing with customers and Tom Frost and Bob deLuca transfer customer calls to me.

Dackerman had been an analytical chemist for 16 years in a clinical analytical laboratory. He had started at ILI in November 1964, and he liked it better than analytical chemistry because it involved a lot more activity. The job involves "watching our inventories of supplies as well as deliveries of completed devices. When I need to make a promise to a customer, I study the situation in assembly and I can get a pretty good idea of when the devices will be coming to final test."

Dackerman stated:

The problem on the flame photometer discussed earlier first appeared down here. It does not seem to be an electronics problem. It is more of a plumbing problem. The problem actually came up four weeks ago and it was interesting that it did not come up until we had produced more than 1000 instruments. So we had to say to ourselves, "Now what has actually changed?" We did recognize that we had gone through five changes. One was that we were using older parts that had been around awhile. Second, we had moved the device from one department to another, but with the same people. Third, we had accidentally eliminated a cleaning operation. Fourth, we added cadmium plating to that section of the pipe. Five, we had changed to use plexiglas on the base but this did not seem to be part of the problem.

Anyway, when we get into these situations, we simply have to put our ideas together and try out and experiment until we are able to locate the problem. What really happens is that in the rush to get into production or to meet customer promises or to improve certain problems, we get a tremendous sense of urgency around here. We are always trying to get into mass production. Thus we sometimes make changes without the time to check out everything. Changes that seem minor can cause problems. We just can't think of everything.

ILI sales had grown very quickly and there had been literally hundreds of engineering design changes during each of the past five years. Because of these design changes, it was not always physically possible to keep up in the drafting and engineering departments, and therefore, many changes were made that were not recorded other than in the memory of the operators and the senior mechanical engineer. In September of 1966 a concerted effort was being made to get more information on paper and to develop a more formal recording system.

Quality Control and Production Engineering

George Guest was in charge of quality control and calibration. He also acted as the production engineer for the manufacturing operation. He had come to ILI from Raytheon and had been involved in electronic production and manufacturing engineering for approximately 15 years.

Regarding the current crisis on the model 113, he said:

We have had simultaneously a rash of field failures with electronic filters, which occurred about the same time we changed the group that made the filters. The potting material on the chopper had been changed to one with a lower dielectric constant, and we discovered the insulation resistance then decreased with age. But I also read an article recently about glass tending to hydrolyze. It picks up water and this shows up as low insulation resistance. We have noticed that the material for our printed circuit board seems to pick up moisture and then its insulation resistance gets low too. So we are trying to see about the possibility of getting our boards very clean, because dirt on the board makes an ionic solution on the surface, which can actually cause up to one-third of a volt change.

Of course, we are having trouble on this night shift. We had started the night shift back in February and we had some women there who were moonlighters until June, but we then decided that the moonlighters just didn't work out very well, so we have got housewives to come in and work during the evenings. We are still in the sorting stage of picking out good ones from the not so very good ones.

Another problem is trying to decide how much inventory to keep in parts, and we are getting all kinds of shortages. But if added to safety stock, this costs an awful lot of money. It is very difficult to predict parts usage because of the field attrition of subassemblies. We know the filters and choppers are failing in the field, using up the available supply in the plant. The more field failures and the rework we have to do in the plant, the more we wear out the circuit boards that we are operating on. So one problem just leads to another. In this business you have simply got to start operations slowly and watch everything closely and pick up every problem as it occurs.

In August the model 113 had been transferred from the first shift to the second shift. There was no overlap, because it was felt better to make a clean break. Guest felt that it was a good idea because all of the subassemblies would then be built on the second shift. "We have a hard time keeping up with the different parts involved. The line supervisors are supposed to be in charge of meeting the schedule. And theoretically all of the parts necessary for any schedule are in stock. It is the stockroom responsibility to see that all the parts needed are there."

In early September Jim Currie, an industrial engineer, was hired. His initial assignment was to review the manufacturing operations and take a rough cut at estimating standard times. The company hoped to use this data for determining product costs and uncovering possible major production inefficiencies.

Assembly

Jim Silva was the assembly shift supervisor in charge of the flame photometer. He had started with ILI in December 1963, made a lead assembler in September 1964, and a shift supervisor in June 1965. He had had military experience in the Marines, and then had two terms in Electrical Technician's School. He said:

The biggest factor is the availability of parts. If we can get the parts we can usually build the product, but we really have some problems in the stockroom. There is an awful lot of confusion there about what is needed, and we are always running out and getting behind. The stockroom is messy, and the changes in stock minimums and maximums are difficult, of course, to keep up. There is so little space and sometimes parts come in that they don't know are in. Our other biggest problem is simply a lack of people right now. Absenteeism isn't too bad, and the people we have are trying to do a good job, but we simply need more of them, and we are not able to hire them.

THE OPERATIONS VICE PRESIDENT—REGULAR ROUTINE

In the first week of every month Webster's group had a production meeting. They started the meeting with a discussion of the order forecast and reviewed the past month's results and reasons for any problems. They then discussed the next month and set some quotas as to what could be produced and what problems had to be overcome. They discussed the allocation of the trained people and established bases for weekly schedules.

On Mondays at 2:30 the line supervisors gathered in Webster's office to discuss production progress. These meetings lasted an hour to an hour and a half. They were attended by the line supervisors, George Guest, the electrical test calibration technician, Webster, Dackerman, and Bob LeMay, who was head of the stockroom area. "Our effort in these meetings," Webster said, "is to air the problems and to try to resolve them."

On Monday, Wednesday, and Friday an operations report was put out which showed on a summary sheet the production results on each product against promises, and progress for the month. Webster then got involved in the areas where there were problems. He assigned special task forces to problems and he worked closely with these task forces.

He also walked through the final test area in both the morning and evening, coming to and going from work, to see the number of instruments in final test. He kept up to date on the production each day by studying the daily billing report from the treasurer's office. He also spent considerable time coordinating the work of production with engineering, both in regard to introducing new products and in improving old ones. He spent considerable time on "people problems." "I do everything I can to help develop my supervisors. For example, this week it was necessary to sit down with two of the newer supervisors and let them see how they could stop doing all the work themselves by doing better planning in advance."

Organizational Changes

Webster commented on two organizational changes he planned to institute as soon as possible. The first was that he intended to transfer the flame photometer assembly line from Jim Silva to Bernie Ward, a recently hired, but experienced line supervisor. There were about 40 people involved. In making this change he felt that the first-line supervisor would be strengthened and a portion of Jim Silva's time would be freed for use on a new product line.

Second, he planned to establish a task group of five members on a project basis for the day shift. It would include a senior, experienced wirer, three other women who were experienced in assembly and calibration, and one man. He planned to use this task force by having them move into an area in which production troubles were being experienced. They would apply their experience and their know-how and help to find out what the problems were and get them straightened out. Then they would move on to another trouble spot. When the task force was not putting out fires, they would work on a variety of small special jobs that were somewhat more difficult than ordinary jobs. For instance, they would help to start in new products, acting as a pilot line for each new product as it came out from engineering.

A PROPOSED CHANGE

The president, Thomas Frost, was very concerned about the situation in the production department. Because of the lack of experience throughout the department, he felt that the men there had many good ideas, but that their answers were not always matched by their results. He commented on the fact that many instruments seemed to cycle through the assembly operation in final test again and again, but never got fixed up and shipped. He commented that he had seen many instruments that were 90% done and then not touched for a number of months.

In the present emergency, Frost had decided that perhaps it might make good sense to transfer the responsibility for the blood gas analyzer, model 113, temporarily to the chief engineer, David Sanderly. He felt that Sanderly was good at working out bugs in production and that, since many of the problems seemed to be engineering-related, the entire line might simply be put under his authority for a month or six weeks, and perhaps this would straighten things out.

Sanderly was not reluctant to take on this responsibility, and he explained some of his philosophy and ideas about the current situation to the casewriter. He made the following points:

One. The stockroom is a sick area. They make too many mistakes. They order the wrong amounts, the wrong items, and much of this is due to the crowding and the rush, but also some stupid mistakes. The order quantities are supposed to be set by George Guest, but they are also set by the stockroom. There are really no formal procedures. Little things get missed, such as how much to order of a new part. They keep raising their minimum levels, which is safe, but it seems to me they have much too much inventory on many items and much too little on others.

Two. Our production department is pretty good at production engineering and product debugging, but they are really not so good at processing problems. For example, they tend to overspecify the process and make it unnecessarily tight. George Guest is an expert at engineering changeovers and their effects, and he is very helpful to us in engineering. He identifies the problems in production and then writes an engineering changeover to cure it. A poorly written ECO would cause more problems than it solves. But George Guest's are good, and I practically always approve them.

Three. In the model 113 blood gas analyzer our shipments are decreasing while orders are increasing, and I think the situation is deteriorating. I am willing to get into it; but if I do, I must have full control. The man in charge of it should report to me. I have confidence in John Duncan and I have confidence in the product, and I think we could even get 100 a month out in October. But now Duncan is very discouraged and desperate. In fact, he is close to quitting. His big problems are in getting people and keeping them, and absenteeism has been terrible, and we have had a terrible history of quality control on the second shift. I don't blame Duncan for being discouraged about managing the second shift. Morale is much more difficult and a lot of his subassemblies are potted by the first shift and then turn out to be no good. This model 113 accounts for half of our sales and two-thirds of profit.

Four. We designed a new circuit board without the chopper and released the information to production in June, but they did nothing about it and then started to use some suddenly in September. They planned a 100% changeover. The new board took the parts cost down by $10 to $11, but the parts had to be tightly balanced and aligned. Now, of course, there have been some problems in debugging, and people in production couldn't build it and adjust it, although our engineering technician in the engineering department could. It seems to look like it can't be produced right now, but we didn't have to get away from the old board all at once. It is the old problem of trying to develop improvements and get them into production without running into bugs on the job.

Five. As we get into this, of course, our engineering group will apply their facilities quickly when they are needed. We will have John Duncan working for us, and he'll let us know just what the problems are. I think if we run that thing, I would take one of my best producers and use her as an inspector on an informal basis because the workers don't really know when they have produced something that is no good. They learn about it a long time later. The operators really want to produce good stuff, but they just don't know what the problems are. Duncan feels that the tolerances are much too tight on the product and that with his low skilled people and the absenteeism, the problems are very, very difficult. I think I could talk with him and show him how critical these tight standards are and that they are really necessary, and maybe I can get him to stop arguing about them. But as far as the people situation is concerned, maybe we could get a kind of a flexible arrangement where on the second shift the women could work less than 40 hours if they wanted to, and maybe this would help us to attract better people.

Six. We have all sorts of problems in the potting room and really poor quality in the epoxy potting. They use the wrong mixtures, the wrong temperatures, and the wrong hardeners; and our specs are kind of rough and probably need tightening up. I would think about paying the potting operator more, maybe get an experienced man for the job.

Sanderly stated that one thing they were trying to do in the engineering department was to develop some basic building blocks such as a power supply, photo detectors, operational amplifiers, and log amplifiers, which could be used for all the company's mainstream products. They would be cheap, simple, and refined, he felt; and this would standardize on parts and make for less original engineering work on new products. The engineering budget was established on the basis of about 15% of net sales and was planned ahead on that basis each year. The engineering organization is shown as

Exhibit 13.4. Frost worked closely with Sanderly on engineering project planning. Frost was always involved with many new ideas for new products and, in fact, Sanderly felt that it was often necessary to drag his feet a bit to concentrate engineering efforts rather than to disperse them too widely.

Frost recognized that there would be many problems caused by getting the engineering department into the problem, but he was beginning to lose confidence in the ability of the production organization to solve it as quickly as the company needed a solution. He felt that the engineering approach might be the best answer to the early improvement in output that he considered critical.

INSTRUMENTATION LABORATORY INCORPORATED

Conventional Analysis

It is clear that the company has been performing remarkably well until recently. The company has been increasing its sales quite rapidly, penetrating the medical instruments market at a remarkable rate, and gaining a major foothold in a very difficult market dominated by such relative giants as Hewlett-Packard and Beckman.

It is equally clear that the present situation is very serious. The company's financing is based on accounts receivable, and until production is resumed and built up, there will be no accounts receivable and therefore no money to meet payrolls. The whole approach that Thomas Frost has followed in financing is under serious jeopardy, and he will have to go out and get in more equity to raise more *depth*. Immediate action is needed.

The situation is difficult in other respects as well, particularly since obviously Sanderly and Webster are not working well together. Both are lobbying strenuously for different approaches that would be at the expense of each other. Production and engineering, often ancient rivals, are clearly at war. Further, the marketing department is also dissatisfied with production and its setup. Finally, reading between the lines, the morale in production is precariously low. Assemblers have come close to the point of giving up, because in the face of engineering's constant effort to put through engineering changes, many people feel helpless and victimized.

Most analysts of this case recommend above all that engineering should freeze designs. To improve the product and reduce costs, Frost must stop them from pushing through so many engineering change orders. Engineering also needs to improve its documentation and records and get itself better organized and under control. Webster is seen by conventional analysts as somewhat weak; but weak or not, he is in an impossible situation where he is constantly interfered with in carrying out any kind of smooth or rational flow of production. Sanderly is seen as the villain of the affair, recklessly and for his own personal needs introducing engineering changes where they are not fully necessary and ramming them down the throat of production. Because Sanderly is one-sixth owner of the company, the inference is that he is much closer to Frost and has Frost's ear. He is, therefore, able to run roughshod over production. Finally, it seems clear to the conventional analyst that production is lowest in the pecking order behind finance and marketing and that finance dominates through Frost's own personal values and thereby his determination to maintain total control of the company and bring in no more equity. It is an overriding basic policy approach that forces production to have a major emphasis on delivery, and this emphasis is wreaking havoc with their need to keep costs down and margins up to provide R & D money and to maintain high quality in a medical instruments market. Production is also seen as playing second fiddle to marketing, and the company is easily considered a "marketing-oriented" company in which manufacturing is criticized on all sides.

As a result of this analysis, the student recommends that designs be frozen; that Frost rap the knuckles of Sanderly or even replace him as essentially irresponsible; that the production job be raised in the counsels and influence the company, possibly replacing Webster with someone apparently stronger; and that more capital be brought into the company one way or another to get out from under the need for accounts receivable financing. The emphasis is to be on quality and smoothness in production, increasing production runs without disruption from the outside, and better documentation and a sane approach on the part of engineering. The development of new products should be allowed to take longer. In effect, the procedures for carrying out all the steps of new product development from the idea through the bread boarding, development of specifications, piece-part design, procurement, test procedures, assembly, testing, and shipment should be accomplished with less overlaps and confusion. In other words, the time for each step should be sequential rather than parallel, even though the product development would take longer. This would allow a much cleaner and less confusing nightmarish new product development procedure which would allow manufacturing to work with a completely clear set of specifications, drawings, and parts list instead of living amidst constant change. Now for contrast, a different kind of analysis.

Manufacturing Policy Analysis

The company has been succeeding in a very difficult market and technology. The company has been growing and penetrating markets and lifting itself by its boot-straps using the following strategy:

First of all, we will compete by a clever technology in which we are ingenious, by our designs, and by our selection of parts such that our instruments will perform and do things our competitors' instruments will not.

We will recognize that competitors can copy our designs and move very rapidly behind us. Therefore, we will be constantly improving our products, squeezing expenses out of the product, tinkering with and adjusting the designs, making field improvements, and eternally scrambling in order to keep six to 18 months ahead of competition. This is the only way a small company like ours can compete with somewhat slower moving but well financed giants like Beckman and Hewlett-Packard. This means above all a number-one strategy, to be top in technology, in product development, and in introducing new products and moving very fast in both marketing and manufacturing to get these products in the field. As Thomas Frost, I own 80% of the company, and I do not wish to give up any more control. I want to finance the company entirely from plowing back profits, which means that for many years it's going to be highly leveraged financially. Accounts receivable financing is ideal, but we must keep up our profit rate, which means squeezing every penny out of the product. Our accounts receivable financing will work fine as long as we can keep up production.

Manufacturing Task

With this corporate strategy and the economics and technology with which we are dealing, we have a major dilemma in the management of manufacturing. The task we have to master is how to get into production extremely fast in a very difficult type of technology where the instruments must not fail in the field and where our financing on accounts receivable absolutely requires on-time delivery. While we are maintaining a high gross margin, we must produce instruments as they are still being designed; and somehow or other, we must control the entire process amidst a rapid, continuing sequence of engineering changeovers. So the manufacturing task is to manage the engineering production interface so as to manage the flow of technology from engineering into the product. It means riding the whirlwind. It means living in a highly disorganized, ambiguous, and changing world. It means rapid problem solving. It means above all, an enormously cooperative, sympathetic, and close communication between engineering and manufacturing.

Seen in this light, the problem is organization. The company has a conventional, functional organization in which production is divided into supervisory units by area; engineering and production are separated, and production has only one manufacturing engineer. If the manufacturing task is to manage this engineering production interface and then develop more rapid and sensitive problem solving and control, this type of organization must be changed. Manufacturing must be organized into more narrowly focused product groups in which each product would have a unit manager who would have production, manufacturing, engineering, quality controls, and perhaps even part of purchasing under their authority. What is needed here is more of a project or matrix type of management, in which the emphasis is on the product and the teams are set up to focus on a product or a small group of products with similar problems and in a similar stage of their technological maturity and development. This type of approach would allow manufacturing to focus on problem solving. It would place engineering and production under one head and stimulate better communication and better problem solving and much more of a focus on meeting the manufacturing task than the present conventional organization.

These two different approaches, the first conventional and the second a manufacturing policy analysis, are in almost complete contradiction. The conventional approach says, "Let's get things cleaned up and operating more smoothly." The other says, "Under the present strategy of the company, which has been working extremely well, production can never be cleaned up and compartmentalized, and we have to organize to live in that kind of world."

Both Webster and Sanderly were victims of Frost's needling style, the conventional organization, and the accounts receivable financing he had insisted on. He pitted these men against each other. Following the case, the company went through four production managers over a period of 10 years, and all struggled against overwhelming odds because of this conflict between strategy and structure. Finally, three years ago the company did reorganize manufacturing, grouping together the functions by product around three project or product set ups and this has worked much better.

The immediate problem was solved as follows:

Frost gave the model 113 to engineering on September 20. Sanderly, overjoyed, worked out his pent-up frustrations over the production situation with an all-out attack on the whole situation. Later he reported:

The company absolutely had to have the shipments. Tom asked me to get into it. Webster had kept saying the situation was under control, but *no* results. I said I had to have full control and Tom agreed. Duncan was demoralized and desperate, ready to quit or be fired. He was in charge of the second shift, of course, and this product was made only on the second shift. Our biggest product with one half our volume—two-thirds of our profit and Don put it on the second shift! We'd had problems in getting people and keeping them for this shift and a terrible QC history. Duncan had many subassemblies from the first shift which were no good. We started on 100 of the old-type choppers, figuring on more trouble with the new ones. I spent half an hour daily over with Duncan.

What did we do?

1. All engineering facilities and skills were applied fast when needed. This probably accounted for about 10% of the subsequent improvements.
2. We decided not to change over to the new circuit as quickly as had been planned.
3. We solved the problems in the chopper by wax (instead of epoxy) potting and careful cleaning.
4. We set up a QC inspector within Duncan's group. I got him to take his best producer and use her as an informal inspector to force a big step-up in quality by giving workers immediate feedback. The women wanted to produce good stuff but just didn't have the knowledge.
5. Duncan had been arguing that the specs were too tight. I showed him why they had to be tight, and he stopped fighting them.
6. We set up a flexible shift in which people could work as little as 25 hours a week. This attracted more and better people.
7. We raised the job grade of the potting job, got a man on it that cost 50% more ($170 per week), but he did a good job.

September production was 77, October 111, November 105, December 116, and January 108. The company has gone on to a magnificent continuing record of growth and profitability.

CHAPTER 14

The
Great Nuclear Fizzle
At Old B & W

The long-awaited transition of the United States electric-power industry into the nuclear age has been slowed by a number of factors, including technological difficulties and public resistance. But a special and unexpected cause for delay has been one company's crucial failure to deliver a single vital component of nuclear power plants. The failure, basically, was a management failure, and on a scale that would be cause for concern even in a fly-by-night newcomer to the nuclear industry. The company, however, was no newcomer. It was proud old Babcock & Wilcox Co., a pioneer of the steam generating business whose boilers were used in one of the first central power plants ever built (in Philadelphia, in 1881). Babcock & Wilcox had an impressive $648 million in sales last year, making it 157th on *Fortune's* list of the 500 largest industries, and it has been engaged in nuclear work in a major way for 15 years, producing, among other things, atomic power systems for Navy submarines.

Moreover, the corporation is one of only five that are engaged in building nuclear power plants in the United States. With consumption of electricity growing by nearly 10 percent a year, the utilities are counting heavily on the new nuclear stations to avoid brownouts and power failures in the years ahead. Poor performance at Babcock & Wilcox is thus one of those problems that could send ripples through the whole economy.

All of B & W's troubles involve a single product: nuclear pressure vessels. These are the huge steel pots—some are more than 70 feet long and weigh

Reprinted from *Fortune,* November 1969, with express permission of the publisher.

more than 700 tons—that contain atomic reactions. They must meet rigid specifications set by the Atomic Energy Commission, and B & W built a $25-million plant at Mount Vernon, Indiana, just to fabricate them. Cockily sure that the Mount Vernon plant would operate as planned, B & W sold its entire projected output of pressure vessels for years ahead. But nothing seemed to go right at Mount Vernon. Plagued by labor shortages and malfunctioning machines, the plant produced just three pressure vessels in its first three years of operation. Late in 1968, after the production snarl reached horrendous proportions, a vice president responsible for the Mount Vernon operation committed suicide in a bizarre fashion.

Last May, B & W was forced to make a humiliating disclosure. Every one of the 28 nuclear pressure vessels then in the Mount Vernon works was behind schedule, by as much as 17 months. For the utility industry, the news from B & W meant intolerable delays in bringing 28 badly needed nuclear plants into service, with all the added expense and problems that would be entailed. Philadelphia Electric Co. estimated that it would have to spend an extra $50,000 a day just to provide from other sources, such as high-cost gas turbines, the power that it had counted on getting from its delayed nuclear units.

CREATING ITS OWN COMPETITION

With so much at stake, B & W's customers could not well afford to be patient. Twenty-one of the pressure vessels tied up in the Mount Vernon Works were there on subcontracts from the two giants of the nuclear industry, General Electric and Westinghouse Electric. Both companies swiftly took the almost unprecedented step of forcing B & W to turn most of their partially completed vessels over to other manufacturers. When B & W, in an ill-conceived gambit, tried to hang onto two of the transferred vessels, Westinghouse took the case to court and won. In all, 14 G.E. and Westinghouse vessels—perhaps $40 million worth—were taken out of B & W's shops. Some of the firms that got the business had never made a pressure vessel before for use in a United States reactor; B & W had managed to create hungry new competitors in its own line of work. Only four G.E. and three Westinghouse vessels remain at Mount Vernon.

The company itself has barely begun to pay the high price of failure. Its earnings last year were still a robust $2.04 a share. In the first six months of this year, losses associated with nuclear work pushed earnings down to 22¢ a share—not enough to cover the 34¢ quarterly dividend. From a 1969 high of 40½ last January, Babcock & Wilcox stock has sagged into the low 20's. At that price the stock is hovering around book value.

The man in the middle of all these troubles is President George G. Zipf (pronounced Ziff), 49, a low-key executive who started with B & W in 1942 as a metallurgical engineer. But the man who bears the main onus of responsibility is Zipf's predecessor, Chairman Morris Nielsen, 65, who chose Zipf for his present job a year ago and handed him his present problems.

BAD BOY FROM BLAIR, NEBRASKA

Nielsen is a flamboyant leader, a big, bluff man with bright blue eyes and a full head of gray-blond hair, who has a gift for salty language. More than one secretary quit "Doc" Nielsen's employ because of his profanity, and more than one executive suffered a colorful tongue-lashing in the chairman's office.

Nielsen got his nickname by virtue of being a doctor's son in Blair, Nebraska, where he was known as "Young Doc." That was as close to earning an academic degree as Nielsen came. As a boy, he himself has said, he was "incorrigible" and was kicked out of school "for being a bad influence on the rest of the students." He then enrolled in a Lincoln, Nebraska, high school and worked part time as an embalmer. "I got into trouble in Lincoln, too," Nielsen told an interviewer a few years ago. "One night I came home with my nose over under my eye. I'd been in a fight and got hit with a pair of pliers. I woke up my old man and he looked at my nose and said, 'You're going to look like a goddamn syphilitic the rest of your life.' My old man used to tell me that there were two steps ahead of me—first reform school and then the pen."

Instead, Young Doc became a steeplejack and ironworker, and in 1924 joined the corporation he was later to head. "I came to B & W by accident," Nielsen has recalled. "I was working at American Bridge as an ironmonger on a job in Chicago, and another fellow and I got drunk. We got on the train and got off at Des Moines. We were walking past this construction job, and a fellow slid down a column and said, 'You looking for work?' We figured we were." It was a B & W job, erecting boilers for central-station power plants, and from the start Doc Nielsen felt at home in the two-fisted company. "Those construction workers were goddamn rough people. They were hard drinkers, fighters, and lived by their wits."

By the time World War II came along, Nielsen was superintendent of marine erection. He supervised the installation of B & W boilers in 4100 Navy and merchant-marine ships during the war. Later he headed the entire boiler division, including manufacturing, and in 1957 became president and chief executive officer.

When Nielsen took charge of B & W the company was already deeply involved in nuclear work. Nielsen's predecessor, Alfred Iddles, had recognized early that B & W would have to prepare for the day when the atom would challenge fossil fuels as a source of energy for central generating plants. Under Iddles, B & W attracted an outstanding stable of nuclear scientists and engineers and in 1956 set up an extensive research facility at Lynchburg, Virginia. One of B & W's first important nuclear jobs was to build Consolidated Edison's Indian Point plant. Another early project was the reactor for the nuclear ship *Savannah*, B & W lost money on these jobs, but it gained the experience needed to secure a corporate toehold in the nuclear era.

Nuclear losses continued under Nielsen, but he improved B & W's overall profitability dramatically. Iddles had run the company as a loose-knit grouping of semi-autonomous subsidiaries. Nielsen centralized and systematized management. Every executive's areas of responsibility and authority were carefully spelled out in manuals that defined company policies and aims in all sectors of the business. Although sales stayed near or below the 1958 figure of $366 million until 1963—this was a low period in the utility buying cycle—earnings climbed year by year. Profits went from $13 million in 1958 to $22 million in 1963. At that point, sales also began to go up, rising 71 percent in the next five years. Profits peaked in 1967 at $33 million, or $2.69 a share (compared to $1.05 a share in Nielsen's first full year).

In the view of his critics, who have lately become numerous, the seeds of B & W's present problems were planted in the years of Nielsen's rich harvests. It can be seen, in retrospect, that he may have been too successful in keeping B & W lean. His determination to keep down the fat sometimes "had the effect of cutting into good red meat," says a former B & W executive. Experienced managers found themselves stretched too thin to cover all their areas of responsibility. Worse, they did not always feel that their authority matched their responsibility—that is, men in the field were held responsible for results that they did not have the power to bring about.

The most biting criticism of Nielsen's regime comes from men charged with nuclear assignments. In their eyes, Nielsen's lack of formal education proved a serious handicap. Explains one former B & W executive: "Nielsen created an atmosphere in which engineers and technical people just didn't feel at home. Their ideas were not treated with respect. They felt that top management didn't understand technical problems and didn't trust those who could understand them."

A TOUCH OF CORPORATE ARROGANCE

From the start, B & W had forseen a long wait before its nuclear work became profitable. Developing the necessary skills and technologies to compete in the nuclear industry has proved to be a slow and expensive process for every company that has tried it, including G.E. and Westinghouse. But what B & W had *not* expected was to lose money on its Mount Vernon Works. When the plant was planned in the early 1960's, Nielsen appeared to believe that he had found a niche in the nuclear industry that offered a quick return. A nuclear pressure vessel, though huge and manufactured to demanding technical standards, is essentially just the kind of heavy steel unit that B & W was accustomed to fabricating with ease.

While the Mount Vernon plant was under construction, United States utilities went on a nuclear-plant buying spree, starting in 1965. At the time, the surge in orders seemed like a lucky break for B & W. The Mount Vernon plant was designed to produce one completed pressure vessel a month, once it was in full operation, and there had been considerable doubt during the planning stages "if we'd ever get enough work to fill the place," a former B & W executive recalls. Orders for pressure vessels poured in, faster than anyone had predicted, and the Mount Vernon plant soon got loaded up with work. It is now clear that management made too little provision for the time it would take to get the new plant operating at full capacity. Says one B & W customer: "I think you have to say that corporate arrogance was involved."

The first delays at Mount Vernon were caused by suppliers falling far behind schedule in providing vital equipment. A linear accelerator, used to detect welding flaws, was not delivered until August, 1966, 11 months late. Even worse, a highly automated, tape-controlled machining center—the heart of the plant as originally conceived—arrived a full year behind schedule, in September, 1967.

THE LURE OF UNSPOILED LABOR

By then, the plant had been operating on a makeshift basis for almost two years. And it had already become apparent that B & W's century of demonstrated competence in the fabrication of heavy steel products had not protected the company from some grievous errors. A principal one was the site itself—a cornfield near the little farm town of Mount Vernon (population: 6200) in southwestern Indiana. The location had been chosen mainly because of its position on the Ohio River, safely above any known flood level, yet reliably accessible for deepwater barges. This was an important advantage because nuclear pressure vessels are so immense that they can best be transported by water. B & W had owned the land for a number of years and had set up a small plant there for making boiler parts.

What Mount Vernon did not have was a pool of skilled labor. This was a serious drawback, because the AEC, for safety reasons, sets rigid standards for machine work and welding on nuclear projects. Late last year a company memorandum reviewing the Mount Vernon fiasco observed: "Production workers required a new level of knowledge, intelligence, and judgment to operate the machinery, perform operations, and maintain the very high quality standards." At the outset, however, B & W took an optimistic view of its prospects—choosing, according to that 1968 memorandum, to regard Mount Vernon as "an unspoiled labor market." Presumably, the company expected to find a more tractable group of workers there than it had at Barberton, Ohio, where B & W's power-generation division has had its headquarters and principal manufacturing facilities for many years.

The company planned to overcome the obvious shortcomings of Mount Vernon's labor pool in two ways: first, through automation—using that sophisticated machining center—and second, through a massive training program that would entice farmers away from their cornfields and quickly turn them into skilled welders and machinists. In one year B & W spent $1 million just to train welders. But almost as fast as men reached the levels of skill required, they left B & W for jobs elsewhere. On September 30, 1968, only 514 of the 1606 hourly employees hired in the preceding three years were still working for B & W; in other words, the company had hired three men for each one it retained. "Turnover of the Mount Vernon work force has been a particularly frustrating problem and a major reason why B & W has been unable to bring its full manufacturing capability to bear on the situation," the 1968 memorandum concluded. Some potential workers proved to be untrainable, others had a "general negative attitude" toward heavy industry, and "some were not able to adjust and therefore returned to their farms."

"IT DROVE US OUT OF OUR MINDS"

Workers who remained with B & W did not prove to be as unspoiled as the company had hoped. Even before the pressure-vessel plant opened, it was organized by the Boilermakers Union (which also represents B & W workers at Barberton) amid charges of unfair labor practices against the management. The plant was closed by labor disputes on several occasions. The most serious occurred when the three-year contract expired in 1967, while equipment was still being installed. The Boilermakers went on strike over wages and work rules, and the plant was down for forty days— unnecessarily long, in the view of President Thomas Ayers of Chicago's Commonwealth Edison, who had pressure vessels tied up at Mount Vernon.

From the standpoint of production, Nielsen won a victory that amounted to overkill. Under the new contract, wages remained too low to stem the flow of workers away from B & W or to attract qualified workers from other areas. The B & W memo cites the "noncompetitiveness of our wage scale" as a reason for the high turnover rate in the Mount Vernon work force.

Even for experienced workers, welding two pieces of eight-inch steel together is a demanding task, particularly in nuclear work, in which each weld is examined by x-ray. When an imperfection is found, the weld must be "mined out" and done over again. In most plants, less than 10 percent of the welds must be reworked, and a rework rate of less than 1 percent is sometimes achieved. But at Mount Vernon 70 percent or more of the welds were rejected on being inspected. "It drove us out of our damned minds," recalls Ayers. "So costly! So time-consuming!" Ayers and other B & W customers say that they urged the company to increase the supervisory force—which regularly worked one and a half to two shifts daily—so that a closer watch could be kept on the welds as they were built up.

In addition to its labor problems, B & W ran into unexpected trouble with equipment. The linear accelerator for x-raying welds was installed in mid-1966 but did not go into full operation until a year later. The tape-controlled machining center was even more of a headache, and began functioning as planned only a few months ago. In this center, huge vessel segments are positioned on optically aligned ways, and then moved a distance of 250 feet while a series of precise machining operations are performed simultaneously, controlled by computer-prepared tape. The concept was a good one, since nuclear pressure vessels are custom jobs, each tailored to a customer's specifications. But "debugging" of the machinery proved unexpectedly difficult. One problem was that the plant was not air-conditioned, and temperature changes threw off the many delicate adjustments that had to be made. In addition, an earthquake—fairly rare in Indiana—shook up the plant last year and it took nearly a week to reset the machine tools. Other start-up difficulties were simply incomprehensible. For example, a vital boring mill was put out of operation for several weeks when a tool broke. There was no spare on hand.

DEATH IN A DRY BATHTUB

The man directly responsible for the Mount Vernon plant was John Paul Craven, vice president in charge of the power-generation division at Barberton. As head of B & W's largest division, Craven was the number 3 man in the company, and was paid $87,000 a year. At one time there had been speculation in the company that Craven might someday become president.

A gentle, upright bachelor of 60, Craven was tall and distinguished looking. An engineer by training, he had been with B & W all his working life, and he had no interests outside his job. For a while Craven had raised roses as a hobby, but after he was made a vice president he gave up roses in order to devote himself more fully to B & W "His work was his whole life," says an old friend.

As the bottleneck at Mount Vernon grew worse, Craven came to feel that neither his customers nor corporate headquarters in New York fully appreciated the difficulties of bringing a new plant into operation, particularly one with Mount Vernon's advanced machine tools. Nor did he believe that he was given the authority, the budget, or the personnel that he needed to fulfill the plant's commitments. Says another of Craven's old friends: "Paul couldn't bear to sit in Barberton and have all the shots called from New York—and then be expected to take responsibility for not producing."

In September 1968, before the seriousness of the pressure-vessel crisis at Mount Vernon became generally known, Nielsen stepped aside as chief executive in favor of George Zipf. For a man destined for the top at B & W's tubular-products division at Beaver Falls, Pennsylvania, near Pittsburgh. This division, whose work is more akin to steel manufacturing than to boilermaking, produces tubing for B & W's own use and for sale to other industrial customers; it accounts for roughly 30 percent of B & W's total sales and more than half its profits. When he transferred to New York as executive vice president in 1966, Zipf had been at Beaver Falls for 24 years, ever since graduating from Lehigh University. He was a stranger to the problems of the power-generation division, and to that division's big corporate customers.

Less than a month after taking over as chief executive from Nielsen, Zipf scheduled a meeting at the Mount Vernon plant with Craven and Austin Fragomen, vice president for manufacturing. The meeting was set for a Monday morning. During the preceding weekend Craven told friends that for the first time in his life he thought his job was getting beyond him. Sometime on the Sunday afternoon or evening before his scheduled meeting with Zipf, Craven took off his clothes and climbed into a dry bathtub in his $250-a-month apartment in Akron's luxurious Carlton House. Then he slashed his ankles, cut his throat, and stabbed himself in the heart with the serrated eight-inch blade of a butcher knife.

After Craven's death, George Zipf took personal charge of the power-generation division, and of the Mount Vernon works in particular. Before long, both Austin Fragomen and the Mount Vernon plant manager, Norman Wagner, resigned. That left Zipf free to put a whole new team to work on the company's pressure-vessel debacle.

THE CHAIRMAN SELLS SOME STOCK

Beginning in 1967, both G.E. and Westinghouse, along with many of the utilities that were the ultimate customers for B & W pressure vessels, repeatedly expressed worry over the Mount Vernon plant's faltering operations. In the fall of 1968, B & W pacified G.E. to some extent by setting up a temporary welding shop on barges anchored at Madison, Indiana, where expert welders from the Louisville, Kentucky, labor pool could be obtained. But for the most part B & W brushed aside its customers' worries with assurances that things at Mount Vernon were not really as bad as they seemed. Even after Craven's death, the B & W management continued to maintain that its optimistic scheduling, with some minor changes, would prove to be realistic. Some utility executives who met with Zipf to express their concern were left with the conviction that he did not appreciate just how serious the pressure-vessel delays had become. On some occasions he seemed to regard his callers as bothersome intruders. "He just sat there like a damned Buddha," reported one customer after such a meeting.

Faced with such frustrations, G.E. and Westinghouse began to consider the drastic step of pulling some of their delayed pressure vessels out of the overloaded Mount Vernon shops. Both companies assigned teams to scout for other manufacturers that might be able to take over B & W vessels and complete them. There were not many potential candidates. Up to then, B & W and Combustion Engineering, Inc. had pretty much divided the United States pressure-vessel business between them. Combustion Engineering had managed to keep close to schedule on its deliveries and had been expanding its Chattanooga machine shops. It had unused capacity. In addition, Chicago Bridge & Iron Co., which had previously done only on-site fabrication of nuclear vessels, was setting up a pressure-vessel plant in Memphis. (On-site fabrication is a more expensive method of constructing pressure vessels, used only when it is extremely difficult to transport the massive units to a site intact.) The G.E. and Westinghouse teams also looked abroad for companies that might be able to take over some of the work.

In April, while B & W's biggest customers were searching for other suppliers, Doc Nielsen—who was retiring on May 1 as an officer of the company but keeping the title of chairman—quietly sold 15,000 of his 20,000 shares of B & W stock. The price at the time was about $33 a share. A couple of weeks later, B & W stockholders got their first official hint of serious trouble ahead. George Zipf revealed at the annual meeting that he expected earnings to drop by 20 to 30 percent in 1969 because of the company's losses on nuclear business. (The actual decline, of course, has since

proved to be much greater than Zipf predicted.) Before long the price of
B & W stock sank into the 20's.

A QUICK TRIP TO COURT

On May 14, less than a month after the annual meeting, B & W sent out
telegrams brusquely letting customers know that the situation at Mount
Vernon was even worse than they had suspected. Zipf and his new team had
completed a gloomy reevaluation of the plant's capabilities, and B & W was
adding two to 12 months to earlier delivery schedules, some of which had
already been stretched past the dates called for in B & W's original
contracts.

On receiving this news, both G.E. and Westinghouse sought B & W's
cooperation in transferring vessels to the other shops that they had scouted
out. B & W agreed to subcontract some of its work to these plants. But an
unexpected difficulty soon arose. Westinghouse had determined that Rotterdam Dockyard Co., a major shipbuilding and steel fabricating firm in the
Netherlands, could take two vessels and improve on the B & W schedule—
provided that the vessels were transferred promptly. Westinghouse located
space on a ship that would be calling at New Orleans on the desired date
and, by paying a premium, was able to arrange for the ship to cancel calls
at other ports and proceed directly to the Netherlands. B & W agreed to
put the two pressure vessels on barges and start them on their way to New
Orleans while it negotiated a subcontract with Rotterdam Dockyard. But
negotiations broke down when B & W and Rotterdam could not come to
terms. To the horror of Westinghouse officials, B & W ordered the barges
back to Mount Vernon.

Westinghouse then decided to pay B & W for the work it had already
done and take over the vessels itself. But speed was required. If the barges
did not continue down the river while these new arrangements were made,
they would miss the ship to Rotterdam. Now Westinghouse found itself at a
strange impasse—it could not reach anyone at B & W who could rescind
the order for the barges to return to Mount Vernon. Nielsen was "not
available." Zipf was "out of the country." Frustrated in its effort to reach
top management and work out an amicable settlement, Westinghouse
reluctantly went into United States district court in Pittsburgh and won a
temporary restraining order to prevent B & W from taking the vessels back
to Mount Vernon.

During the hearing Federal Judge Wallace S. Gourley had a revealing
exchange with John T. Black, B & W's manager for commercial nuclear
components.

JUDGE GOURLEY: . . . on this contract for $2,542,000, what would you say that you expect to make on this:
BLACK: This specific contract?
JUDGE GOURLEY: Yes.
BLACK: I don't expect to make a profit.
JUDGE GOURLEY: You don't expect to make a profit?
BLACK: No, sir.
JUDGE GOURLEY: I don't know why you would want the material to work on. You are not in business to lose money for your stockholders.
BLACK: We do not expect to make it.
JUDGE GOURLEY: In other words, on this contract [for] $2,542,000, you don't expect to make a penny profit for your corporation if you went ahead and finished it?
BLACK: No, sir.
JUDGE GOURLEY: How much on this other one, $2,304,789, what profit could you be reasonably expected to make on this contract if you finished it?
BLACK: I would think that one probably [is] in the same condition.
JUDGE GOURLEY: If you went ahead and finished this, you wouldn't make a cent?
BLACK: I think on direct cost, we would cover our direct cost to labor and shop expense.
JUDGE GOURLEY: I mean after everything, would you or would you not make any money on this?
BLACK: No.
JUDGE GOURLEY: I wouldn't think your stockholders would want you to finish. I certainly wouldn't.

BACK ON THE TRACK

After Westinghouse won possession of the two pressure vessels and sent them off to Rotterdam, B & W raised no further objections to transferring work out of its shop. Indeed it actively cooperated with its customers to get the job done. Westinghouse sent five vessels to Combustion Engineering's Chattanooga shops and two to a French firm, Société des Forges et Ateliers du Creusot. General Electric turned three vessels over to Chicago Bridge & Iron and had B & W send two others to Japan's Ishikawajima-Harima Heavy Industries. In every case, these firms are expected to equal or better the delivery dates set in May by B & W.

With the load at Mount Vernon lightened, prospects look better for the 14 pressure vessels that remain there, including seven for nuclear plants that

B & W itself is building. For example, the Sacramento Municipal Utility District has been notified that the vessel for its Rancho Seco nuclear plant, a B & W project, will be only a couple of months late, instead of the year that seemed likely in May. That means that the vessel for Sacramento is essentially on schedule again, since the delays now expected are no more than could be accounted for by the labor disputes and earthquake that Mount Vernon suffered.

To his utility customers, George Zipf remains very much a man on trial. But now that their pressure vessels are moving along again, some utility executives are convinced that he has quietly managed to put B & W back on the track. One move that has met their approval was the appointment in September of an experienced Westinghouse man as vice president in charge of the power-generation division—John Paul Craven's old job. Bringing in an outsider at such a level is something new for B & W, and one B & W customer believes that he knows what it means: "I think George Zipf is really in command now." If this is so, he will have a lot to do to restore the honored old name of Babcock & Wilcox to its former luster.

THE GREAT NUCLEAR FIZZLE AT THE OLD BABCOX & WILCOX:

Conventional Analysis

When managers are asked, "What went wrong?" the conventional reply is, "Many things went wrong." They cite that the company did a poor job of training and motivating the workers and that this gave the factory low production and high costs. B & W had a difficult time procuring and installing the customized, numerically controlled equipment so they were unable to produce and slipped months behind their orders. They apparently had ineffective work force management policies, for they were unable to retain the workers on which they had lavished substantial training. The company was also foolish to keep accepting orders that were piling up well beyond the planned capacity of the plant. Some managers also fault the company for choosing a location so far away from their headquarters and their cadre of experienced engineers. Others criticize B & W for not setting up enough capacity when sizing the plant. President Neilson always receives criticism for having a highly centralized, autocratic style in management and creating an environment in which engineers believed that they were not appreciated. Many analysts feel that B & W's approach was adequate for routine manufacturing but not for a start-up situation. The company is also faulted for arrogance which led them to take on more work than they could handle.

After all this criticism is leveled, the next logical question can be asked: "How can a successful and highly competent company with an excellent record over the years make so many mistakes and create such a disaster?" In the conventional analysis there are usually two schools of thought in reply. One says that it was the combination of so many things that were new all at once—a new product, a new location, a new technology, new equipment, new workers, new supervisors, new customers, and a new level of volume to be produced. This line of reasoning says that for a given management to handle so many new problems all at once is courting disaster, and that when you have so many things to overcome at once it's necessary to organize a very tight set of controls and set up teams under project or program management.

The second school of thought blames "poor planning" for the sequence of problems that compounded themselves. They say that if the company's planning had been more realistic, more comprehensive, and more detailed, these possible negative outcomes could have been forecast and a great many of the consequences might have been avoided. They argue that an intelligent management recognizes that a good decision simply leads into a new set of problems that is better than the old set of problems and that better planning would have led them to look at the implications of their decisions and then to make subsequent plans to deal with those implications. For example, the new, numerically controlled machine tool should have had particularly detailed planning to take care of its inevitably difficult start-up. And the effort to plan more systematically might have come up with a need for new organization, new controls, and a new approach to work force management instead of adopting conventional approaches from other parts of the company.

At this point, if the instructor probes further, most groups of students, including the most confident and experienced, simply run out of gas. They say, "When you are moving into new plants and new products, it takes a great deal of conscientious planning, and the newness could be handled by better planning." But when they are pushed to say what might have been planned differently, most students and even experienced groups of managers end up lamely stating that good planners plan for possible consequences, building backup systems and redundant systems. They claim that they would never let themselves get into such a hopeless and helpless position as did the managers at Babcock & Wilcox.

But was it simply bad planning that led the company to make so many poor decisions? These were intelligent, successful people, and it seems strange to have had them make so many poor decisions on so many factors all at once. At this point it is helpful to push again and say, "But why did they make so many poor decisions?" The group will then begin to say, "Perhaps it was because they were saddled with the wrong objectives." They claim that the objectives seemed to be to make money and that perhaps the emphasis should not have been on making money for the first year or two. The company should have been building up production slowly and carefully and making sure that problems got solved. Perhaps the objective should have been to learn to solve problems during the first year or two. But they were pushed hard by President Nielson, who for so many years had been investing in the nuclear power business and losing money and then, having seen markets ready to explode, saw glittering gold. Setting up a specialized plant that could turn out these reactors in large quantities and make some money was perhaps his primary objective. So the conventional analysis usually ends on a discussion of objectives, and the class finds itself saying that it's very important to have the right objectives. But how do you know when the objectives are "right"?

Manufacturing Policy Analysis

In the manufacturing policy analysis the analysts start at the other end. They derive objectives from the company's strategic position and its marketing needs and develop a sense of what must be done in manufacturing for the company to be successful. They list the technological and human constraints involved in meeting these objectives.

At Babcock & Wilcox the strategy objective was to preempt the nuclear reactor business by being very customer- and market-oriented over the next two or three years. The company had a running start in the field and had 10 years more experience than anybody else. The orders had begun to pour in. There was no way that they could fail unless they failed to make deliveries and hold AEC quality. The strategic goal of the company, therefore, should have been to earn the position of being the industry's sole reactor supplier because of their technological lead and their reliability of deliveries. Their customers were electric power companies of the United States, an industry in which demand could be fairly reliably predicted and in which the delivery completion of a power station on time was of great importance to the utility to prevent brownouts. Therefore, from the customer standpoint, reliability of the product's delivery, combined with satisfactory quality, was paramount. The technological constraint was the fact that these devices were big and heavy and new and required a great deal of know-how which had to be developed. And the market was exploding, yet the company would have to be careful in how they accepted orders and promised delivery. The company would also have to be careful in the sizing of the plant.

What was *the manufacturing task?* One statement could be that the manufacturing task was to get into production on a new and technologically difficult product in a rapidly expanding market in such a way as to minimize the risk of missing deliveries.

Seen in this light, the "name of the game" was to get started on something new and difficult in such a way as to absolutely minimize risk. Once this manufacturing task is seen, a great many structural decisions begin to fall into place.

The task was to develop this volume and deliver it without fail. If they had stood back, designed the strategy, looked at the technology, recognized the economics, and then very carefully defined the manufacturing task, they would have prevented these problems. The task had to be defined. They should have asked, "What kind of structure do we need to accomplish this task?" The manufacturing task question is, "What do we have to be especially good at? What is going to be especially difficult?" They had to be especially good at delivery commitments, and what was going to be especially difficult for them was the new technology, the new growth, and the new products.

The name of the game, therefore, was control and avoiding risk. If they had seen it that way, would they have set up a new plant hundreds of miles from their basic technical know-how? Would they have set up a plant where they would have to hire green labor? Would they have imposed on that plant the heritage of that heavy-handed organization and structure? Would they have imposed on that plant tight-fisted labor policies? Would they have put into that plant a centralized bank of equipment through which every single reactor had to pass? Would they have employed a process flow where one failure could bottleneck the whole plant? Of course, the answers are "No."

With these questions answered negatively, quite a different set of structural decisions would have been made. It would have been better to have set up the new plant closer to the home office and the locus of accumulated technical know-how. They would have produced this new and difficult product with experienced labor and relied less on training. They would have probably set up production in an existing facility with experienced supervision; they would have made room by moving out an old, established product into a new plant. The organization would have shifted to push decisions down the line and delegated as far as possible and created a problem-solving, project-centered type of decision-making aparatus. The equipment and process technology would have been selected to minimize risk. The plant would have been designed not only with much greater capacity but with redundant or alternate methods of production in contrast to the perfect bottleneck they created. And they probably would have gone ahead with more conventional equipment in the effort to minimize risk.

To summarize, the manufacturing policies and structure would have been designed entirely differently if the company had explicitly stated their manufacturing task and then set up their plant and its entire system to accomplish that unique task.

INTERNATIONAL MANUFACTURING

International manufacturing is steadily growing more significant in the corporate strategies of many firms. The question often raised by managers assigned to manage international production is, "What is going to be different? What must I look out for?" The following three chapters offer some answers to these questions from research abroad. The emphasis is particularly on the manager assigned overseas, but each chapter deals with the inevitable and often troubling set of issues concerning what is done at headquarters versus the overseas plants and how these decisions can be effectively allocated.

CHAPTER 15

Managing
International
Production

In their efforts to manage international production operations expatriate
managers in Chicago, New York, Madrid, Frankfurt, Karachi,
Bombay—the world over—are wrestling with problems such as the
following:

- How to deal with vendors who are habitually late in delivery and
  marginal in performance but are nevertheless the best vendors available.
- How to minimize investment in inventory and prevent stockouts—when
  replacement of a missing item may require four to six months; the cost of
  local working capital is 12% to 20% per year; and it is difficult to hire
  stock clerks, especially in underdeveloped countries, who can keep
  accurate records.
- How to maintain a fair, motivating wage and salary rate in the midst of
  inflation, secrecy regarding practices of other companies, and traditional
  patterns of compensation such as automatic annual increments and
  "dearness allowances."
- How to select and train employees in the face of (1) language differences
  and often a low general-education level, (2) difficulties in testing applicants' potential, (3) the necessity of relying on new or weak lower-level
  supervision for the bulk of recommendations and training, and (4) high
  penalties for mistakes made (such as heavy compulsory severance pay to
  employees discharge).
- How to choose between (1) equipment or processes characterized by high
  initial cost, automated features, high maintenance, and low labor cost;

and (2) alternatives with lower initial cost that may require more direct labor and tighter control in terms of quality and supervision. Such decisions are often complicated by unpredictable future costs and markets.

The decisions needed to solve these problems call for the skills of the administrator, engineer, economist, political scientist, anthropologist, and historian. Few, if any, problems can be solved in terms of only "efficiency," or "economics," or "culture," or "management principles." To be effective in international production, managers—both at home and abroad—must have special skills and broader social and political perspectives.

In contrast to the lack of attention being given to production by international headquarters, manufacturing managers abroad have long been aware of the difficulties and complexities of managing manufacturing facilities in alien environments. In conducting the research on which this chapter is based, I visited 30 production plants of United States subsidiaries in seven countries. One clear impression emerges from these visits: The managers of these operations, American and local, are gamely grappling with significantly more difficult problems than those encountered in domestic operations. For example, here are three short typical cases.

Plant A

A United States parent company purchased a majority interest in a successful, foreign-owned company located in Europe. An experienced European was transferred from another location to become managing director. As he became familiar with the firm's operations in areas such as production scheduling, quality and inventory control, purchasing, personnel, and cost accounting, he expressed concern over what he felt were excessively informal and erratic procedures. He requested the temporary assistance of various staff experts from the Chicago headquarters.

These men were appalled to find production scheduling virtually nonexistent, to the extent that shifting overloads bottlenecked one section of the plant while other sections were nearly idle. Salary procedures were highly irregular. Certain favored employees (sometimes through under-the-table deals) were paid more than their supervisors. Product costing was nil; it was impossible to know which products were profitable.

When the headquarters executives in Chicago were apprised of these irregularities, they became increasingly uneasy. Each new revelation of problems seemed to lead to two or three more. They became convinced that the entire management needed a thorough housecleaning.

By this time, however, the new managing director and five headquarters staff men abroad had become more familiar with the local management and their rationale. While still pushing for changes to "modern management practices," they had developed more respect for the host-country nationals and recommended less urgency in pushing through drastic changes. The home office continued to be disturbed at the prior evidence of poor local management and grew even more disquieted over the apparent fact that their professional staff had "gone native." In short, the three groups—home office, overseas managers and local people had become involved in a fitful tug-of-war over what United States procedures to install, at what pace, and who should be calling the shots.

Plant B

A United States vehicle manufacturer in Turkey had a successful first year. The operation was based on the importation of 85% of the parts required. Foreign exchange had been guaranteed by the Turkish government. But economic conditions deteriorated, and foreign exchange became unobtainable for four years. The American manager and his staff of eight American department heads decided to mark time, conducting only maintenance and clean-up work while they tried to gain government support to acquire foreign exchange.

After this failed, they attempted to make and sell several simple agricultural and road-construction products that required no imported parts. This proved somewhat less than successful. Marketing the new products was difficult, and production delays owing to vendor inadequacies, scrap, low production efficiency, and inventory losses further hampered results. One by one, the Americans returned home discouraged and antagonized by everything Turkish.

A new American plant manager, reflecting the views of the home office, called a halt to most of the attempts to develop new products and take in subcontracting, saying, "I do not want to run a variety store." A policy vacuum developed. No final decision was made as to what the plant should be doing. The plant was only two days away from closing when foreign loans to Turkey made exchange available again for vehicle production.

Plant C

A United States company's plant in the Far East encountered repeated mechanical breakdowns apparantly due to employee sabotage. American and local managers alike were unable to link any incident to a particular employee. It gradually became clear that the sabotage was located in areas under the control of four supervisors who had been promoted from the ranks. Apparently the employees were "out to get" these supervisors.

The sabotage was so cleverly done, however, that it seemed impossible to do anything other than to hold the supervisors responsible. Although non-supervisory employees were warned of immediate dismissal and attempts were made to communicate how serious and costly these incidents were, the sabotage continued. The plant manager felt that his only choice was to dismiss the supervisors who were "unable to control" their employees and safeguard employer property. But new supervisors soon experienced the same problem.

In the meantime, the plant's cost and productivity record was one of the poorest of the corporation's worldwide plants, in spite of low wages and an American-developed incentive plan that had been successfully applied in many other parts of the world. The Americans involved were baffled and frustrated by the "irrational and stupid" behavior of the employees. "They have the best jobs and pay they've ever had; they have far better standards of living than their neighbors in the village here. And yet they are crippling our production and failing to cooperate to the extent that we are losing money."

COMMON CONCERNS

These formidable problems not only have affected the profit and growth of overseas enterprises, but in some instances have threatened their survival. The problems described in these cases are not unusual. Their seriousness is indicated by the fact that in some instances companies have "pulled out" and closed down plants. Executive turnover in overseas production work appears to be much higher than in domestic plants. Even in the operations one would ordinarily call "successful" (such as plant A), there are many perplexing problems to the managers involved.

The declining trend in return on overseas investments, coupled with the inherent difficulties in managing foreign production plants, adds up to a need for improved insights and practices. But the task is not simple. Managers involved often feel that precedent, or experience, is rarely applicable from one country to another. Virtually no body of knowledge, discipline, or conceptual framework is available to assist the production executive. Basically two things are required:

1. A clearer understanding of the problems by both overseas and head-quarters managers. Headquarters managers need a better grasp for the actual problems faced overseas as well as an enlarged awareness of the profit potentials and long-range benefits of plants that are run better.

2. A framework for thinking that will enable overseas executives to divide their problems into manageable groups. Otherwise they seem so complex, shifting, and amorphous as to elude solution. The complexity of managing production operations in foreign cultures and economies urges the development of some unifying concepts and a framework in which one can think more effectively and with more flexibility.

In this chapter I hope to help international production managers acquire both a clearer understanding of their problems and an analytical framework in which to seek solutions. I will:

1. Suggest some of the sources of problems inherent in an international manufacturing operation.
2. Identify three recurring issues that underlie many of the problems facing those in international manufacturing.
3. Show how a broader, more global view of their problems can be obtained.
4. Offer specific advice on promising approaches to take and tendencies to avoid.

SOURCES OF PROBLEMS

Which forces in an overseas environment cause problems? Here is a list of 11 such factors, some of which may appear rather obvious at first glance, but which, nevertheless, involve subtle effects:

1. Operating environments in host countries differ from the home country in terms of culture, politics, and economics.
2. Production processes must be carried out by a work force composed of foreign nationals.
3. Management must be by foreign nationals under top management from the home country or by home country managers sent abroad. In either arrangement problems arise.
4. Distances between overseas plants and home offices present logistic and communications difficulties.
5. Overseas partners or investors, when involved, further complicate the already difficult process of establishing objectives and policies for the overseas plant.
6. Since selling abroad is different from selling in the home country (i.e., product specifications vary, demand and price are less stable, and

goods are less available) the production system simply cannot function in the typical way.

7. The production function demands an emphasis on time, costs, efficiency, and precision—an emphasis that often runs counter to patterns in the local culture.

8. The long-term as well as the short-term future is often more difficult to predict abroad, expecially for the American forecaster. This is particularly true in the underdeveloped areas but also to a certain extent in Europe, where the economic picture has been closely tied to political arrangements such as the Common Market.

9. Dealing as a foreign investor with overseas governments is fraught with problems of delicate relationships and voluminous paperwork especially in the emerging Middle East and "nonmarket" socialist countries.

10. The expatriate company must work in the spotlight of the foreign nation's public opinion and government attention. Sensitive, nationalistic feelings in many countries create political and public relations pressures.

11. Many countries are in the midst of rapid economic and social changes. Thus the expatriate firm must be especially concerned with the establishment of precedents and with public, government, and labor relations, since freedom, resources, and continued existence of the guest depend on the sanction of the host and acceptance by the public.

BASIC ISSUES

To cope with such problems, the first requirement is that those involved, expatriate managers and foreign nationals alike, enlarge their views to develop a sense of perspective. This broader perspective may be provided by the recognition that certain basic issues underlie most international production-management situations.

I observed these issues in every one of the 30 plants I visited. Their essential pervasiveness is further attested by interviews with headquarters executives involved with South American and Common Market areas which were not included in plant visits. Specifically, the issues are:

1. *Environmental adjustment.* How should we adjust to a new cultural, economic, and political environment?

2. *Exporting know-how.* How much of our company's technical and managerial expertise can and should be applied abroad?

3. *Organizing the multinational manufacturing corporation.* How much

control versus autonomy? How should we handle communication and information systems? What role should the home-office staff play?

These are the key issues in managing international manufacturing operations. Let's look at each in more detail from the perspective of a manager in a United States company.

Environmental Adjustments

The overseas plant is in a political and economic environment which is generally unfamiliar to United States managers. Labor laws, tax laws, and regulatory requirements, obviously, are different from those in the United States. But more important, the role of the government in foreign countries is often more dominant than in the United States. Basic business decisions and daily operating requirements are affected. International United States businesses usually get into trouble if they object to such control "on principle" and try to "fight city hall," or in ignorance, fail to staff so as to handle government contacts properly.

The problem is more difficult than it appears to be at first. The obvious answer would seem to be to hire some competent local men who know the political environment to handle governmental relations and requirements. Unfortunately, this does not often succeed, since there is a chasm between the foreign national and the American corporate management in their understanding of the corporation's policies, objectives, and ways of doing business.

Routine paperwork can be handled by the knowledgeable foreigner. But years of experience are usually necessary before decisions made at higher levels can be transmitted by means of the foreign national to the government without some misunderstanding of the original intent occurring through the "filter" action of the foreign manager. In four of the companies visited, new foreign managers at high levels so incurred the wrath of their corporate headquarters for mishandling of important government relationships that they were forced to resign.

The economic environment poses quite different, but equally difficult, problems. Rapid changes, such as those occurring in Europe over the past five years, make forecasting difficult. An economic "cost mix" that differs from that used in the United States requires a new rationale for decisions about equipment, process, make-or-buy, and economic order quantities. The corporate headquarters staff must judge plans and requests by different criteria for each country, taking into account not only the specific mix of costs but local quality and material-procurement problems as well.

Exhibit 15.1 The Cultural System as It Affects Production Management

Differences in these cultural factors	. . . affect people's values and habits relating to	For example, the local employee might feel that	. . . and this would tend to affect approaches in these (and other) areas of manufacturing management
I. Assumptions and attitudes	Time	Time is not measured in minutes, but in days and years	Production control, scheduling, purchasing
	One's proper purpose in life	The only purpose that makes sense is to enjoy each day.	Management development
	The future	The future is not in man's hands.	Short- and long-range planning
	This life versus the hereafter	Life and death are completely ordained and predetermined.	Safety programs
	Duty, responsibility	Your job is completed when you give an order to a subordinate.	Executive techniques of delegation and follow-up
II. Personal beliefs and aspirations	Right and wrong	I give the boss inventory counts which please him or her.	Inventory control system
	Sources of pride	A college degree places one higher in society for life.	Selection of supervisors
	Sources of fear and concern	Jobs are hard to get for a person laid off, regardless of the cause of layoff.	Layoff policy
	Extent of one's hopes	Without the right education and social class, advancement is limited.	Incentives, motivation

			Labor relations
	The individual versus society	The individual's wants and needs must be subordinated to the whole group.	
III. Interpersonal relationships	The source of authority	My crew doesn't like the new process. It won't work.	Quality control
	Care or empathy for others	I'd rather give my salary raise to my supervisors than have to tell them they are not to receive raises themselves.	Merit reviews
	Importance of family obligations	I had to stay home because my father was sick.	Absenteeism
	Objects of loyalty	Friendship is more important than business.	Work-group relationships
	Tolerance for personal differences	If you don't agree with your boss, he or she will be insulted.	The decision-making process
IV. Social structure	Interclass nobility	I'd refuse to work for a person without a trade school certificate.	Promotion from within
	Class or caste systems	People with my standing don't move heavy objects such as typewriters.	Job scriptions—flexibility of job assignments
	Urban-village-farm origins	The company must take the place of the village in caring for its people.	Fringe-benefit programs
	Determinants of status	Elderly people have wisdom. They deserve the most important jobs on big machines.	Equipment selection

Moreover, the factors involved must be considered not just for the present; they also must be estimated for the future.

Cultural Differences

Conflicts caused by the collision of differing cultural systems are abundant.[1] Such conflicts result in technical and organizational problems as well as in human relations problems. Exhibit 15.1 suggests some of the varieties of impacts that cultural differences have on manufacturing operations.

Manufacturing in diverse cultures brings a new dimension to many conventional decisions in production management. Effective systems, control procedures, and choice of equipment, for example, all depend on the values, habits, and attitudes of employees and supervisors. Countless decisions made with little reflection at home become vastly more complicated abroad. The complexities arise within the factory from the intermeshing of technological systems (usually based on product or process requirements), the local social or cultural system, and a whole set of management policies, systems, and procedures. This collision of technology and culture is present regardless of the number of United States managers on the scene; but the collision between local customs and management practices can be attributed to the involvement of American managers.

Baffled by the "illogical" behavior of local executives and workers, many American executives tend to react to one of two extremes:

- *The "main streeter."* "This is an American business and these locals are going to have to learn to think and do business the American way. After all, we in the United States of America have developed the most efficient businesses and the highest standard of living in the world."
- *The Yankee "gone native."* "When you're in Japan or India or France, you've got to adapt. Forget our American ways—they just don't apply. When in Rome. . . ."

Surprisingly enough, it is necessary to point out (*a*) that neither position is correct, and (*b*) that certain facets of the local culture should not be ignored any more than should certain elements of the United States corporation's know-how and expertise be left in the United States. This leads us to be second basic issue.

---

[1] See Edward T. Hall, "The Silent Language of Overseas Business," HBR May–June 1960, p. 87; and Dudley L. Miller, "The Honorable Picnic: Doing Business in Japan," HBR November–December 1961, p. 79.

Exporting Techniques

How, when, and where should we export the corporation's industrial techniques? Do we use our regular wage plan? Do we install an economic order quantity decision rule in scheduling? Do we use preventive maintenance?

The outcomes of these decisions often present further problems. If the firm decides to adopt the techniques it has used in the United States, there may be situations where they do not fit or where foreign-national managers chafe under a strange approach. And if the decision is to "do it the local way," an advanced or well-tested technique may be ignored and the performance of an entire operation allowed to suffer.

Manufacturing in a different culture and on a smaller scale offers an easy rationale for leaving at home potentially useful technical concepts and managerial techniques and practices. This is particularly so in the areas of work force management, production control, and procurement, which are generally under local supervision and require a heavy input of local "feel."

The next step in the logic of many companies is to leave this field of management entirely to foreign managers. The flaw in this reasoning is that these areas depend heavily on lower and middle levels of supervisory management which are apt to be especially weak in the overseas plant. A rich body of skill and knowledge of the parent company is thereby unapplied, and as a result falldowns in these areas are legion.

The opposite extreme is less frequent, but by no means rare. Some international companies insist that the foreign subsidiary follow the parent's own manufacturing processes and procedures to the letter. A predisposition toward "doing it our way" usually leads to a large number of overseas Americans, visiting staff, and a tightly run control system.

It would be a mistake to conclude that avoiding these extreme positions averts all problems in the transference of industrial techniques. For even with an ideal balance, there are many alternatives and degrees of effectiveness in the methods of transmission of knowledge, the use of home-office staff, the development of foreign managers, and the mechanisms of control.

Organizing Multinationally

The third basic issue is one of organization. Nearly every company I visited sensed the difficulty of developing an effective organization. Distance, culture, growth, and change, all add to the normal organizational questions of allocating responsibilities, authority, and control, and handling communications in any multiplant operation. Two focal points may serve to highlight the organizational problems

1. *What contributions should be expected of United States home office staff?* Determining the number and type of people to assist the overseas operation is only part of the question. Most companies have technical specialists who either review process and equipment requests or, given the basic requirements from abroad, select the equipment and process themselves. A smaller number of companies have production control, personnel, procurement, time study, training, and quality control staffs who serve the overseas plants on a request or regular audit basis.

There is a tendency to belong to a "school of thought" on this question:

One school says, "An American company must use many Americans from the headquarters staff in its overseas plant until the foreigners can be trained in the American way. We must have a complete staff to indoctrinate our foreign nationals and sell them on the idea of learning efficient and practical methods of business as rapidly as possible."

The other school says, "A home office staff is too expensive, and no one group is going to be able to understand local problems and conditions throughout the world, anyway. It's best to decentralize and let your local managers figure things out for themselves."

2. *How much control and direction should there be from the home office?* What type of decisions should be delegated abroad? Should the headquarters staff for overseas operations be advisory or decision making? These decisions are difficult enough in the management of domestic, geographically decentralized operations. And abroad, where the differences in cultural, political, and economic environments are frequently very substantial, great confusion and strong differences of opinion reign.

These differences lead to more serious consequences than just hurt feelings. They frequently are the cause of poor decisions or downright indecision. The host-country manager claims, "We are not trusted. We know our country and its needs. But the Americans seem to feel they have all the answers." To this, the typical American headquarters reply is, "The foreigner is often impractical. He dreams of great growth and glory, but he just doesn't get things done. Can we turn the foreign plant over to locals and allow them to determine important policy? Don't we have a responsibility to our stockholders to hold the reins tight?"

SEEING THE GLOBAL PICTURE

What new approaches or insights might prove helpful to international business executives in dealing more effectively with the problems plaguing them?

It is my belief that the development of a sense of objectivity about these problems is a vital first step. A broader understanding of the forces that complicate the job of the international manufacturer would include:

- A deeper awareness that managers of overseas plants are caught up in the complexities of four interacting systems—the technological, cultural, political, and economic systems in which they operate—and that they must learn to understand and cope with all four.
- A realistic appreciation that managing a group of overseas manufacturing plants is not essentially identical to managing a set of branch plants at home.
- A concept of the approach to achieving a desirable balance among home- and host-country production procedures, practices, or techniques.

Interacting Systems

Exhibit 15.2 presents one possible framework on which executives might build their own understanding of the major factors in the technological,

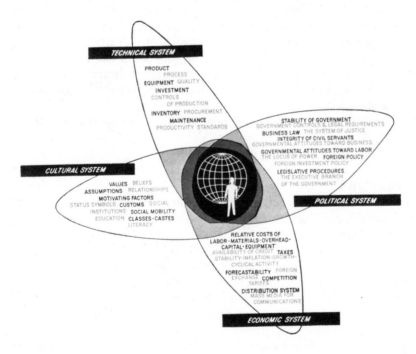

Exhibit 15.2   Four Intermeshing Systems in Which the International Production Manager Must Function

cultural, political, and economic systems in which they operate. They must be able to recognize the demands of these systems on their decisions and behavior. They must learn to view each system rationally, to recognize interferences and conflicts, and to perceive possibilities for adjustment, change, and compromise among the four systems.

Many people who are experienced in international management recognize those factors that are *fixed*, those that are *changing* or changeable, and those that are the *most critical* in each of the four systems.

Sophisticated international production people not only seek to understand the interworkings of these four systems; they also learn to isolate the permanent elements from those they can influence, and they address themselves to the latter. In so doing, they view their situations as dynamic, rather than static. They have the patience that comes from the recognition of change, and the impatience that derives from seeing that apparently immobilizing factors need not be deterrents to progress and efficiency.

Overseas versus Domestic Operations

In spite of obvious cultural, economic, and political differences existing between the foreign nation and the United States, many American corporations tend to view the overseas plant as just another domestic branch plant, different only in its being more remote. This misconception leads to policy struggles as well as to the tendency to supply too much control and too little assistance. Let us compare briefly the differences between the domestic and foreign production operation.

In the case of the domestic branch plant, headquarters usually provides:

- Engineering and product specifications.
- Cash for meeting operating plans and capital budgets, after approval by the home office.
- Policy direction and control affecting products, prices, basic manufacturing processes, plant and equipment, make-or-buy, manufacturing organization, and long-range plans.

Branch-plant personnel handle "local" decisions and operations such as labor relations, local procurement, work-force management, production control, cost and quality control. In these management areas, the headquarters staff frequently provides only a degree of coordination to the various branch plants.

The approach to branch plant management used in domestic plants is often adopted in the management of overseas plants. But such an allocation of responsibility and authority between headquarters and overseas plants usually does not work so well. This is because:

- Domestic branch plants have ready access to corporate headquarters expertise when they request it or need it. Overseas plants, separated from the headquarters by thousands of miles and situated in a particular milieu of culture, economics, and politics, often do not receive the staff help needed in operations and yet are often dominated by the home office in the establishment of basic manufacturing policy.
- Multinational organizations require a specially tailored, total management system. Intelligent policy decisions cannot be assured when they are made for a plant 5,000 miles away by people who visit infrequently. And local operating decisions cannot always be made wisely by local managers with limited experience in efficient plant operation.

The tug-of-war over policy determination is another result of applying United States domestic branch-plant management approaches to overseas plants. The home office wants policy settled at headquarters. "We have the global picture. The local plant must accept this." And since foreign nationals often feel that their experience is being ignored, they find it difficult to give wholehearted support to the demands of headquarters.

Unfortunately, the world is full of policy errors made by United States headquarters, and unfortunately also, the men in overseas plants generally do lack the global picture (and, occasionally, seasoned judgment). Hence, it is foolish to let this "either-or" tussle go on.

The tug-of-war over policy should cease, not just because of the poor human relations involved, but because people in both locations have a great deal to contribute. The position holding that "New York decides policy" results in poorer decisions. Instead, local plant managers and managing directors should be held responsible for initiating and recommending policy decisions and planning ahead, and for results obtained. The local managers' recommendations on policy should ordinarily be accepted if they are judged adequate for the job. They must be supplied with the facts of the situations at other plants in order to broaden their views. And a central management staff at the home office should coordinate the multiplant system without dominating it.

Mix of Know-How

The successful exporting of corporate know-how is a problem of balance. The appropriate exporting of a process, a product, a management system or control, all depend on the requirements and demands of the four interlocking systems described in Exhibit 15.2

A company may find parts of the wage system it uses in Peoria worse than useless in France, yet valuable and highly motivating in South Africa. The willingness and fortitude to think precisely about each new situation is mandatory if (a) the best of the company's experience is to be effectively combined with local practices, and (b) the given facts of each local plant are to be taken into account.

Also, the function of the corporate staff should be considered in the light of each situation. Managers can begin to get better yardage out of staff groups if they will challenge conventional platitudes such as "local problems should be left to local people."

Procurement, work force management, production, and maintenance are usually considered local problems not worthy of corporate concern. This carryover of conventional branch-plant management practices is based on a shaky premise—adequate lower-level and middle management is available locally. In the final analysis, the operating decisions and actions in these "local" areas are carried out by middle management, and sufficient numbers of capable people in these levels are apt to be scarce for many years.

By contrast, middle-management know-how and skills in the United States, for example, are especially well developed. We have learned a great deal about factory supervision, procurement, and production control—to mention only three areas. These skills and techniques could be and should be adapted to overseas local problems.

Some companies do have effective headquarters staff people dealing with their equipment or process decisions. But these companies usually do not provide equal staff help for functions that are frequently more important— labor relations, production and quality control, work force management, and procurement. As a result, in many parts of the world unfortunate precedents in labor relations are being set with no benefit of the trial-by-fire experience gained in the parent company. "But labor relations is a local problem" is the protest. This is so; but with a less timid approach and with competence in understanding local culture, labor relations specialists can adapt corporate know-how and furnish mature guidance.

Headquarters executives are needed who so thoroughly know their fields that they can adapt and teach tactfully and flexibly in a foreign environment. Today there are not enough executives with these skills. But when the home office staff is seen as a group whose mission is to teach, innovate, and collaborate rather than export company know-how indiscriminately, such people will be developed to fill the recognized need.

TWOFOLD ADVICE

Successful management of overseas production operations calls for adaptive thinking. For example, the degree of control that appears proper for one product and one management in one country is not likely to hold for a second plant or another product in a different country. This will perhaps seem so obvious as to be gratuitous. It needs saying, nevertheless, because there is a natural tendency for key executives in each corporation to settle for their own stock answers to given questions and problems of international production management. Different companies handle these issues quite differently; yet each tends to be unaware of the validity or even the possibility of other approaches.

What advice can be distilled from this research? The following suggestions are intended above all to question the reliance on certain stereotyped convictions repeatedly encountered. The ideas offered here come in two forms—one negative, the other positive.

Tencencies to Avoid

Do not send managers abroad who are just "available." This mistake stems from a failure to appreciate fully the first basic issue cited—adjusting to unfamiliar environments. As seen in Exhibit 15.2, the job of the overseas production manager involves more organizing and broader skills than might at first appear. Managerial strength, as defined by headquarters, must be tempered by a capacity for growing in cultural, political, and economic sophistication in order to handle adquately the complexity of the four interaction systems. Those who are technically strong, but poor organizers, frequently fail under the additional demands of the international environment.

Avoid concluding that "since labor is cheap and the most critical problems are environmental, therefore efficiency and productivity are not essential for us." If this point of view is adopted at headquarters, as it so frequently is, labor relations, production control, and procurement may be viewed as inconsequential problem areas to be left to inexperienced local people. One typical result: unfortunate precedents are established in arrangements with workers, and mediocre pace and output are accepted as normal. During the time that the market is unsaturated and profits are good by corporate standards, this may be of minor concern. But when tomorrow brings the tightened conditions of competition and labor (as declining profit rates now suggest is already occurring), such companies and their management cadres trained under relaxed conditions must start somehow to reverse some of the precedents set by loose management control.

Do not believe that in international manufacturing operations you cannot plan ahead. "How can we plan ahead when the economic and political situations in each country are so unpredictable?" the refrain goes; "the only sure thing is that any plans we'd make would have to be scrapped. We try to keep loose and play it by ear!" This attitude arises from a lack of clarity in distinguishing between a domestic branch-plant complex and an international organization—an organizational problem expressed under the third basic issue above. With this assumption, manufacturing planning does not get done. Many companies are not prepared to deal with the problems of organizing for operations in unpredictable environments—foreign exchange fluctuations and shortages, inflation, money supply shortages, cut-price competition, politically fomented labor unrest. Overseas planning must be directed toward what to do and how to do it if such and such happens. Planning for facilities, organization, and operations is made more, not less, essential by the uncertainties of international operations.

Promising Approaches

There are some positive actions that can improve the operations of many international companies:

Managers must recognize that the different stages of growth of a plant in another country require different contributions from headquarters and from its managers abroad. Typically, the talents required change over time. At the start, the roll-up-the-sleeves, practical, adaptive executive is needed; later, the staff specialist is required.

Contrary to generally held expectations, the start-up phase of the plant is often easier to handle than later stages. This is because selection and training of the work force are apt to be less difficult than is commonly assumes; there is often an initial period when each worker and supervisor is eager to please and most hopeful of commensurate rewards; there is likely to be a honeymoon period with the government, the community, and sometimes even with suppliers.

Managers should accept the idea that there are nearly always some elements of a company's managerial competence that can be exported. Expatriates can contribute to foreign operations if they can handle cultural barriers and human relationship problems sensitively, and if they are properly educated and coached. Increased sophistication in matters of culture, economics, and politics is essential for competence in international management. Broadened understanding in these disciplines heightens a manager's interest in another country and its people. Thus, once begun, such efforts tend to be self-sustaining.

Managers must realize that management assistance for foreign subsidiaries of international organizations must be tailored to local conditions. Many overseas plants are especially short of middle managers who are competent in the how-to-do-it skills of production scheduling and control, personnel management, procurement, and quality control. In these cases the headquarters must supply skilled trainers to teach the essentials of production management and to help avoid poor precedents, low productivity, and higher costs which become more serious over time. Other plants may need top-management assistance to do better planning, revaluate basic policy, or improve overall organization. A few plants may be best left alone.

Though a central manufacturing staff group poses so many problems that it is frequently rejected, *a core of internationally trained experts whose services can be requested as needed can be vital to the development of foreign nationals and the overseas plants.* The problems connected with a central manufacturing staff (expense, work load, career problems, and the usual stresses in line-staff relationships) can be minimized by the use of some expatriates from other countries and by making the staff more of a service function, available on request, and less of an arm of central management.

Management of international production is growing in importance, as heightened competition in the developed areas and new opportunities in the emerging economies force top-management attention to this area. Situational thinking, with fewer extreme positions on the difficult issues, framed against a broader context of understanding, can help to ease the sense of struggle at home and abroad and improve the return on investment in manufacturing subsidiaries throughout the world.

CHAPTER 16

Manufacturing
Abroad

There is nothing new about managing geographically decentralized organizations across international boundaries. Roman emperors, worldwide religious orders, colonial systems, and the British Admiralty faced these problems hundreds of years ago. In commerce, the East India, Hudson Bay Trading, and the Balfour-Guthrie Companies operated profitably long before the post-World War II flood of investments abroad. These enterprises faced the same task as modern international corporations: achieving effective operating controls and policy direction from remote headquarters.

Companies manufacturing abroad must deal not only with the problems inherent in domestic manufacturing, but with additional issues arising from the facts of international existence. International manufacturing management differs from the strictly domestic because three sets of problems are encountered when a corporation with headquarters in one nation owns and operates a production facility in another nation. These are:

1. Problems that arise from operating in an environment differing from that of the corporation's home base
2. Problems that stem from delegating management functions to foreign nationals
3. Problems that result because the ownership and headquarters are in a different country from the plant

The purpose of this chapter is to delineate these management problems and to explain their significance. Suggestions for dealing with these challenges in a variety of international settings are addressed to managers located at the overseas plants as well as to those at the corporate headquarters.

ENVIRONMENTAL PROBLEMS

It goes without saying that a company manufacturing abroad operates in a different environment than it does at home. It is not so immediately evident, however, to what extent the foreign environment actually affects plant operations or requires managers to modify domestic production management practices. The effects of the environment are often subtle and far-reaching.

A manufacturing plant may be viewed as a system. The system is composed of *workers* and *equipment* carrying out a *process* of transforming *materials* into a marketable *product*. The ingredients of the system are guided and coordinated by a set of *policies and rules* designed to optimize productivity and profit. When one part of the system changes, therefore, adjustments may be necessary in other parts of the system to keep it in balance.

The environment in which the production system operates affects costs, availability of materials and equipment, skills and attitudes of workers and managers, acceptable quality, and price of product, to mention several broad categories. Therefore, a production system must be designed for its environment.

A specific example of how the foreign environment may invalidate a transferred production system is furnished by the manufacturer of an electrical-mechanical product in the Middle East.

Equipment and tooling had been largely imported from Europe. After six months of barely profitable operations, cost analyses indicated that the two primary factors in the company's poor showing were the high cost of local financing and inventory losses. The equipment and tooling were designed for relatively long runs, which resulted in high average inventories of parts. Because local capital was scarce, interest rates were about 2% per month (approximately four times greater than the United States rates and three times greater than those of Europe), which made a carrying cost of 24% per year. In addition, poor material handling, storage, and record-keeping systems were causing an abnormally high loss and damage of parts in inventory. Hence, the total carrying cost of inventory was nearly three times that in Europe. And because the annual usage requirement was about one-fifth of that experienced in Europe, the net result was an economic order quantity of about one-fourth of that for which the process tooling and equipment were established.

Thus, a change in interest rates and skills in materials handling and inventory control—both of which are environmental factors—caused a domino effect throughout the production system. To reduce inventories and lower costs, shorter runs were necessary. Engine lathes, for example, would have been more appropriate than turret lathes, which required different skills and training on the part of workers, setup men, and supervisors. Quality was adversely affected by shorter runs; loads on equipment increased; and production scheduling became more crucial. The managers faced the necessity of making wholesale changes in the entire system to make it more profitable and competitive.

If environmental differences are understood in advance, many of them can be taken into account and the production system designed to be appropriate to the circumstances.

Of course, manufacturing abroad often involves adapting to environmental changes that even though identified in advance, are apt to seem volatile and difficult to predict. The starting point is a thorough analysis of the environment. For this purpose, a listing of major environmental factors and some of their primary and secondary effects may be useful. The effects of these environmental factors may be many and the particular effects shown in Exhibit 16.1 are merely examples.

The cultural system is more difficult for most administrators to delineate than the economic, political, or technological environment, because values, beliefs, and philosophic assumptions are intangible. They are nevertheless as real as more easily measured differences such as interest rates or foreign-exchange controls.

Guidelines for Environmental Adaptation

Analysis of the experiences of many companies suggests the following guidelines for achieving congruence of a firm's production system with a foreign environment:

1. Describe the environment in as precise and explicit terms as possible, using the outlines in Exhibit 16.1 as a checklist. The facts may be collected and assembled from a wide variety of sources: historical and anthropological literature about the country or area, discussions with personnel from other companies, marketing and staff personnel in the foreign country, government sources of both the home country and the foreign country, and legal representative overseas. These data should be assembled and analyzed, preferably under the direction of the manager who is or will be responsible for the overseas operation.

Exhibit 16.1 The effects of an Environment on a Production System

Environmental Factor	Some Primary Effects	Which In Turn May Affect
Economic		
Cost of		
Interest	Inventory, choice of equipment	Scheduling, labor skills, supervision
Materials and supplies	Procurement organization	Make-or-buy decisions
Labor	Equipment decisions	Training, wage system
Equipment	Technological strategy	Capital versus labor intensity, number of shifts, tooling
Taxes	Net profit	Return on investment
Utilities	Plant location	Choice of process
Local availability of		
Foreign exchange	Ability to import	Make or buy, scheduling
Capital	Ability to borrow	Inventory policy
Workers	Selection, training	Labor relations
Subcontractors	Investment requirements	Technical skills required
Materials and supplies	Plant location	Equipment, maintenance
Technological level		
Skills and knowledge of labor	Equipment and process	Training, supervision, maintenance organization
Supervision	Worker productivity	Labor relations
Engineers	Technical independence of overseas plant	Costs, quality, reliability of process
Middle management	Numbers and skills of expatriates needed	Needs for headquarters-staff services
Communications services	Customer, distributor, and vendor relations	Plant location, local offices
Vendors' skills	Quality, delivery	Amount and type of vendor assistance needed
Utilities	Reliability of service	Standby equipment
Transportation	Warehousing, inventory requirements	Planning, forecasting
Equipment, spare-parts availability	Plant downtime	
Marketing situation		
Purchasing power	Size of market	Planning, inventory
Competitive prices	Operating margins	Scale of plant
Distribution channels	Delivery requirements, customer-service requirements	Cost-control system Scheduling, inventory controls
Political		
Laws pertaining to foreign investment	Taxes, incentives, risk	Start-up process
Government attitudes toward foreign industry	Government cooperation with company	Middle-management organization
Permits, licenses, paperwork	Need for people trained to handle government liaison	Lead times, schedules

Exhibit 16.1 (Continued)

Environmental Factor	Some Primary Effects	Which In Turn May Affect
Government regulation of		
Manufactured content	Equipment needs	Costs and capital (required)
Prices	Operating margins	Manufacturing strategy
Working conditions and		
fringe benefits	Labor costs	Equipment strategy
Foreign exchange	Make or import	Increased local flexibility
Quality	Reduced freedom to change product specifications	Quality controls
Government involvement in company relationships	Labor relations	Increased concern with precedent
Employment of foreign nationals. . . .	Management development	Headquarters assistance
Process and equipment	Use of secondhand or local equipment	Maintenance
Plant location	Labor supply, transportation	Choice of process
Expansion	Expansion timing may not be ideal	Excess capacity or limited capacity
Profit repatriation	Financial policy	Modify objectives of local plant
Competition	Umbrella over prices	Dependence on government
Distribution	Channels established by government	Finished-goods stocks
Suppliers	Government monopolies	Quality and delivery from vendors
Political strength of economic interest groups, unions, farmers, business	Political climate re. taxes, regulation, unions, importing	Procurement, labor relations
Social		
Educational levels	Selection	Training
Urban/agricultural populations	Continuity of employment	Dollars invested in training
Population mobility	Plant location	Housing needs
Attitudes toward business	Quality of managers available	Headquarters assistance
Union strength	Supervisory techniques	Grievance procedures
Position of minorities	Interpersonal relations	Hiring practices
Democratic institutions	Worker attitudes	Supervisory practices

2. Contrast the environmental conditions with conditions at another location where a company production plant is operating. The latter plant should be one whose operation is both familiar and generally considered to be successful. Identify differences, using specific data and examples to highlight the differences.

3. Identify those foreign conditions that are essentially static or persisting and those that are in the process of or likely to be subject to change.

4. Identify and describe the company's technological requirements and basic policy constraints that must be considered as "givens," not subject to significant latitude or management choice. These facts can be considered as a company environment that it takes wherever it goes. They include minimum specifications on materials and products, identification of segments of the process that cannot be subcontracted or require critical company control and know-how, proprietary information, and key policies relating to products, ownership, quality, and finance which the company considers inviolable.

5. Design the production system. This is, of course, the most difficult step, because it requires synthesizing a practical and concrete plan from a combination of dozens of facts and variables. A critical question is where to start and in what order to consider the different parts of the plan. The decision sequence should lead from markets and strategy to product to process, thus making the most basic and critical decisions first. The production system can then be built around the process. When the process is determined, the equipment, organization, work force, procurement, control and planning systems, and the like can all be designed around that process. The key environmental forces—marketing, economic, political, and social—affect all the production system decisions; hence, each decision must be checked out not only for internal congruence with the rest of the system but for external congruence with each environmental factor.

A conceptual scheme for this analysis is shown in Exhibit 16.2. The approach shown may be followed in the original design of a production system or in the reappraisal of an overseas manufacturing operation. Eight sets of decisions are shown, taken in order from top to bottom. In general, the arrows indicate a logical flow of thought and decisions—those on the same line can be worked out as a set, in parallel, and decisions on a lower line should typically follow all those on higher lines.

The simplicity of this format is not intended to suggest that the process itself is simple or that there are short cuts that can guarantee good results. Instead, the diagram's purpose is to indicate an orderly approach to a problem of considerable complexity.

Typical Problems Encountered

This discussion of the impact of foreign environments on manufacturing concludes with a short description of some typical problems encountered in several key management areas of international production operations, together with some lessons from experience.

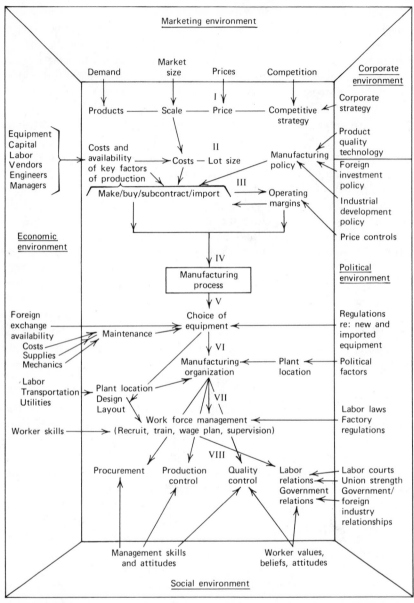

Exhibit 16.2   Sequences and Environmental Influences in Production System Design for an International Manufacturing Plant (used by permission from the Division of Research, Harvard Business School)

Equipment and Process Decisions

The most common mistake in choosing equipment and processes is to copy them from another plant, typically a domestic plant. In so doing, the company ignores a different cost mix, and often a different product specification, lot size, maintenance capability, scale of production, and labor and supervisory training demands as well.

Such mistakes often come about because of one or more of three contributing causes:

1. Original equipment decisions are usually made at headquarters by engineers who are not always familiar enough with the environment abroad to specify appropriate facilities.
2. Production managers consider equipment decisions "technical" and delegate them to engineers without realizing that equipment and process decisions largely determine the makeup of the entire production system and thereby involve far more than technical aspects. Designing from a distance, engineers sometimes tend to "play it safe," overspecify, and apply the same equipment they have used elsewhere instead of flexibly adapting the process to the new environment.
3. Overseas manufacturing plants are frequently understaffed in industrial engineering talent. Reequipment and process improvement are apt to be done "by the book" instead of tailored to fit the environment.

For example, at a plant in eastern Europe a superintendent ordered a new piece of equipment he felt would mean savings. It was approved by the headquarters because it had been used in other locations. When asked how long it would take to pay for itself, the superintendent said, "Oh, I'm sure that it will pay for itself very soon." On-the-scene analysis indicated that the machine could not possibly pay for itself in less than eight years.

Inadequate industrial engineering is most frequent where labor rates are low. But capable industrial engineering is needed even where labor is cheap to increase productivity from relatively expensive equipment and to develop economic processes which are appropriate to the requirements of the plant's total environment.

Manufacturing Organization

In different environments, different parts of the organization become more or less critical. Organizational structure can place emphasis where it is needed; assigning a key function as a full-time activity of one manager who reports to the top executive gives it attention and raises its status. But it is expensive to give each function its own executive, and similarly, every function cannot report to the top. Hence organizations must be designed to fit the situation.

One environment may place a premium on effective management of the maintenance function. For example, if spare parts are limited in supply, skilled mechanics are rare, and the economics or technology requires the use of closely linked equipment, when one machine fails a large part of the plant has to shut down. Tire plants in India, for example, are dependent on capable maintenance management.

Frequently, organizations are not adapted to environments abroad but are transplanted as they are from one country to another. Many companies tend to use the same basic organization worldwide. Other companies let the head man at each location set up his own organization, but often this does not result in an organization that fits the environment, for the executive organizes the plant in accordance with his own previous experience and biases.

Work Force Management

Many companies have found that the initial recruiting, selecting, training, compensating, and supervising of workers in a foreign country are simpler than expected. Surprisingly, the problems often seem to magnify after the first several years, particularly in the process of improving productivity and quality levels through training and first-line supervision.

It has been proved repeatedly in many types of manufacturing, from Brazil to France to India, that workers can be taught how to operate highly complex machinery with adequate proficiency in three to six months. But adjustment to the discipline, time demands, and necessity for cooperation essential to daily industrial life has frequently proved more difficult and time consuming than learning manual skills.

Appraising worker morale and productivity through the filter of a strange culture via indigenous supervisors is a further challenge. It is difficult for managers abroad to know what is going on.

Yet productivity must increase to meet growing competition and narrowing operating margins. This requires developing more advanced skills in the work force and more effective supervisors. The harried expatriate and his inexperienced middle management often need trained assistance from headquarters.

Overseas managers generally receive little help from the home office in handling this type of problem. Headquarters can hamper the process by exerting too much control over specific personnel policies and practices, while simultaneously offering inadequate transfer of knowledge and experience from one location to another.

Labor Relations

A well-developed sense of perspective is a prime requisite for effective labor relations abroad because company-worker relationships appear to grow and evolve through stages which are difficult to recognize at the time they occur, although clearly discernible in retrospect. The stages are influenced by a wide variety of factors:

1. Cultural attitudes and beliefs of workers and managers.
2. The political environment for labor unions.
3. Structure of labor and industrial laws affecting workers, wages, bargaining, grievances, health, and safety.
4. Precedents established in country, area, and factory.
5. Company policies and practices in work force management, especially wages, grievance handling, supervision, and training.

My study of many plants in eight countries suggests that an overseas plant's labor relations tend to pass through five stages over a period of time:

Stage	General Characteristics
1. Family style	Company strong and organized relative to workers. A paternal management deals with employees as individuals.
2. Skirmishing	Protests from workers. Grievances, union organizing, immature worker organization.
3. Open battle	Both sides take ideological positions. Strikes, sabotage, use of power by company and workers.
4. Postwar	Acceptance of workers' and management's rights. Relationships structured with clear procedures and precedents.
5. Industrial peace	Recognition of mutual interests. Strong, mature leadership.

The length and intensity of each stage depend on the factors listed above, and in particular on the company's labor practices. In some plants, for example, it has been possible to bypass the open-battle period.

Managers in stage 1 often do not realize that as workers become accustomed to factory life some form of industrial protest[1] is almost inevitable, and they fail to prepare for it. They see labor relations as a "snap," with labor docile and unions weak. They are disappointed and antagonistic when workers later become "ungrateful" and "union-minded."

---

[1] See Clark Kerr, John T. Dunlop, Frederick H. Harbison, and Charles A. Myers, *Industrialism and Industrial Man* (Cambridge: Harvard University Press, 1960).

In periods of skirmishing or strife, managers with a sense of perspective can recognize that more peaceful relationships can be developed as labor organizations mature and both company and workers accept each other's "rights" as natural and normal, and as adequate and satisfying procedures are worked out for handling grievances and negotiations.

Controls of Production

Many companies assume that in countries where the scale of operation is often small and the costs of labor are relatively low, the careful control of costs, quality, and inventories is "frosting" and largely unnecessary. Frequently, therefore, controls of production are loose and excessively informal by corporate standards.

In reality, overseas environments actually require exceptional competence in the control of production. Newly trained workers who lack a sense of product quality and mechanical intuition may make quality control especially difficult. Limited capacity of relatively expensive equipment, price controls, the necessity of using local materials, and increasing competition often add up to a requirement for better cost controls. High interest rates, long lead times, limited local capital, and lack of adequate quantitative orientation on the part of inventory clerks and production-control supervisors require close attention to inventory control in many overseas locations.

Production controls, by their very nature, must be largely delegated to lower and middle management, whose skill in handling a myriad of details largely determines the effectiveness of the system. Further, a surprisingly high degree of sophistication is required to develop special systems for economic conditions differing from those of the home country. Transplanting domestic systems will usually not suffice. For this reason, headquarters and overseas staff assistance is especially needed to develop systems, approaches, and lower- and middle-management skills. Here is another area where a "local problem" cannot be delegated solely to local people.

Procurement

Procurement problems are commonplace and often highly troublesome abroad. Even in Europe, vendors frequently fail to satisfy the needs of foreign manufacturing plants. The problems generally center around reliability of delivery promises and quality standards.

Sometimes the problems are culturally derived. The vendor's notions of adequate quality and the importance of time differ from those of his customer. Or the problem may be one of adapting to specifications which are unfamiliar. Frequently, there is inadequate competition, and the vendors simply do not have sufficient incentive.

Procurement, for these reasons, is often a management area that calls for more attention and expertise than is necessary in a domestic operation. Development of vendors may take years of special attention by an experienced and expert team. This is expensive, but nationalistic laws very often require local purchasing. Top management must recognize that procurement problems have been one of the most frequent causes of major failures and problems in overseas manufacturing.

DELEGATING MANAGEMENT FUNCTIONS

Inherent in manufacturing abroad is the necessity of entrusting much of the management of the plant to foreign nationals. Daily decisions in production scheduling and control, procurement, and supervision of the work force must be made by foreign nationals regardless of their experience and capabilities. In domestic branch plants, new lower and middle managers can be supported and closely supervised by an ample number of more experienced people from the parent corporation. Abroad, because of cost, distance, and nationalistic pressures, it is usually not possible to cover the plant with enough headquarters expatriates for sufficient years to train a competent local team.

The central problem is inexperience—inexperience in manufacturing in general, in the particular industry, and with the specific company. No one nationality has a monopoly on effective management of manufacturing plants any more than only one nationality can efficiently run a turret lathe or assemble electronics components. But there are ingredients in the experience of a competent manufacturing manager that take time to acquire and assimilate.

Some of these ingredients are present when a trained and experienced manager goes to work for a different company, but even he or she requires time to learn the particular customs, policies, and ways of the new firm. If the new company is a foreign-based firm, the amount to learn is generally much greater.

Simarlarly, the requirements for new learning are enlarged if the manager's experience has been in another industry, and further expanded if he must adapt to industry from a prior post in government, military, or other nonfactory occupation. If the candidates are from a non-Western culture, the requirements are greatest of all, because certain elements of Western culture—particularly its emphasis on time and personal responsibility—are usually assumed in the management of an international firm.

Pictorially the adaption requirements are shown in Exhibit 16.3 with each adaptation building on those below it.

With all these adjustments to be made by local managers, it is no wonder that expatriate production managers are typically disappointed over the performance of their subordinates. Local managers are often criticized by headquarters and expatriates for one or more of the following attributes:

1. Being idealistic and impractical.
2. Magnifying their position, status, and responsibility out of proportion to reality.
3. Working too little.
4. Failing to follow through and take responsibility.
5. Carelessness about time.
6. Technical incompetence.
7. Showing poor judgment.
8. Paternalism in their personnel practices.

Many of these criticisms are imprecise labels open to various interpretations and meanings. Many represent the frustrated complaints of expatriates who have been unable to communicate satisfactorily with their subordinates or counterparts, do not understand their behavior, and therefore condemn their performance. Such criticisms are natural, but they are also unfortunate because although frequently justified, they accomplish little but building resentment and mutual dissatisfaction. Hence, it is not surprising to find foreign nationals equally critical of managers from the home country.

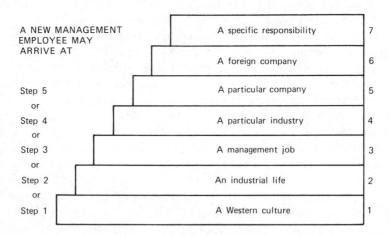

Exhibit 16.3   Seven Steps in a Manager's Adaptation of His or Her Job

Selection and Development

To move beyond mutual criticism, managers of foreign manufacturing need special skills and insights in selecting, managing, and developing their local managers. Specifically, the expatriate manager has four problems:

1. Determining how effective his local managers are going to be.
2. Minimizing production problems and failures during the learning period.
3. Maximizing the development rate of the local managers.
4. Dealing with his own frustrations and difficulties during the maturing period of his managers.

Neither the approach of "when in Rome, do as the Romans do"—adapting to foreign nationals, respecting their methods of managing, delegating fully—nor the approach of "this is an American company; they must learn to do things our way" is an effective way of dealing with these four problems. Instead, it is more practical to think about the problem in a different frame of reference.

Several ingredients appear essential in developing workable ways of handling these four problems. Basically, they all depend upon the manager improving his or her understanding of local managers. This is a complex task which calls upon many disciplines: anthropology, psychology, political science, economics, and organizational behavior. The critical ingredients are:

1. To recognize, identify, and isolate how particular foreign managers, as individuals, behave and work.
2. To determine which deviations from conventional or expected company, industry, and managerial behavior are actually important and which are merely surprising or annoying.
3. To develop specific ways of dealing with important shortcomings and differences on the part of local managers.

The first calls for some specific approaches to analyzing individuals' behavior. The managerial grid[2] is one good approach. A questionnaire[3] developed by Mason Haire and associates is another example of a useful tool. This analytical pattern examines managers' beliefs and values: (1)

[2] See Robert R. Blake and Jane S. Mouton, *The Managerial Grid,* (Houston: Gulf Publishing Company, 1964).
[3] Mason Haire, Edwin E. Ghiselli, and Lyman W. Porter, "Cultural Patterns in the Role of the Manager," *Industrial Relations* 2, No. 2 (February 1963).

leadership beliefs, (2) beliefs about the manager's role, (3) motivations and needs, and (4) the degree of satisfaction of these motivations or needs achieved by the managers. Finally, a study of managers in terms of Exhibit 15.1 (p. 256) can also lead to useful insights.

The common element in these approaches is that expatriates (or headquarters executives) attempt to understand their managers instead of criticizing. Group discussions and training sessions are used by some companies to help develop the skills of understanding in their managers.

Evaluating the effects of the differences in managers is the second ingredient. This, too, is difficult. But much is accomplished by the attitude of questioning and searching rather than condemning.

Culturally derived differences between expatriates and foreign national managers are not all bad; many expatriates tend to criticize foreign managers for any divergencies from their own conventional behavior. Differences in dress; in religion; and in beliefs about the future, optimism, democracy, and the uniqueness of each individual are relatively immaterial to managerial performance, although they may be annoying and disturbing. By and large, these differences are because of lack of Westernization (step 1 in Exhibit 16.3). For example, the fatalistic managers who do not believe that their own energy can bring about change may need close and persistent supervision, but properly led, they can become efficient at carrying out assigned tasks.

Differences due to lack of industrialization (step 2 in Exhibit 16.3) are more serious, yet somewhat more susceptible to change. Industrial life has imperatives of time, cooperation, self-discipline, and consistent application of effort and attention to details that are not demanded by nonindustrial occupations—farm, government, education, or military. These imperatives are built into the very nature of manufacturing. A manager new to industrial life in any country has much to learn and many old habits and outlooks to change.

A third important area of analysis is the amount of pertinent industrial management experience a manager has had (steps 3 and 4 in Exhibit 16.3. Experience in a copper mill may be scarcely applicable to a job in a food processing plant. But new skills and knowledge may be transferred in due course with application and training.

In summary, the "foreign" differences that matter are more apt to be inadequate industrial experience and disciplines and less apt to be lack of Westernization, even though the latter characteristics may be more difficult to change and more readily apparent. To help managers develop, superiors must carefully attempt to identify their deviations from truly important habits, attitudes, and beliefs. This approach is more likely to net results than labeling them "impractical" or "irresponsible."

Coaching Relationships

The final ingredient necessary for dealing better with local managers is the development of coaching relationships to replace superior-subordinate relationships. It is becoming a cliché to state that the expatriate must be a teacher and a coach, but the practice of listening (as a good teacher would) is an administrative technique that is useful not only for developing managers but for communicating acceptable and accepting attitudes to them.

The process of coaching and teaching involves the expatriate in many details, and it provides information that can help him or her prevent mistakes while training a local manager. It is not a "let him sink or swim" process, but one in which the expatriate becomes involved in all aspects of the job, observing, listening, and explaining.

It should be clear now that members of the headquarters staff can and should be very useful in the early years of any new foreign plant. Their role, too, must be in coaching and training, becoming involved in all manner of local operating problems and details. This violates the rule that a staff manager should stay out of details, a rule that is often invalid overseas where a plant has managers who simultaneously have many steps to climb in their adaptation process.

OWNERS AND PLANT IN DIFFERENT COUNTRIES

The third source of problems arises from foreign ownership. The international corporation has objectives and policies that make up its total strategy for growth and competition. The local plant must fit into this strategy and conduct its operations in a way that will benefit the corporation as a whole. But the local plant must also shape its policies and practices to be congruent with the needs of the nation in which it is located. This is a fact that is frequently repugnant to corporate managers who resent government interference, but it is a fact that cannot be avoided. For example, the nation may insist that the plant manufacture 90% or more of the plant's needs, whereas the international corporation may wish to consolidate the sourcing of certain items in one location to gain economies of scale. International manufacturing requires the constant reconciliation of these points of view.

Geographical decentralization across international boundaries also introduces problems of organization, control, and communication between headquarters and branch plants. Policy and corporate know-how must be transferred across political and cultural interfaces so that the corporation and its plants benefit from each other, cooperate and prosper.

Overseas manufacturing problems center around who determines manufacturing policy, how control is obtained, and the headquarters services needed abroad.

Circumstances that are peculiar to the locality, nation, or culture must be taken into consideration at the corporate policy level. Hence manufacturing policy questions (such as whether the plant should expand, diversify, make a larger fraction of its total product, and the like) can rarely be answered unilaterally by the corporate headquarters. For example:

An American corporation turned down a capital appropriation requested by its subsidiary in India for a major diversification because the forecasted return on investment was less favorable than alternative uses of the corporation's funds. The company's Indian management argued that once India's capacity for the commodity was adequate, the government would not permit other companies to invest in competitive facilities. Nevertheless, the headquarters rejected the appropriation, a competitor built the plant, and the company was blocked for many years from a major diversification that would have improved its competitive position.

Two kinds of problems arise because the owners and plant are in different countries. The first has to do with the compatibility between the international corporation and the host government and conditions in the foreign country. The second deals with problems of administration at a distance across international barriers.

Relations with Foreign Governments

Problems often erupt because the plant's policies and operations may not serve the international corporation and the foreign nation equally well. For example, the foreign government may require the use of local materials which are expensive or off-grade and which increase costs to the point where the firm cannot compete in the nearby export market.

Something must give in these conflicts. Sometimes governments can be persuaded, but more often, the international corporation must adapt. A number of United States firms have pulled out of countries rather than accede to apparently unreasonable government demands. This has usually proved to be shortsighted. In the long run, the country's markets remain and grow, and the government is forced to moderate unwise economic policies.

Analysis of corporate experience abroad suggests two critical conditions which should be met before a company decides to invest in a manufacturing plant abroad:

1. The company's needs and plans for the plant should be congruent with the long-range requirements of the host nation.
2. The company's anticipated investment and returns should be realistic in terms of the competitive conditions existing or forthcoming in the industry in the host country.

The first condition involves these manufacturing considerations:

(a) Products and markets served.
(b) Plant location.
(c) Equipment and processes.
(d) Make versus buy; local versus import.
(e) Labor relations—personnel policies.
(f) Use of expatriates.
(g) Local financing of work in process.

The second condition is concerned with the corporation's assessment of the competitive situation in the local industry. In particular, the company should carefully examine the operating margins available and projected— that is, the difference between prices and costs of materials, labor, and manufacturing equipment. This spread must be adequate to cover marketing and administrative costs and profit. Its breadth is a good clue to the possibility of successful competition. It will reveal the emphasis necessary on each *part* of the production system if it is to be viable.

In seeking compatibility between corporate strategy and local conditions, it has proved valuable to recognize as realities foreign government objectives and competitive conditions that are difficult to change. Usually, the international corporation must do the adapting.

Administering the International Manufacturing Corporation

In manufacturing the broad problem of international administration boils down to three key issues:

1. The nature of home office control.
2. The nature of home office support.
3. The nature and type of the communications between the home office and overseas plants.

Although the issue of home office control is usually debated in terms of "centralization" versus "decentralization," this dichotomy is rarely mean-

Exhibit 16.4   Selecting the appropriate degrees of headquarters' involvement and command

Degrees of involvement	Degree of command				
	A. Observe and advise if requested. Approve capital budgets.	B. Observe and offer unilateral advice. Approve capital budgets	C. Command per B plus approve annual budgets on capital and operating expenditures.	D. Command per C plus require policy plans and decisions to be submitted for advance approval.	E. Command per C plus require approval of any deviations from budget and any changes in operations or procedures.
I. No headquarters involvement. Reporting is only on broad overall basis and infrequent.					
II. Involvement in general policy, objectives, strategy, long-term planning. Receives frequent information on overall results.					

III. Involvement per II plus more detailed reports on results. Participate in short-range planning. Participation in general approaches for achieving aims, i.e., organization, general systems.		
IV. Involvement per III plus participates in procedures, specific approaches, and local controls. Reports more detailed and frequent.		
V. Involvement per IV plus regular deep involvement in specific operating decisions, schedules, manpower, expenses. Constant information required.		

ingful in conducting international manufacturing operations. Situations differ in terms of key variables in manufacturing, the nature of the environment, and the developed abilities of local executives. Appropriate controls and influence from headquarters are entirely different from one plant to another. It is a mistake, therefore, to attempt "a philosphy" or take a position on how much or what type of controls "our company" should exert. But unfortunately, many companies do attempt to apply one universal approach to this facet of international management.

In contrast, it appears more sensible to examine each situation in terms of critical variables: the competitive situation, the aspects of manufacturing most vital to success (procurement, work force productivity, equipment maintenance, etc.), and the strengths of the overseas management relative to the task. The inputs needed from headquarters are those necessary to fill the gap between tasks required and skills available abroad.

In tailoring headquarters administration to the needs at each foreign plant, it is necessary to establish where and how decisions should be made, ranging from broad policy and planning to specific operating decisions. The "where" and "how" affect the amount of headquarters control. But the concept of "headquarters control" is too vague to be very useful. More precise terms are needed.

In fact "headquarters control" can be divided into two key facets: *involvement* and *command*. A headquarters can be highly involved but exert only minimum command over a foreign plant if it keeps in close contact with progress and problems abroad and if its charter allows it to offer advice which the local plant is free to accept or reject. No one combination of involvement and command is "right" for all situations. Exhibit 16.4 describes and graphically represents the range of possible combinations of involvement and command. This matrix is not intended to be definitive but to demonstrate the possibility of different headquarters-plant relationships in each functional area of manufacturing. A company should explicitly decide what combination is best for each functional manufacturing area— manufacturing policy, procurement, work force management, equipment and process, labor relations, and controls of production. These decisions should be reviewed annually to ensure that the chosen point in the matrix for each area (and the entire set of administrative practices that follows from each matrix point) is in keeping with the action situation.

CONCLUSION

The quality of the job performed by the headquarters staff is a critical ingredient to success in manufacturing abroad. In many cases, it is the single most vital requisite to improved production performance overseas.

This conclusion grows out of analysis of the experiences of international firms in handling the three principal sets of problems discussed in this chapter. The environmentally derived problems are moderated by tailoring the production system in its original design and subsequent adjustments to the total environment. This is a demanding task calling for situational thinking and many skills. Managers assigned to overseas plants can play a major role in this task, but they need the specialized support and unbiased analytical outlook of a trained headquarters staff.

In each functional area discussed (procurement, work-force management, etc.) the overseas plants typically need more headquarters assistance. Leaving "local problems to local personnel" has often been a mistake, for foreign managers generally can benefit from accumulated know-how relating to operating problems and systems. The expatriate manager is seldom able to transmit this experience in more than one or two areas.

For the same reason, problems arising from the necessity of delegating management functions to inexperienced foreign nationals can be mitigated by the use of a headquarters staff to assist the overseas management in the massive coaching and training job often needed.

Problems in administering the international manufacturing firm center around achieving compatibility between corporation and foreign nation while competing successfully. Developing the overseas company's plans and competive strategy so that they are congruent with the needs of the firm as a whole and its host country requires a breadth of viewpoint that a home office staff can develop by repeated experience throughout the world.

The control issue is clarified by separating control into two ingredients— involvement and command. The thrust of this discussion is that headquarters should emphasize more involvement and less command. In fact, a headquarters actually controls overseas plant managers very little. Attempts at control are normally resented and confuse the assignment of responsibility. Thus less command is more realistic and appropriate when accompanied by more responsible involvement.

The complexity of managing foreign operations demands broad training, insights, and experience. Managers must be particularly competent and mature to be effective either as expatriates or in headquarters manufacturing positions. To succeed in international business, a company must be willing to assign a full share of its best talent to manage its manufacturing.

CHAPTER 17

Technology Abroad

In the manufacture of most products the producer has a series of process choices to make. The costs and implications of each choice affect the equipment needed and the entire production system. Choices of equipment and processes are the result of a firm's technological strategy, its objectives, and policies relating to the use of technology. This chapter is concerned with technological strategy in the management of international manufacturing.

A production system centers on the process used for transforming materials into the finished products. A process may be carried out with one or more alternatives of equipment. The particular equipment selected places its set of demands on labor skills and attitudes, supervision, industrial engineering for tools and manufacturing techniques, materials and supplies, maintenance, production scheduling and inventory controls, quality control procedures, and so forth.

Each of these ingredients in a production system is affected by the environment. The economic environment affects costs and availability of labor, equipment, and materials. The cultural environment affects attitudes, values, and motivation of workers. The political environment is sensitive to nationalistic pressures, which may influence what the plant makes and how it makes it.

For these reasons a firm's technological strategy is both an independent and a dependent variable, independent in that it is the starting point for the whole production system and dependent because the production system itself is affected by the environment. To be effective and viable the demands and ingredients of a production system must be congruent with those of the environment. It follows therefore that a successful technological strategy should be derived in part from a realistic assessment of the total environment in which it is to operate.

Analysis of the technological strategy of the U.S. firms in this study indicates that in practice the choice of process and equipment is seldom influenced by a systematic study of alternatives and their congruence with the total environment. Processes and equipment are seldom developed or selected expressly for a particular set of circumstances in an overseas location. Instead, the technology is more often exported unchanged from the domestic operation.

This approach is not without its advantages. It requires less engineering time, and it is a low-risk strategy because it exports tested technological methods with which the company has had experience. But its disadvantages are that it is a gross or crude fitting of technology to circumstances and its fit may be random. It is safe but often expensive. The price is paid chiefly in cost and low productivity of the production system as a whole, including costs not only of direct labor and equipment but of inventories, overheads, and customer service. When operating margins are ample and competition is minor, it may be a good strategy. But as competition grows and margins narrow, technological strategy needs to be more precisely tailored to maximize the fit of the production system to the critical environment factors.

TECHNOLOGICAL STRATEGY—DOMESTIC AND INTERNATIONAL

In domestic production the choice of equipment and process is a highly developed area of management decision making. Manufacturing process alternatives grow out of product designs. Industrial and manufacturing engineers choose the most economic and feasible process and develop or select the equipment and plan the plant layout for the entire manufacturing sequence. The facility may be engineered as a system composed of various interlocking elements. The entire system and each of the elements are worked out considering possible choices of process and equipment so as to produce the product at the proper quality level at the lowest cost.

Various technical elements enter into the choice of equipment: the technology of materials, tools and processes, time and motion study, cost of the equipment and its operations, skill and safety requirements, setup time requirements, probabilities regarding maintenance and repairs. These technical aspects are combined with the management decisions pertaining to the appropriate meld of labor and supervisory skills and controls of production and quality, with judgment and analysis of uncertainties always taken into account. It becomes clear that this is a complex area of decision making. An extensive body of theory and practical knowledge has grown up around this area of plant management, for it is susceptible to tangible measurements and quantitative analysis.

In addition to technical elements in the choice of equipment and process there are also engineering economics ingredients dealing with costs. In developing an understanding of the economy as it is affected by businessmen's decisions, economists analyze the rationale of the typical choice of equipment or process. Labor-intensive and capital-intensive alternative processes are compared by the economist, using various criteria, before recommending the final process in terms of its impact on the business and, on a macroscale, the nation's economy. In the economist's model, the businessman calculates the amount of capital and the amount of labor required at different rates of production, and, depending on the cost of capital, the cost of labor, and other less tangible factors, makes a rational decision on the process to employ in the plant.

Unique Choice

Exporting a given process for use abroad requires careful reappraisal. The scale of production and the total market size are likely to be lower than (or at least different from) that of the domestic plant; the costs of money, capital, and labor are different both absolutely and in relative proportions; the skills of operating, supervising, and maintaining an operation are probably less developed; sometimes the product quality required may be different from that in the United States. Technical changes in the process may therefore be indicated, with subsequent changes in the surrounding production system.

Since a different mix of ingredients abroad might be expected to result in a unique choice of process and equipment, it seemed odd that most of the companies I have studied appeared to have invested less careful analysis and study in their choice of equipment and process overseas than at home. This was in spite of the fact that the same analytical approaches[1] to the problem which are used domestically could, essentially, be applied abroad. If this had been done, the decisions resulting would presumably have been different. For example, the relative advantages of labor-intensive versus capital-intensive processes as pointed out by many economists would have been apparent in developing economies with labor surpluses. Analyses of this kind were largely ignored by practitioners in the companies visited.

Overseas decisions pertaining to choices of equipment were typically simplified by international managements who allowed these decisions to be

---

[1] Engineering process analysis in combination with engineering economics and industrial engineering principles.

largely dictated by one or more of these factors: (1) what the product called for in a technical sense; (2) what the engineers making the process and equipment decisions were accustomed to using domestically; (3) what equipment could be most easily obtained. Limiting the factors in this way vastly reduced the number of alternatives considered. The relative simplicity of this method of making decisions is in sharp contrast to economic theory and conventional domestic practice.

CONTRIBUTIONS OF ECONOMIC THEORY

For years economists studying industrial development have devoted considerable time and publication space to the issue of capital-intensive versus labor-intensive processes. For example, in an article entitled "Capital Intensity in Industry in Underdeveloped Countries," the authors point out that the determination of the appropriate choice of production process is a key issue in any program of industrialization.[2] For individual plants it involves a choice between different manufacturing alternatives. At an overall national planning level it may involve choices between establishing different industries. The authors develop a case for labor-intensive policies in developing economies based on their bringing about (1) increased employment; (2) decreased capital requirements; (3) wider distribution of purchasing power; (4) lower skill requirements in maintenance, equipment operation, and management; (5) reduced setup and breakdown time due to use of less complex labor-intensive equipment.

Economists are often divided over which of the two directions is better for industry in a country to follow. In contrast to the U.N. Bulletin cited, some economists recommend capital-intensive policies for developing economies because they result in high efficiency and therefore a larger amount of production, higher national income, increased savings and investment, and hence a greater surplus for capital formation.

Such diversity of opinion sometimes produces pressure on managers in a developing economy toward one type of process or the other, depending on the school of economists in power. For instance, in India some of the new steel mills have the latest equipment and processes, partly because the national government wants "modern" steel plants and partly because capital-intensive theorists feel that this is the most efficient approach to steelmaking. They argue in effect, "Just because India has a labor surplus, they should not have an old-fashioned plant." But at province or town

[2] U.N. Bureau of Economic Affairs, "Capital Intensity in Industry in Underdeveloped Countries," Industrialization and Productivity Bulletin Number 1 (April 1958).

levels, pressure is often placed on companies to use processes that involve large numbers of people rather than a capital-intensive alternative.

Inflexibility in Management Thinking

Business researchers as well as managers are also frequently divided on this question and attempt to influence businessmen to their own school of thought. Richard D. Robinson, in his *International Business Policy*, recommends that the American businessman give much more attention to the possible imaginative development of labor-intensive equipment in plants in developing economies.[3]

My survey likewise demonstrated that there has been a singular inflexibility on the part of a substantial number of American companies in their *productive processes*. A member of the export division of an electrical appliance company observed that he had designed a plant for Chile which the company's engineering department had estimated at $190,000. He added, "I had it down to about $40,000." He then went on to explain that, of course, his experience in manufacturing was about 30 years behind him, but perhaps that was why he could think in terms other than the most modern manufacturing innovations.

A tractor company executive spelled out another difficulty: "We know how to make 10,000 tractors a year, but not 500. In Mexico we are doing things by hand that we'd never do here." In planning the Mexican assembly layout, the vice president had asked the company engineering group for a "low-cost assembly line." The engineers evolved a line costing $175,000—to build 16 tractors a day. The engineers planned on a paint room, a drying room, and other elaborate installations that were taken more or less for granted as part of any American assembly line. Besides other changes, the vice president ordered the use of a tent for a paint room and a hand sprayer. The result was that $50,000 investment in paint facilities was reduced to $750, and the overall cost for the assembly line from $175,000 to $29,000. The vice president added, "Our people simply can't think in these terms."

Analysts of manufacturing policy abroad draw on the thinking of anthropologists, economists, and engineers in recommending more flexible thinking on equipment decisions to take into account the economic needs of the country, the skills and attitudes of employees, and short- and long-run cost ingredients. Professor Jan Tinbergen points out that often both the industrial planning authorities and the engineering experts have seemed to be unaware that there is a choice of technology in planning for industrial

---

[3] Richard D. Robinson, *International Business Policy* (New York: Holt Rinehart and Winston, 1964), p. 180.

activities.[4] He states that undue emphasis is often given to purely technical aspects of equipment and manufacturing selection process and that consideration of national prestige has frequently led to unnecessarily ambitious facilities. A high degree of mechanization is often employed to avoid dealing with larger numbers of workers and their families, housing, and utilities needs.

Indiscriminate Selection of Techniques

In making the same point, the authors of "Capital intensity in Industry in Undeveloped Countries" suggest that managers and engineers are often so convinced of the superiority of familiar, mechanized techniques that they do not seek labor-intensive ones, although alternatives may be available.[5] They admit that there are certain industries for which Western blueprints can and should be used almost without change. For example, in chemical process industries, equipment choices are typically determined by technical requirements for certain reactions and processes which cannot be operated efficiently on a small scale. Units now operating in highly industrialized countries can be copied with relatively few changes, with the qualification, however, that highly trained engineers are generally required to erect and operate such plants.

But in most other types of industry the authors assert that equipment designs can often be adapted. It may be desirable to decrease the size of the equipment and demechanize it to make possible a reduction in both the capital expenditure and the length of the training required to obtain operators, maintenance men, and foremen. Many of the mechanical industries fall in this category as well as some of the chemical processes.

These authors feel that fresh thinking should be devoted to the specific requirements of industry in the underdeveloped countries. They point out that recommendations of engineers proceed largely from technical considerations and that there is evidence that in many cases there is a ready, almost indiscriminate, resort to mechanization.

R. F. Eckaus states that among equipment and process proposals by engineers

There are few, if any, which entail alternative factor (labor and capital) combinations. Government policies, however, seldom recommend or are explicit enough to

[4] Jan Tinbergen, "Choice of Technology and Industrial Planning," U.N. Department of Economic and Social Affairs, Industrialization and Productivity Bulletin Number 1 (April 1958).
[5] *Op. cit.*, p. 142.

guide technicians in the field and there are major gaps between government policies and industry practice. In many cases the choice may be nonexistent or at least severely limited, but there are a large number of industries where alternative factors and combinations are applicable in major processing operations. Much research is needed in order to determine the proper mix. It is necessary in order to reveal the possible technical combinations to achieve a much higher degree of disaggregation than is currently practiced or appears feasible.[6]

Much of the discussion of this subject by economists may seem irrelevant to individual managers because it refers to the choice of planners of a developing country as to whether to seek labor-intensive or capital-intensive industry. But the part of the discussion that deals with process alternatives at the theoretical level could be effective in influencing industry.

Importance of Theory

Theoretical economics are in fact more important to industrial managers than is usually realized. Company managers should pay attention to the policies and the thinking of economists and government officers concerned with national industrial development policy. It is wise for a company to give every possible assistance in the achievement of national objectives if their stay in a country is to be satisfactory. Several companies studied benefited both politically and in better technological strategy from a purposeful sensitivity to recommendations of top government planning people.

Instead of fighting against "hopelessly academic and unrealistic government planners," as some managers consider most foreign government economists, some companies have taken a more positive attitude by inviting them into their plants to explain the necessity for company decisions that had been made and to listen to their points of view. Experiences like these indicate that effective efforts can be made to win government officials to a company's point of view. Such communications may also help in making sounder government policy recommendations.

A second and probably more important reason for considering theorists' views of equipment decisions is that they offer a point of view that often has merit and should not be dismissed as merely "theoretical." Choices of equipment and process available in most industries are less limited than industrialists usually infer. Economists who suggest more company research and innovation in seeking alternative industrial processes tailored to fit each particular environment are realistic more often than not. Industrial nations

---

[6] R. F. Eckaus, "The Factor Proportion Problem in Under-developed Areas," *The American Economic Review* (September 1955).

export familiar processes and techniques (many of which require engineering and maintenance skills not available abroad), but the evidence indicates that they seldom export a most vital industrial tool—the attitude and frame of mind which constantly seeks improvement. Economists who criticize American industry for sending ill-adapted processes abroad have little difficulty in marshalling evidence to support their position.

Inadequacies in the Economics-Oriented Position

In fairness, now, to the international firm, we must also criticize some of the economists and theoreticians who complain that international companies envision only a fraction of the alternatives possible in establishing processes. Using the capital-intensive, labor-intensive dichotomy they cite that there is more than one way to make a radio, to assemble vehicles, to package food, or to compound pharmaceuticals. Companies are criticized for "playing it safe."

But economists who conceptualize the choices as labor-intensive versus capital-intensive tend to overlook or minimize some less measurable or quantifiable factors, which can be very important. There is a wide gap between the theory of tailoring a production process to the environment and the actual, detailed plant design. Someone must tailor the process, and it is a problem to get the right people in the right place. Equally important is the fact that for some products or processes alternative choices are not readily available. For any new process the startup and "debugging" problems are usually considerable, especially abroad. Special equipment may cause problems which are not readily solved by recourse to past experience. And judging from maintenance problems experienced abroad, maintenance of specially designed processes would often be a nightmare. Although the conservative practices of United States firms overseas may run counter to economists' theories, they take into account some practical realities which could prove critical if overlooked.

The notion of designing processes to fit the environment is sound in a conceptual sense, but it is in fact too gross a generalization to be very useful. The experience of United States firms overseas dramatizes the necessity of anticipating problems and reinforces the wisdom of using tested processes while suggesting fruitful approaches for moving (as economists suggest) toward better adapted choices of equipment and processes.

Equipment and Process Decisions

Companies tend to use basically the same processes and equipment abroad as currently or previously employed in the United States. Often the equipment abroad will be of a type used in the domestic plant two to 15 years before and now outmoded by its scale or the labor-saving features of new models. The primary reason for not innovating abroad appears to be that these decisions are usually made by technical people employed to use their knowledge and experience to recommend processes that work and will consistently produce proper quality. Companies are often under time pressure to meet tight schedules. They lack the time and pressures to develop new processes tailored to the specific economics and practical realities in each different industrial location.

The general tendency observed is toward too much mechanization rather than too little. The following factors help to explain this orientation:

1. The engineering orientation involved in equipment decisions.
2. The prestige factor, from both the company and the national standpoint.
3. The trend toward increasing mechanization in the United States.
4. The tendency toward copying processes known and proven in the United States.
5. The lack of time and impetus toward fresh study of the problem abroad. Often those responsible for equipping the new overseas plant have not been able to visit or observe conditions in the foreign location.
6. The argument, sometimes specious, that cheap labor is not really cheap, and that high quality and production are most easily assured by more mechanization rather than less.

By and large the decisions on equipment and process abroad appeared to be made on practical bases rather than on economic considerations of cost of labor and cost of capital. Noneconomic factors such as availability of equipment in different countries, the problems of repair, maintenance, quality, vendors, supervision, labor skills, setup, and production planning and cycle time factors received most of the emphasis. Companies interviewed on this question tended to explain their equipment decisions primarily on the basis of technological considerations, the need for achieving quality and keeping maintenance to a minimum, with relatively little consideration of the economics of a wide variety of alternatives and the industrial engineering aspects of different manufacturing approaches.

The technological ingredient tends to dominate United States equipment and process decisions, whereas the economic and industrial engineering elements are more often neglected. For instance, in machining a part on a turret lathe there is frequently considerable choice in the order of different steps, the tools to use, the frequency and methods of checking results. The skill level of the operator is also open to analysis and choice.

In these decisions on how to use the equipment and to carry out the process, more basic industrial engineering work is needed abroad. American industrial engineers have been carrying on such analysis for at least 60 years. The trade-offs between labor and capital, which are a large part of the question, are seldom looked at in detail abroad. There are additional and equally important problems of improving the balance of assembly lines and the related items of equipment in materials handling, scheduling, and quality effects.

Most American companies abroad have taken a practical and safe approach to these problems by delegating plant design to the home office engineers. As a result their process and equipment decisions have been worked out with less emphasis on maximizing total productivity and more on achieving adequate quality and continuous production. Instead of devoting time and attention to developing more economical approaches with an equal assurance of quality and continuous production, they tend to try to accomplish it with equipment alone.

Bounded by the major equipment decisions of home office engineers, overseas plant managements tend to delegate the important detail of designing specific operations and processes to foreign middle managers. But they, in turn, tend to delegate these "technical decisions" to the home office.

THE USE OF INDUSTRIAL ENGINEERING ABROAD

Why is the time-proven process of industrial engineering innovation not usually applied well abroad? The basic process of industrial engineering takes apart an industrial process, examines all of its ingredients (practical, human,[7] economic, technical), and works out a combination that will result in lower costs for achieving the necessary quality. This type of research and development has been a key to the achievement of productivity for which American industry is famous. Nevertheless, we tend to set up overseas facilities with relatively little emphasis on the achievement of productivity. Time and again new plants have been established abroad by more or less directly lifting processes from the United States.

New equipment is often ordered with virtually no economic analysis, frequently justified by hope for some future labor savings and buttressed by the fact that United States plants have proven the technical feasibility of the equipment. However, the analysis of savings and improvements from projected new equipment and the planned payback of the investment, analysis rigidly demanded in most United States plants as part of the appropriation process, is often omitted abroad.

---

[7] Modern industrial engineering typically encompasses the social and human factors as well as those of the old-fashioned "efficiency expert."

The remark of a plant manager in India is typical. He said in reference to a new machine that was being ordered, "It will be economical, I am sure." The order for this equipment had already gone in; it had been approved without any economic analysis of its payback. A quick calculation by the researcher indicated that the payback time on this particular equipment would be at least five years and probably closer to ten.

A number of reasons help to explain this phenomenon. First, the American companies rarely send industrial engineers abroad. They do send engineers with a technical emphasis, but relatively few companies have a home office industrial engineering staff that does on-the-scene work to improve the productivity of overseas plants. Citing a problem in improving the productivity of a certain operation, a plant manager in the Far East stated, "We will not get help on this problem from the home office because they are a *technical* staff and this is a plant *operating* problem."[8] He perceived that the *technical* staff was involved in engineering decisions affecting quality and producibility but not in improving productivity.

Second, the lack of "disaggregated" analysis of equipment and process abroad appears to be due to the shortage of middle management experienced and competent in this sort of detailed analysis. In general, middle management consider decisions in this area as "technological" and therefore leave them to someone else. In fact, the achievement of productivity involves a much broader area than the technological. It requires a thorough on-site analysis of the problems in the process and the equipment as they affect and are affected by such factors as labor skills, setup, supervision, worker attitudes, quality specifications, maintenance and production control.

Finally, there is an absence of American top management attention and effort. "Technical" problems are delegeted to "experts." To a large extent this inattention may be because labor costs have been generally low and operating margins substantial in comparison to American plants. Therefore, in contrast to American operations, top management has not emphasized "squeezing the fat out" of the overseas process to gain a few more cents on the dollar.

Unfortunate Precedents

This type of reasoning seems essentially faulty and shortsighted. Competition is increasing abroad; as a country industrializes, there is typically more competition rather than less; there is a tendency for profit margins to

---

[8] Author's italics.

narrow over the years; labor costs generally increase as labor organizes. Unfortunate precedents are being established in permitting low productivity.

One problem causing low productivity that I have seen in plant after plant in both undeveloped and developed countries is an unbalanced assembly line. Foreign managers often appear to believe that the best way to organize work is on an assembly line, apparently a symbol of modern industry. Workers are positioned in an assembly line with virtually no time and motion study analysis of the actual operations at each station.

The assembly line in a packaging operation in South Africa is typical. Twenty-four operators were on the line. Most of them seemed to be working at a rather leisurely pace. Toward the end of the line one operator was operating a mechanical closing device. He was working at fever pitch, limited by the location of his supplies and a fumbling step in fitting two parts together. The entire line was paced by his work. Yet his job could have been readily facilitated by a simple, inexpensive fixture and some rearrangement of his work-place layout.

Misleading Standards

Overseas plants are generally less productive in terms of the output per hour than plants in the United States with the same equipment. Apparently such inefficiency is permitted because management has not considered it vital to work at improving productivity in labor-intensive operations. The labor costs involved are usually small by American standards. Since management expertise is limited and the home office typically offers little or no advice, it is almost inevitable that production operations will be sloppy.

An additional problem is that of learning to set up and operate small-scale plants. Many manufacturing investment propositions have been turned down because too large a capital cost was foreseen in the face of possible market uncertainties and unfavorable political conditions. Some of these decisions might have been affirmative if more imaginative effort had been invested in planning the operation.

Richard D. Robinson noted in his research:

Virtually every management, other than those already heavily involved in foreign manufacturing, commented about the difficulty of going abroad because of the small national markets. It seems, however, that the real difficulty in many cases did not lie in the small national market, but rather in the inflexibility of the company itself in terms of product, manufacturing processes, and organization.[9]

[9] *International Business Policy, op. cit.*, p. 143.

Willys Jeep Company furnishes an example of a more flexible approach. The U.S. company owned a 25% interest in its plant in Turkey and the capital invested was Turkish.

The Turkish owners and operators were extremely resourceful in setting up the overseas operations. They were assisted in this by an imaginative American, who helped to establish a plant along the shore of the Sea of Marmara 30 miles from the nearest industrial resources.

In setting up this plant, the American established simple processes tailored to the situation which had never been used before. For instance, in the paint spray operation, he completed a satisfactory paint spray tunnel at a cost of only $2000. American engineers interviewed stated that this was fantastic, that it was impossible to do a decent auto paint spraying job for a capital cost of anything less than $25,000. If $25,000 had been projected originally, this type of plant would never have been built.

PRACTICAL PROBLEMS FACILITIES

Equipment decisions encompass more than the major process decision. A "right" equipment choice may be "wrong" if the equipment is not subsequently operated properly. There are choices of how to operate the equipment or assembly line, decisions on maintenance, and the effect on quality—which are apt to be just as important as the major process decision typically made at the home office. The former decisions must usually be made abroad, and they, too, need intelligent industrial engineering analysis.

The Start-Up Phase

Some typical problems that must be taken into account in getting an operation underway are reflected in the comments of the production manager of a pharmaceutical company in Pakistan:

We had problems on every piece of equipment. It was necessary for me and the American to spend several months working with the supervisors and the operators on this equipment, using dummy material at first, to work out the processes and to get the "bugs" cured. It was not that the equipment was new or different, but simply learning its operation, its maintenance, and training the workers took us a long time.

Time must be allowed for the start-up phase in scheduling initial production from overseas operations. Considerably more time is usually necessary than in most domestic start-ups, even when using well-known and tested equipment. In another American company in Pakistan the start-up problems were underestimated. Delays in the construction of the building forced the production group to go through the inevitable break-in problems under severe time pressure. When the plant itself was ready and workers could finally be hired and placed at work on machine tools, many problems developed in achieving good quality machine work. Production techniques and processes had to be worked out so that the parts actually fitted together. Scheduling and coordination skills were also underdeveloped and the entire organization had much to learn about working together as a cooperative unit.

Many of these difficulties had not been anticipated because the same machines and tools had been used for identical operations in Germany. After four months of operation the stockrooms of finished products were virtually empty, and the first units were just beginning to trickle out of the new plant. Top management foresaw at least three or four more months of reduced sales and operating losses in order to get through the start-up period.

Building and construction problems were legion in every underdeveloped country visited. Industrialists in the United States have grown accustomed to knowledgeable and experienced contractors who can work with little supervision. When men who had been involved in the establishment of new plants abroad were asked "What would you do differently?" the first answer was often "We would have given the contractor much closer supervision."

A tire plant in India is a good example. In spite of the fact that the American company sent over experienced construction engineers to work with the contractor, there were numerous problems and many delays. The company managers complained that the contractors simply could not read blueprints, and that the quality of the concrete, the electrical work, and the mechanical and plumbing work was consistently poor. In many instances work had to be taken out and done over. There were difficulties in concrete forms; the electrical subcontracting dragged on months late; there were problems with licenses, documentation, and other government clearances. The production manager had to spend a large portion of his time on the building and the construction process instead of on the hiring and training of workers and supervision. There were still many sections of the building uncompleted when the company finally had to move in and start production. This sequence of problems came about, in spite of the fact that they had used a group of contractors that had the best reputation in Pakistan, due to the problems of communication and variations in standards of adequate and acceptable construction.

Other examples from Turkey, Nigeria, Spain, South Africa, and India are numerous. For instance, an American company experienced months of delay in building a new plant near Bombay. Achieving the quality they required in their electrical and concrete work was particularly time-consuming. A large part of this particular problem was due to difficulties in procuring materials. The Americans praised the architect, but the building was delayed by a three-month strike of the roofers. Delays in importing equipment due to problems in import licensing further postponed the eventual startup of production.

Problems with Secondhand Equipment

In many cases the companies I have studied have made use of secondhand equipment in locations where labor costs are low. The decision was sometimes made because secondhand equipment could be obtained in the foreign country without importing. When used equipment was available, the foreign government was generally reluctant to grant licenses to import new machinery. In other cases secondhand equipment was sent overseas by the parent company on the assumption that the economic environment of the new overseas plant called for an earlier stage of mechanization relative to United States plants. The assumption was that older equipment was generally more simple, required a higher input of labor, and was easier to operate and keep repaired.

Of course these assumptions are not always reliable. Although the authors of the article in "Industrialization and Productivity"[10] point out that simpler equipment that requires "relatively simple skills, less maintenance, less management and organization, will result in fewer breakdowns and waste, an increased use of machinery and decreased downtime," this is not true in all circumstances, especially when the simple equipment is secondhand. And even when new, an ordinary lathe, for example, requires more skill on the part of the operator for certain jobs than does a more mechanized turret lathe or an automatic screw machine. The more advanced machines require considerable skill on the part of a setup man, but once set up the machinery does the work and relatively less skill is required on the part of the operator.

Nor can it be assumed that second-hand equipment will require less maintenance. Maintenance requirements may vary both in respect to the frequency and the complexity of maintenance. New, complex machinery may take less maintenance but involve work at a more sophisticated level. Older, simpler equipment may take more frequent maintenance even though it would be considered elementary work to the skilled tradesman. But abroad, trained maintenance workers are often a rare commodity.

[10] *Op. cit.*, p. 142.

Several companies that had used considerable secondhand or specifically designed or developed equipment abroad felt that in the final analysis it had been unwise, and they would not do it again. A pharmaceutical plant in India, for example, employed mostly secondhand equipment in combination with locally designed processes, largely because it had been able to obtain it cheaply and would not have been allowed to import new equipment. Because of shortages, several supervisors had developed ingenious rigs and processes, but there were repeated difficulties because this equipment proved marginal in its ability to maintain the necessary quality.

The plant manager several times referred to his marginal equipment as his major problem:

These problems affect us seriously; each machine has its own defect. We are able to overcome these difficulties by taking extreme precautions. We know our machines and process equipment so it doesn't hurt us very often. But for instance, our ampule filling machine does not necessarily provide uniform quality and accuracy. And the ampule sealing machine does not give uniform quality in its sealing. Our solution preparation filtration methods and our vacuum set-up are both poor. Many of these things could result in problems, and we are always on edge that our quality may suffer because of the marginality of this poor equipment.

At a tire plant in India the installation of a labor-intensive bias unit that was 41 years old created several problems. The maintenance manager felt that the use of secondhand equipment had not been wise because there were so many breakdowns, some of which tied up the whole plant.

The equipment also placed additional responsibility on the workers, which in turn meant that the supervisors had to be more competent. Unfortunately, as is often true in developing countries, trained and reliable supervisors were relatively nonexistent, and this placed a relentless load on United States expatriates in this particular plant. They had to be everywhere at once because the labor-intensive equipment would not hold specifications and automatically pace production without their watchful attention.

Maintenance Problems

The frequency of maintenance problems overseas suggests that tested and trouble-free equipment should normally be a higher-priority objective than that of employing more labor and reducing initial capital outlays.

The maintenance function was often at a relatively low organizational level in the plants visited. It was frequently a second or third duty of an operating executive and, overall, given less attention than it deserved and required.

Typical problems in managing a maintenance operation in undeveloped locations were recounted by a chief maintenance engineer who had been sent to India from England. He found that equipment serviceability was badly affecting productivity. His predecessor had had to spend the bulk of his time handling breakdowns in the factory. Even the quality of repairs was shocking. He found his men brazing instead of welding; they were inept at welding; they were even using mismatched nuts and bolts.

He felt that the men's attitude toward tools was "nonsensical." They took poor care of tools and seemed to have no feel for which ones were correct to use. They sometimes used a pipe wrench on nuts instead of a proper spanner wrench. The maintenance and repair people had no concept or feel for the strength of materials and safety factors. There was "a sloppy attitude in regard to engineering problems. They tend to accept half-baked jobs. The maintenance organization was poorly organized."

He also pointed out a shortage of materials for proper repairs. There was no stainless steel, no high carbon steel, no bronze for bearings, and they often had difficulty in obtaining the necessary perishable tools and supply items. (They had recently discovered, however, by an aggressive search effort that there were actually many items available locally that they had struggled along without for years.)

They did not have an adequate supply of spare parts for the machines. Bearings, for instance, had to be imported; they were able to find some equivalents after extensive searching. They lacked nuts, springs, lock washers, and they found that no other companies seemed to stock them or use them. In addition, the Indian master mechanic was not up to his job. "I had to fire him," he said, "He worked hard but he had a grasshopper mind. He did not organize the operation, and in spite of the fact that he had been a sea-going engineer he was extremely sloppy about everything."

The quality of replacement parts, which were fabricated locally, was "terrible" in terms of tolerances, dimensions, finishes, and materials. But after many rejections from vendors, the company was able to increase the quality it received. Some vendors even refused to quote, but finally the company was able to develop better suppliers, although deliveries of spare parts continued to be a severe problem. The maintenance engineer went out to see these vendors, for he considered purchasing a very significant part of the maintenance job.

This manager had been able to achieve considerable improvement during the year he had been in the plant. He said that his men had learned to do a good job on routine tasks but that new jobs still created snags.

One approach he had used in improving the operation was to be much more selective in the hiring of maintenance men. He personally interviewed all candidates, asked them semipractical questions through an interpreter— for example, to identify metal, to set a micrometer at 0.487. He also had them do a few operations, such as filing parts to make them fit. He was able to discover which of those interviewed were "relatively practical." He found, too, that by "placing pressure" on his men he was able to increase the amount of work that was accomplished. He could then weed out the many men who could not take the pressure. There had been a 30% turnover during the past year.

The advice of the plant engineer, who was returning to England in a year or two, was that his successor should have "good practical engineering and design experience, but particularly he should be a good organizer. A man needs 20 years of experience to set up in a place like this because there are so many problems." He would advise his successor to contact the expatriate engineers of other companies to get opinions of the competence of the local talent and to hire and train his own maintenance men and foremen rather than relying on their prior experience. "There is a real problem here in that the local tradesmen don't like to get their hands dirty. In addition, we've had problems because our maintenance men make their helpers do much of the work. Their refusal to do many simple operations themselves slows down the work."

Culturally based problems further affected the maintenance organization. For example, because the operators of machines refused to clean them, the sweepers performed this work. Thus in effect the sweepers ended up doing whatever maintenance was done on a daily basis, which amounted to very little.

Because of the large number of maintenance problems over the years this company had worked out some administrative improvements, such as learn- ing the causes of breakdowns on different pieces of equipment through better record-keeping. By training, pressure on supervision, and gradual weeding out of employees, they had cut time from 16 hours for making a mold changeover to two hours (a record of 50 minutes had been set by one maintenance man).

The chief maintenance engineer said in parting, "Don't let American management send second-class people to a place like India. They have got to be first-class people and unusually competent at home if they are going to succeed here. The people at home have no idea what it is to run a plant out here."

Nevertheless, these same types of maintenance problems are found in many parts of the world in a variety of forms. To the responsible manager these problems are troublesome and annoying, and in several instances machine breakdowns due to inadequate maintenance significantly affect production output. Simply keeping better records, more systematic lubrication, and preventive maintenance often can pay off in fewer breakdowns and longer equipment life.

One cannot avoid the sense that some of the chief maintenance engineer's complaints were due to the violation of his vocational norms. His standards of the "right way" to do maintenance work, developed throughout a disciplined career, were flagrantly desecrated in India; his reaction was one of near revulsion at the inept, casual, apparently careless procedures he observed.

The seriousness of maintenance failures depends on the process which can determine the priority given to this function. Over the short run the effect of shoddy practices is not so costly in light industry (where the process depends less on continuous flow or linked mechanized steps) as it may first appear. Disrespect for tools and a temporary patch instead of a permanent repair is more important in heavy, equipment-centered industry.

Lack of replacement parts and skilled first-class mechanics, coupled with the typical firm's reliance on the functioning of its own equipment (since there are generally fewer standby sources) add up to an enlarged dependence upon the maintenance function in the environments of developing economies. Equipment requiring a high degree of maintenance skill and attention should generally be avoided.

CONCLUSION: DECISION-MAKING APPROACHES

Technological strategy decisions culminating in choices of original processes and facilities abroad are frequently dominated by the home office technical staff. People in such positions are naturally concerned with their reputations and aware that it is easy to criticize equipment if it produces only marginal product quality or is inadequate in its output. They also know that they will not be involved in the operation of the equipment. There is a built-in tendency for them, therefore, to overspecify, overdesign, overinsure quality and capacity, and often overmechanize.

It is curious, however, that once the plant has been set up, replacement and expanded capacity decisions in the companies studied were seldom initiated or analyzed by home office engineers. Instead, after the plant is operating, the facilities are turned over to the local plant managers; when more equipment is necessary, the plant managers usually make the decision. Typically these plant managers had relatively little knowledge of possible alternatives and virtually no training in engineering economics. Relatively little "know-how" in industrial engineering is made available. Like maintenance, industrial engineering is usually on a "do-it-yourself" basis abroad.

American managements are sometimes prone to dismiss the writings of economists as academic and to feel that technological factors limit the process alternatives far more than they do, in fact. Too few alternatives are recognized and studied. To a large extent a lack of organizational emphasis and the apparatus for making effective equipment and process decisions is responsible for this state of affairs. Increasing pressure for lower costs and higher quality may tend to change this in time, but already the opportunities for developing more economical processes and equipment are considerable. An increased emphasis on industrial engineering and improved maintenance management could be fruitful in many plants.

The experience of an American food-processing plant in Spain furnishes a good example of the contribution of the industrial engineering point of view. Faced with inadequate capacity due to increasing sales, the managers tentatively decided a major expansion was necessary. However, before going ahead they learned, through an extensive industrial engineering analysis of their entire system, that by breaking three bottlenecks they could increase production by approximately 15% using the same facilities. An incentive plan was established to reward continuous production and penalize downtime. This placed further emphasis on total equipment productivity, allowing the company to meet growing market demands and delay an expensive expansion program.

In this chapter I have offered three conclusions from research abroad:

1. Dominated by a technical point of view, international manufacturing firms often appear to be conservative and limited in their vision of possible alternatives.
2. Economic theorists could help broaden the typical industrialist's point of view with their notions of adapting technological strategy to the environment, but economists' contributions are frequently too gross and aggregated. They tend to leave out such practical considerations as start-ups, problems with labor-intensive processes, and maintenance.
3. The industrial engineering approach is too infrequently employed abroad. Since it is situational and pragmatic as well as broad in its notions of a production system and total productivity of the system, this approach offers both an outlook and the mechanics for an improved handling of technological strategy decisions.

The industrial engineering function, available domestically, is typically weak or absent overseas. The gap between economic theoreticians and practical industrial decision makers could be filled by an able industrial engineering staff encompassing both the broader alternatives seen by the economists and the practical, conservative requirements emphasized by industry. Industrial engineers are trained to develop processes and methods to fit the environment. This is precisely the gap that must be filled overseas.

The culprit in the technological strategy area is the decision-making process itself. Decisions on both original and replacement equipment and equipment maintenance are too often considered "technical." But wise decisions go far beyond this dimension into marketing, finance, human, and political factors which may be just as important. Equipment and process choice is more a matter of technological strategy than a mere technical calculation. A longer-range, multidimensional outlook is needed; however, it cannot be provided by only specialized engineers and technicians, able as they may be. Industrial engineering is management oriented rather than technically oriented.

Too often managers act as spectators and never get involved. Facilities planning is a proper and vital arena for managers' responsible participation through the use of industrial engineers, who speak their language and bridge the gap between technological and economic theory and daily practice.

PERSPECTIVES

Chapter 18 deals with management development. I discuss the development of effective manufacturing management, men and women who are general managers in their perspectives, outlooks, and skills rather than highly specialized. The chapter describes some trends in business schools and manufacturing firms.

Perspectives
on
Operations Management
for
Educators and
Practitioners

The decade ending in the early 1970s was rough for American industry and it was an equally rough period for those teaching in the field of production and operations management (POM).

In industry we suffered high costs, mediocre quality, automation and start-up fiascoes, "blue-collar blues," Lordstowns, a "brain drain" in failing to attract our able young into industry, and innumerable situations in which the manufacturing function became a competitive millstone for the entire corporation.

In the POM field at graduate schools of management the decade was marked by declining student enrollments; loss of market share in courses offered, research grants obtained, and doctoral students attracted; widespread criticism of the field and its courses as irrelevant, dull, and "technique-y"; a pervasive sense of discouragement, and frequent ideological debates over whether the content and future of the field should be quantitative or nonquantitative. In some schools POM was removed from first-year MBA required courses and relegated to the status of electives. In a few schools POM had faded out altogether.

Somewhat mysteriously, however, in the last four or five years the process has reversed itself with enrollments growing, student ratings climbing, new courses being developed, and POM being lauded as contributing an element of the concrete, physical, and tangible world to the gradually more conceptually weighted Masters in Business Administration (MBA) curriculum mix. The hard-nosed facts of schedules, costs, and quality levels have apparently become important to business survival in enough industries that students, faculty, and deans receiving and locking on to such signals coming from the business environment have begun to see POM as vital and relevant.

The turnaround has been remarkable. As usual, industry led the way and academics scrambled to keep in touch with what was happening. What was happening is that industry was being faced with increasing competition, shorter product lives, more new products, more technological innovation, larger-scale investments, more integrated investments, rising risks and dangers in consumer liability suits, shortages, more stringent government controls such as OSHA and EPA regulations, consumerism, and a whole new flock of problems centering on changes in the content of the work force and its mix of expectations and demands.

Back at the schools of management we have belatedly attempted to cope and contribute. But we have been saved more by these changes than by any great clairvoyance and subsequent shifts in our research, teaching, or areas of interest.

We have an opportunity to learn from this experience and whether we learn the right things and take appropriate action will have a substantial influence on production management in the next decade.

Let me suggest that we have learned that we are no one single discipline or family of techniques. We are operations problem solvers and operations systems designers, which takes a vast array of talents and point of view. As the outside environment got rougher, we learned once more from the enormous complexity of operations management that its problems are far from solved and that mathematical, economic, statistical, behavioral approaches are all rich in their potentials, but inadequate and impotent separately and that the POM area is one in which we need both differentiation and integration, specialists and generalists, quantitative and qualitative approaches. As operations problem solvers, we function best by being constantly oriented to and concerned with current industry problems. We succeed when we seek techniques for our problems, not vice versa. Our orientation must be outward and our ability to adjust rapid.

I first attempt an explanation of what has been happening to POM and why and then suggest what this means to our future, closing with a description of promising opportunities fast opening up for POM faculties.

1. *Causes of the lean years and the recent recovery.* What happened that led us to the brink, survival level and some POM faculties indeed becoming extinct? And why are we now apparently recovering and in many schools actually prospering? I think the factors divide into external/environmental and internal/academic factors. Of the two, I think the external/environmental side has been more important.

2. *External/environmental factors.* POM's vitality as a subject area is especially susceptible to and affected by the economy, social needs and concerns, and problems in industry. Our medicine may be strong and taste bad, and therefore it is only taken when the patient is pretty sick. Regardless, let me cite a number of recent changes that have enormously affected the responses to our offerings.

To start with, we have moved from an economy of affluence and surplus to an economy of marginal competitive ability and frequent scarcities. Our costs are high and rising. Our balance of trade is poor, and the dollar is weak. Our production quality is highly variable. Productivity is now of national concern. It is no longer taken for granted that we are the number one industrial nation in terms of productivity, quality, ingenuity, and leadership in applied industrial and production engineering.

Our POM heritage and tradition of attention to details of planning and production; the gospel of efficiency; the old virtues of saving, thrift, economy, and "waste not want not" were lost on the affluent student, corporation, and economy of the 1960s; and POM floundered. My colleague across the wide Charles River, John Kenneth Galbraith, wrote in "The Affluent Society" that our production problems were over. But we POM instructors banged away in our classrooms about time studies, work simplification, and quality control when we were still storing up gold at Fort Knox, selling steel and electronics abroad, and producing looms and machine tools for the whole world. What MBA student cared about industry when factory problems were easily solvable by old, routine techniques, industrial engineers, and engineering specialists? Sure, we had some interesting labor problems, but no one could do much about them without 20 years of experience and the patience of lots of slowly accumulated seniority. Not the stuff for an MBA.

Time and circumstances have changed all that. Once again productivity, costs, efficiency, smooth flows, and competitive quality are important. They used to be for industrial competition—now they are important for national survival. The dramatic rise of the place of service industries in our economy—in most of which human efficiency is vital for success—has opened up a whole new sector of opportunity and challenge for business managers and entrepreneurs. Our students' interest is being caught. Yet success in the factory or service industry is even harder to achieve today than before because of a pack of changes in social demands and expectations.

Here again chang s in the external environment hurt POM in the 1960s but now seem to be running strongly in our favor. Reasonably docile, work ethic oriented workers who did what they were told, bargained collectively, and followed the union contract and the steward's orders, have been infiltrated significantly by the newer generation of workers with a different set of goals and expectations. The MBA of the 1960s was not particularly turned on or intrigued with the management of people. This was either seen as a slow way to get to the top or avoided as being too fraught with nasty and unpleasant encounters with "stubborn" workers and "emotional" foremen.

As a symbol, Lordstown ended any excuse for managers, MBAs, colleagues or deans to disclaim interest in or the importance of industry and people in factories and service operations. Problems of organizing jobs and work, scheduling, control of productivity, and reliability have once again become vital and interesting. A shift in the content and nature of jobs with increasing mechanization also brought a need for more knowledge workers—highly trained, skilled, and specialized, with new, difficult problems relating to their selection, training, motivation, compensation, and supervision. The factory is no longer "Dullsville" because shorter runs and product lives and more customer specials have added interest, variety, and complexity to what was once becoming a routine and repetitious job. Investments now tend to be in larger chunks, at bigger price tags, with bigger risks, and involving more integrated, planned, and delicately coordinated operation sequences and human uses of human beings. Planning and organizing have come to be more critical, and as this trend has advanced new sectors of management have opened for the MBA (as opposed to the technologist or strictly industrial engineer).

These changes have spawned a new generation of people in management as well as a new generation of workers—blue-collar and white-collar as well. But it has not been all roses or an unmitigated professional paradise. Not only have there been the blue-collar blues and seething discontent among older and younger workers and foremen but there have been a whole host of economic and technical problems in all industries. Major bugs and equipment disasters, computer fiascoes, inability to adjust to changes in volume and product shifts, higher costs, low productivity, foreign competition, low returns on massive investments. Such problems have attracted more professionals in industry—professional production controllers, quality control experts, industrial engineers, accountants, maintenance engineers, personnel people—all with their own professional societies, norms, cultures, aims, values, and objectives. Most of these are in conflict. This new breed needs managing, and to the MBA the challenge of managing professionals is quite a contrast to the task of managing large numbers of generally less formally trained employees characteristic of the 1960s. The task of the 1960s required considerable experience and a kind of cunning bred by years of experience. Today these skills are still important, but there is also a need for broad general management training to manage professional specialists and professional managers.

BACK IN ACADEMIA—RESPONDING TO EXTERNAL CHANGES

So the economic, social, industrial, and technological environments are all, in my opinion, changing so as to increase the perceived significance, profit and loss importance, and interest and attractiveness of the POM area to managers and future managers. But back in academia we generally respond slowly. We are not so dull as wholly to miss the changes going on externally, for the echoes of those changes have been loud. But changing over our own equipment and process technology so to speak does not come any more easily than in factories and service industries.

Why are we so slow to tune in, focus the picture, interpret it, and change the direction of our work, our research, and our courses? Our individual professional training impedes change, for it is with us all our lives, creating biases, knee-jerk reactions, areas where we feel skilled and areas where we feel insecure. Our internal security and seniority systems protect the old, entrenched success of yesterday.

The pressures for academic respectability are strong and often quite debilitating. The elders push the young to carry on and develop the elders' research in more depth. The great research interest of one 5- to 10-year period thus gets milked for another 5 to 10 years. It appears to be sheep-like behavior, but there is more economic and social pressure to it than merely imitation. The young must publish and their work, whether innovative or not, must be acceptable to their elders and leaders. Since it must be "rigorous" and "solid" to get published, the pressures and payoffs for doing more of the same old thing in more detail are far greater motivators than the risk-prone disincentives of carving out rough taxonomies of new problem areas that need exploring and describing but cannot be very rigorous at a new stage. So the old group does what it learned and feels good at and forces the youth to imitate.

In our academic world we are also sluggish in our curriculum response to changes in the business scene. We tend to be cautious about adding new courses, dropping old ones, and innovating in our existing ones. We must ask, "Where does the new material come from? How much of my time, a scarce resource, will it take? How can I get two to three months in the field which I need to develop a course? Will the students rate it high? Will it affect my reputation if it does not go so well at first? Will it have a discipline and rigor:" "Just what is it, Professor Jones, that you will be teaching in that new course you are proposing to this committee?"

We must ask about the POM area in particular and why it is that we have been, I think, particularly slow to respond effectively to the demands and opportunities presented by outside changes and needs. It seems to me that four aspects of our POM heritage and culture have rendered us relatively inept at picking up signals, learning from experience, and adapting to change.

Stodgy Reputation

First of all, we have been hurt by being the area that pioneered the whole development of a scientific approach to administration. Starting with Frederick Taylor, the field of production management initiated measurements, standards, empirical research, controls, human engineering and so led to the study of management as an approximate science. This hurt us in the 1960s because 50 years of research, analysis, and development of concepts, techniques, and principles led our various publics and colleagues to believe that the problems of industrial production management had been largely solved. Many said that nothing really new had come along in POM in the last fifteen years. We were seen as unexciting and unchallenging by our finance, marketing and organizational behavior competitors and as dully exacting by our students. We had plenty to teach but it was mostly old hat.

Some of us believed that our industrial problems were more or less solved by known techniques, others did not; but the net result was that we tended either to fall back on our well-proven notions and principles or scramble a bit desperately for any new ones. The effect was a kind of schizophrenia and inability to look outside to develop inside.

Ideological Warfare

At the same time that many were criticizing POM on the grounds that it was thoroughly worked over and unexciting, some innovative and exciting new tools and techniques began to be developed—mathematically based quantitative approaches to scheduling, inventory control, physical movements and flows.

These new ideas and applications of rigorous quantitative techniques came to us as a whiff of oxygen to an exhausted athlete. There was the new excitement, the future of the field, salvation from growing second-rate—enormous challenge coupled with the clear potential of academic respectability. And the tools were much needed in industry, had massive potential applications, and could produce superb improvements in operations.

Sadly, however, we let this new set of superlative breakthroughs hurt us in several ways. It hurt us most seriously because it divided us into two camps. Individually and as schools we became typed as either "quantitative" or "nonquantitative". The quantitative types called the others old-fashioned and reactionary. The nonquantitative called the quantitative people specialists or technicians who "don't really understand the realities of life."

The ideological warfare was unpleasant. It was also harmful in that it tended, I believe, to compartmentalize thinking and slowed integrated progress in the field. Worst of all, the ideological conflict thoroughly confused everybody (outside POM as well as inside the embattled garrison) as to who we were, what we were about, and where we should be going. Some said that the field *was* the new concepts and techniques, that their study and application was the way of the future and the long-sought body of knowledge and discipline. Others said, "No—not so," but offered little else in the way of excitement or alternatives.

It was a time of ferment, at least, and progress was made in the quantitative sector, but it was also a time of near disaster for many POM departments, for the bulk of MBA students showed little interest in what we had to offer; we were damned for any bugs in computerized-modeling experiments, and our competitors in marketing, finance, and so on looked at the combination of our poor results, confused identity, and the low interest of managers in our wares with the polite, disdainful smiles of one's betters. We suffered in reputation, productivity, and in not attracting many of the young to our classrooms and our doctoral programs.

Confused Identity

A third factor in our adaptive capacity as an area is that poor, confused sense of identity. How do we know what environmental factors are relevant to our future when we do not know who we are now? Are we industrial engineers, manufacturing engineers, efficiency experts, production and inventory control specialists, operations researchers, technology analysts, applied mathematicians, or what? What is the discipline base of our subject—engineering, economics, mathematics, psychology, or something else?

The answer is now clear that we require the use of a variety of disciplines in a rich, cross-disciplined approach. We became hung up over our parentage and the particular traditions and beliefs we each assimilated at some impressionable time in our lives. All this has given us a group identity problem and communication difficulties. Our diverse orientations, the product of quite different upbringings, has tended sometimes to make us a bit edgy with each other, not so sure of our colleague's motives, and certainly less than fully trusting. This hurt our internal decision-making processes and frequently left us imbalanced in the mix of skills in our departments when one side "won" and came out ahead.

Grasping at Straws

In our sense of insecurity we tried too hard, we got too involved, we reached out for any new notion or technique that would seem to lift us out of our slide to oblivion. We reacted badly in a crisis, leaping to overdrawn, simplistic conclusions. Some concluded that the future lay in going back to standards, time and motion, and industrial engineering. Others protested that in operations research and the computer lay our one best hope for the future of the field. I personally said that manufacturing policy, relating our work to corporate strategy, was the way out of our predicament of what to teach and how to teach it. In pristine ideological arguments we laid waste our powers.

From our past difficulties and the subsequent turnaround, what have we learned about who we are, how we function best, and how we can prevent a repetition of what happened in the 1960s?

FRESH OPPORTUNITIES

In contrast to our struggles for survival a few years ago, we are now surrounded with an unbelievably rich new set of opportunities. I am speaking of opportunities for research and course development for which there is a growing need. If intelligently and energetically developed, these opportunities will provide us a decade of powerful agenda and powerful results. These opportunities have surfaced because they reflect real and difficult problems in industry. We are surrounded by superb opportunities in every direction, and I have never seen it that way to that extent before. The environment outside and inside has moved our way to the point that we are simply bursting with things to do that have great promise.

1. *Leadership in the study and teaching of technology.* There is great public and industrial interest in understanding technological change and managing it much better. How do innovations develop? How can good ideas be spotted? How can billions for R & D be better managed? How does a particular technological change impact on each sector of an industry?

2. *Management of service operations.* Here is another booming opportunity. More than a third of the students at the Harvard Business School are taking such a course as an elective in the second year of the MBA Program. Our first year has more and more service operations cases as well. One reason it is such a natural is that many students can see themselves as smaller businessmen and women in such operations. Another is that managers of such operations are very interested in help and ideas, having cases written, and getting closer to the business schools.

3. *The operating manager.* Another substantial opportunity to meet a need is also a natural for POM. Everyone is teaching about strategy and policy and the big top-level decisions top managers make. But who is teaching about how a manager operates, day by day and week by week? Who is teaching about the skills and attitudes of an effective operating manager? Who is helping MBA students get off to the start in their first five years which may get them to the policy level? Students are concerned about this. We started with 58 in the first year this course was offered and over twice that number have signed up for it each year since. It grew to 475 in 1977.

4. *Urban operations.* Government services are natural for POM approaches, and there has been considerable interest in our course in the management of urban operations since it was started four years ago. The cases are dramatic and interesting: costs per ton of solid wastes of Town A 50% that of Town B only 12 miles away; massive government projects for improving the environment. This is a great area for attracting today's students.

5. *Logistics and distributions systems.* The POM faculty is working more closely with logistics and transportation faculty and getting occasionally involved with retail distribution and service industry logistics. It is natural to combine this with a production and inventory control course, and we believe that a combined course can appeal to more students and make a greater contribution.

6. *People at work.* Not human relations, not labor relations, not personnel management but kind of a mixture, with operating problems of a factory or service industry, cases have to do with blue-collar blues, job content and job design, new approaches for turning on people at work and finding in a factory or corporate organization a sense of belonging.

7. *Manufacturing policy.* Bringing corporate strategy to meet face to face

with the realities of production is an exciting eye-opener, and if the industries are kept up and the material is fresh, a sure winner because the decisions are critical and the payoffs big.

8. *International operations management.* This is a comer and another winner—exciting and challenging, lots to teach and lots to learn and belongs in every curriculum.

Generally in POM what works and goes well is fresh field material, plenty of field trips, visits to the classroom by executives, and liberal use of video tapes showing actual shots of operations, people, and layout. We have learned that when the student can *visualize* the situation he can grasp it and grapple with it and enjoy it; when he cannot, he turns off. The difficulty of teaching POM can be cut 90% with the use of the reality of trips, field work, projects with companies, and video tapes.

POM has been taught to teach and we have found that a good POM instructor is an unusually good teacher of most anything. In a tactical sense, required courses should be taught by superb teachers, teachers who would stand out in any area. The POM area should become known as a developer of the best teachers in a graduate school of business and it should use this focus on top grade, general management-oriented teaching as a major weapon in its own development within the school.

THE FUTURE

To summarize, I have said that POM is alive and well again. We have had a close call with extinction, and some great schools have pushed POM under. But for the survivors of this shake-out things have not looked better in 20 years. We have new interest, new publics, new challenges, enormous opportunities on all sides. And we have excellent people—people who have learned to accept each other's talents and interests and ideologies with the genuine mutual respect of researchers and teachers who need each other.

As the sheriff (or Indians or bad guys) goes tearing down the wrong canyon and we sit briefly safe, gathering our breath and thanking our stars for our amazing escape, we have got to say, "What have we learned (or should we now learn) from this experience? Or, if you feel you are still in the process of survival, how can you *make it*?" I would offer several observations:

1. An area or department—like a company—will prosper only if it is marketing oriented. You must offer what students want and respect their wants, and you must offer what business and the economy signals it

needs. We cannot often afford to teach today what we researched yesterday or what no one but us finds interesting. We must constantly keep our radar turning and respond to, even anticipate our markets. We are in business to provide a service, to make a contribution, not to nourish our own intellects or quest for academic respectability. Market oriented is problem oriented.

2. We must not only tolerate diversity, we must seek it and use it as a competitive weapon, for POM is above all else an *integrated area of management*. It is people and equipment and technology and flows and materials. We need every scrap of knowledge and technique and judgment to survive and prosper. But POM is not a set of techniques any more than marketing is a set of market research techniques. It is a combination of knowledge and skills and attitudes. We need people with top skills in personnel, technology, flows, mathematics, research, case-writing, organizations, and with both operating and policy points of view. We can serve as an integrating factor in a curriculum if we can learn to thrive on diversity within our own group and learn to overcome the communication problems usually encountered when different cultures are thrown together.

The seeds for each new year in a company are planted in the present. The same is true for us. Our present improving situation can become the basis for a great new era for us if we can be the masters of ourselves, keep market and problem oriented, and cooperatively nurture the opportunities all around us into a whole new level of contribution to our students and our schools.

This chapter has been all about POM, for we have learned to find ourselves by losing ourselves in the problems of our society, our economy, and of our schools. We will survive only if we address those needs.

What is the future of POM? The question is unnecessary, for the future of POM will take care of itself if we focus outside on the needs of our ultimate constituency—the businesses of this country and of the world.

Index

325

congruence with operating systems, 84, 85, 87
economics, 96
of equipment and processes, 81-97, 245
and manager, 81-97
product, 227, 228
requirements of, 91, 273
risks, 92, 245
technological change, 81, 92, 321
see also Equipment and process technology
Time and motion study, 16
Tinbergen, Jan, 295
Tools and techniques, of production management, 4, 5, 7, 13, 15, 16, 17, 19

United Nations, Bureau of Economic Affairs, 293
Urban operations, 321

Willys Jeep, 302
Work force management, 33, 52, 53, 78, 110, 112, 113, 123, 245, 321
blue collar blues, 40
international, 264, 276
labor relations, 3, 277
selection, 13, 249
training, 249
wage policy, 10, 19, 249
Work simplification, 16

Zenith Radio, 143